FORMS OF POWER

Gianfranco Poggi

Polity

Copyright © Gianfranco Poggi 2001

The right of Gianfranco Poggi to be identified as author of this work has been asserted in accordance with the Copyright, Designs and Patents Act 1988.

First published in 2001 by Polity Press in association with Blackwell Publishers Ltd

Editorial office:
Polity Press
65 Bridge Street
Cambridge CV2 1UR, UK

Marketing and production:
Blackwell Publishers Ltd
108 Cowley Road
Oxford OX4 1JF, UK

Published in the USA by
Blackwell Publishers Inc.
Commerce Place
350 Main Street
Malden, MA 02148, USA

ISBN 0-7456-2474-X
ISBN 0-7456-2475-8 (pbk)

A catalogue record for this book is available from the British Library and has been applied for from the Library of Congress.

Typeset in 10 on 11.5 pt Sabon
by SetSystems Ltd, Saffron Walden, Essex
Printed in Great Britain by MPG Books, Bodmin, Cornwall

This book is printed on acid-free paper

Contents

Preface

1   *Homo Potens*   1

2   Power Forms   15

3   Political Power   29

4   Ideological / Normative Power   58

5   Religious Power and the State   74

6   Creative Intellectuals and the State   97

7   Economic Power   123

8   Business and Politics   141

9   The Economic Costs of the State   159

10 Military Power   180

    Epilogue   203

    Notes   205

    Select Bibliography   212

    Index   217

Preface

This book, like others I have written, is an attempt to seek a wider public for a number of themes that I have been discussing in my university lectures for many a year.

As long ago as 1965, having been charged with teaching a course in political sociology at Edinburgh University (together with James Cornford, at the time lecturer in politics there), I turned for advice to Juan Linz, who had often assisted me most generously in my progress as a graduate student at Berkeley and then as an assistant at the University of Florence. I told him that I did not want to focus my teaching on the then fashionable theme of 'political behaviour', and was looking for alternative topics. Juan replied that there were two important themes that most political sociology courses unjustly neglected – one was the modern state, and the other the relations between political power and other forms of social power.

That was, for me, a momentous suggestion, for in due course I was to write two books and various essays on the state, after repeatedly making it the theme of my teaching. I also followed Juan's second piece of advice, and from the late 1960s on, over many years, in numerous English-speaking universities – not just Edinburgh, but in the universities of California (Berkeley), Victoria (British Columbia), Washington, Harvard, Sydney, Virginia – I focused my political sociology teaching on the relations between different forms of social power.

For a variety of reasons, however, I hesitated for some time to *write* about this theme. I only decided to do so, almost thirty years after I had taken it up in my teaching, in 1993–4, while holding a fellowship at the Wissenschaftskolleg in Berlin. Thanks to the Wissenschaftskolleg's most supportive hospitality, I was able to complete a book-length manuscript, but then allowed it to lie fallow for a few years. In 1998, however, I drew on that manuscript in producing a much smaller book on the same topic, in Italian – *Il gioco dei poteri* (Mulino, Bologna, 1998) – and decided to prepare for publication the Berlin manuscript (written in English) as a whole. I completed this task (undertaken after being appointed to a chair at the European University Institute in Fiesole) while holding a fellowship at the Humanities Research Centre of the Australian University (Canberra), for whose hospitality I am most grateful.

The book, I suspect, bears the marks of its origins as a course of lectures taught for the first time in the now remote 1960s. It defines its topics in what may appear an idiosyncratic manner, and explores them in an essay-like rather than systematic fashion; furthermore, it pays only occasional attention to literature that discusses aspects of its theme, particularly if that literature was the product of the last two decades or so. (I never like expressly to discuss other people's writings when teaching a class, preferring to leave it to students to deal with that themselves). But I hope that the book now presented to readers conveys some sense of the significance of the phenomena on which it touches.

I am grateful to Dr Sebastian Rinken, a former researcher at the European Institute, for his assistance on the draft of this book and to Elizabeth Webb, my secretary at the EUI, who kindly assisted my efforts in finalizing the manuscript.

I dedicate this book to the memory of a dear friend, Luciana Pepa (1938–1999).

Gianfranco Poggi
Fiesole (Italy)

1

Homo Potens

Our subject

This book deals with social power chiefly as it manifests itself in differentiated forms, each embodied in distinctive institutions, that is, in relatively
self-standing sets of practices, resources and personnel. It is particularly
concerned, on the one hand, with the ways in which such embodiments
emerge, and, on the other, with the tendency of those differentiated
institutions to bargain or struggle with one another for advantage, to
increase each its own autonomy at the others' expense.

I shall explore this theme in a selective and non-systematic manner,
examining only some aspects of it. One reason for this preference (among
others) is that a systematic approach is not easily adopted in this thematic
area. In particular, it would be good to approach our theme starting from
a widely shared, generic concept of social power or indeed of power in
general. Unfortunately, no such concept exists. What does exist, however,
is a largish body of literature – a great number of essays, a sizeable number
of books from the disciplines of sociology, political science, social psychol-
ogy and philosophy – where numerous, overlapping and generally inconclu-
sive attempts are made to generate agreement on a given understanding of
the notion of power.[1] Typically, each author recalls some classical presen-
tations of that notion (Hobbes's *Leviathan* is a favourite beneficiary, or
perhaps victim, of such exercises), then reviews the related contemporary
controversy, then proposes and variously justifies his or her more or less
distinctive contribution to the theme. There even are anthologies assemb-
ling a number of such contributions,[2] the more recent of which often
remind the reader that the notion of power has been authoritatively
characterized as being 'essentially contested'[3] – as if social scientists needed
such a fancy justification for squabbling over how to define their terms.

It is not my intent to add to this literature, which tends to focus on
topics (such as the relation between power, intention and interest, or the
roles respectively of force and consensus as the grounds of power, or the
question of how to ascertain the existence of a power relationship and of
how to measure it) in which I have little interest. As I have already
suggested, my concern is much more with diverse institutional embodiments of the power phenomenon, and the relations between such embodi-

ments – a theme that has held my interest for decades, and the significance of which was emphasized, in the mid-1980s, by Michael Mann.[4]

Unfortunately I cannot arrive at that theme without attempting a preliminary statement, however brief, on what 'power' should be taken to mean, and on why there should be power among human beings. Furthermore, while I feel little inclined to deal with such an assignment in the standard fashion – line up the usual suspects and possibly a few unusual ones, sort them out into a few clusters by reference to their similarities, adjudicate their contrasts, present personal answers to the key queries – I find it convenient to signpost my approach to that theme by referring to a few entries from the literature that I mentioned earlier.

I do not claim that my selection of these entries is the outcome of a close, critical examination of that literature, and that the arguments I shall introduce are demonstrably more significant than those I have instead neglected, or fit together into a particularly cogent discourse. I am simply sharing with the reader what seems to me a plausible conceptual itinerary to my main topic, emphasizing the contributions of authors whom, over the years, I have found useful in seeking to establish to my own satisfaction (and that of my students) what one might reasonably mean by 'power', and by 'social power' in particular.

Herbert Rosinski's contribution

Let me begin with an argument inspired chiefly by Herbert Rosinski's *Power and Human Destiny*.[5] This book appeared in 1965; its author, a German scholar long active in the United States, and known chiefly as a specialist in military history, had died three years earlier, leaving the work unfinished and unedited. He had written it largely from within a German intellectual tradition, that of 'philosophical anthropology', which at the time had very little resonance in English-speaking countries. (Things have not changed that much, considering the not hugely dissimilar fate, in the 1980s, of the American translation of a masterpiece from the same tradition, Arnold Gehlen's *Der Mensch*).[6] At any rate, *Power and Human Destiny* attracted very little notice, and apparently quickly passed into total oblivion. This is an undeserved fate, for, in my view, if what one seeks to articulate is a very broad concept of power (as I am seeking to do in the first instance), the book's argument appears most relevant.

Rosinski, to begin with, does mean what his title says. That is, he considers power a phenomenon that belongs to the very essence of the human species, which characterizes its very position in the order of nature. In fact, humans – to adopt a noteworthy formulation of Helmuth Plessner, another contributor to the German philosophical anthropology tradition[7] – are 'ex-centrically positioned' in that order. Considered purely as parts of nature, human beings possess biological equipment apparently insufficiently adapted to the rest of nature; humans are unable to sustain their own existence *except* via a form of activity distinctive to the species, and grounded of course in its biological equipment, but not completely programmed by it. In this context, that form of activity – we might call it 'action', and propose *Homo agens* as a kind of primary characterization of the species – amounts to a kind of self-programming. That is, through action, the species on the one hand avails itself of the relative indeterminacy of its position in nature, on the other hand surrenders that indeterminacy by finding expression, unavoidably, in *determinate* – that is, limited and of definite scope – arrangements and preferences.

We may clarify this by considering a few other characterizations of the species, all of them more usual than *Homo agens*, but in my view compatible with it – for instance, *Homo sapiens, faber, loquens, ludens*, or *videns*. They are all enlightening, but each points up only a potentiality, that is, the capacity to know, make, speak, play or see, and thus leaves open a very important series of questions – respectively, what does the human being know, what does it produce, how does it speak, which games does it play, what does it see. Only the answers given to those queries settle, for a given human group, the position it takes in nature.

In other terms, in order to survive the human species must *make a difference*: make a difference to nature, which will not sustain it unless intervened upon by the members of that species themselves; and make a difference to itself, for the manner of that intervention will in turn shape the mode of existence of those men and women, impart to it a more or less distinctive bias, and differentiate it from the mode of existence of other men and women.

The widest meaning of 'power', then, is the *ability* to make such a difference; and this ability must be seen as belonging to the very essence of the species. *Homo potens*, indeed, is an expression that might appropriately be added to more usual species listed above. It focuses on the fact that, by its very constitution, the human being is uniquely enabled, or condemned, to self-*determination*, in the etymological sense of assigning boundaries (*termini*) to itself and locating itself in the world. If power is thus understood, the human being is implicated in power through and through; and the phenomenon of power turns out to be closely associated with that of liberty, although on the face of it liberty and power may appear to be intrinsically at loggerheads with one another.

In his opening chapter, Rosinski emphasizes a somewhat narrower meaning of 'power', bearing again on the human species's relation to the rest of nature, and I shall follow him in this preference. This meaning focuses on the fact that from very early on (see for instance the myth of Prometheus, the hero who stole fire from the gods of Olympus) the human intervention in nature takes the form of gathering, controlling and deploying natural energies; here, power in a sense becomes the human ability to turn nature against itself (by burning bits of it, in Prometheus's case) in order to make it serve human interests. The energies in question are to begin with those built into the human skeleton and musculature by nature; but they go on to encompass the calorific energy of plants and trees, the motorial energy of animals, and so forth. This energy-focused concept of power has been developed by Richard Adams.[8] It is apparently straight-forward, but it has some interesting implications, bearing on a broad theme I shall repeatedly emphasize in this book – the contradictions and dilemmas attendant upon power, in *all* its manifestations.

Gehlen, for instance,[9] points out that over the millennia, as the prime energy forms stored and deployed by humans developed from their own muscular energy all the way to nuclear energy, this progression in the absolute amount of natural power at the service of human beings was accompanied by their increasing intellectual and emotional estrangement from the sources of such power. The more the progression advances, the less we understand its successive objects, at any rate in the sense of being empathetically aware of what is going on as we put each new energy source to use, and the less we can plausibly take a caring and nurturing attitude toward it. Thus, for instance, we have a less keen sense of what goes on when we burn fossil fuels than when we burn wood; and our ability to comprehend, and thus to control, nuclear energy rests on exceedingly sophisticated and abstract knowledge of natural processes very remote from intuitive understanding, which relatively few people can master intellectually, and with which probably nobody can empathize.

Rosinski, whose sustained concern with what I have called the dilemmas and contradictions of the power phenomenon largely inspires my own, focuses it specifically on power as a critical feature of the relationship between human beings and nature, and particularly, again, on the storage and deployment of natural energies. Integrated by additional consider-ations, his treatment of this topic can be summarized as follows.

Dilemmas and contradictions of power in general

In the first place, the accumulation of power tends to become an end to itself. For a familiar example, let me invite the reader to look at me right now, at work (using the term loosely). The computer I am using is a superb machine, into which the makers have built what is by any standards a lot of power – the speed of the processor, the size of the memory, the complexity and sophistication of the operating system, the quantity and variety of the software it gives me access to. As it happens, however, I use the machine almost exclusively for word processing, and for this I need at most 20 per cent of its speed (I know this because that was the processor speed in the first computer I used, which performed quite efficiently exactly the same operations); besides, I never have any use for most of the bells and whistles of my fancy word processing package, let alone the rest of the available applications. Thus a lot of the machine's power is useless to me, as I suspect it would be to the great majority of other users; yet I long nursed a passionate desire for this machine, having previously learned to despise and to feel humiliated by my previous one, despite its adequacy for my needs; and I am desperate to acquire a still more powerful one, which I will buy as soon as I can afford it. I have, in other terms, become hooked on power. The design of my car, the number of electrical plugs around my house and of the attendant gadgets, my yearly expense for fuels of various kinds, testify to the same fact; and the same things can probably be said, quite plausibly, of my reader.

In the second place, in most cases the accumulation of power (still meaning here the storing of deployable natural energy) entails dangers, many of them directly related and (at least) proportionate to its uses. Consider here the case of a character from one of James Thurber's stories, which I read long ago and which unfortunately I have been unable to locate. The character is one of Thurber's numerous eccentric relatives, an uncle – a total recluse, but obviously a man of genius, for during his years of isolation, thinking and tinkering away in his attic, without any communication with the outside world, he has invented all manner of wondrous things, beginning with the wheel. As the uncle's lonely, relentless search for scientific and technical advance veers in the direction of chemistry, his admiring and devoted relatives become very anxious; and rightly so, because at the end of the story he turns his hand to developing explosives, and blows himself up.

Let me stop playing with homely examples – real or fictional – and remind readers of the wreck of the *Torrey Canyon* tanker and the ensuing ecological disaster of 1967, or the Chernobyl disaster of 1986. What is at work is in each case a redoubtable 'fix' which, with reference to social power arrangements, Cicero sharply pointed out in a discussion of a Roman magistracy, the tribunate. He wrote: 'I would say that there is something evil inherent in this magistracy; however, without such evil it would not be possible for us to benefit from what is good about it.'[10] Possibly echoing this source, Rosinski writes, in a passage encompassing both power over nature and social power: 'All power, all capacity to exercise effort and to influence the course of events, is by nature ambiguous, "open", and neutral or indeterminate in its implications. Were it not equally potent for good or for evil, it would not be power at all.'[11]

A closely related point is that power accumulations, whatever their positive significance, have negative side-effects. Our awareness of this third aspect of the power phenomenon has been much increased over the last few decades, but the intensity and visibility of the damage inflicted on the environment by human artefacts tended to increase our hold upon natural resources. Over the last few decades, the Three Mile Island incident, for instance, or the wreck of the *Exxon Valdez* tanker, have made this point most dramatically; but this same point is implicit also in the slower, more insidious impact that (as we have become aware) large dams have upon their natural settings, by destroying the habitats of animal and vegetable species, and sometimes by unbalancing irreversibly the geological structure itself of the environment. In 1963 both this point and the previous one were evidenced by what happened in a locality in the Italian Alps. Over the years, the building and subsequently the existence itself of a big hydroelectric dam had set in motion slow, hidden geological shifts which suddenly resulted in a huge landslide down the side of a mountain. As a gigantic mass of rock toppled into the artificial lake formed by the dam, a large quantity of the lake's water overflowed the dam's rim and instantly poured into the valley below, where it destroyed a village, Longarone. The dam in fact held (if it had not, the damage would have been immeasurably more severe) but both the environmental danger represented by the power accumulation upstream and the irreversible erosion of the dam's setting were strikingly demonstrated. The current Chinese plans for damming up the Yangtze river hold promise of further such damages, multiplied tenfold.

A further point barely needs mention. Power over nature generates dependency; the more a human group invests in mastering the resources of its natural environment, and the more it counts on them to satisfy its needs, the greater the stake it acquires in the maintenance of those arrangements and the greater the damage it can suffer from their disruption. The American historian McNeill makes this point in an essay where he notes that during the twentieth century American agriculture reached spectacular levels of mechanization that made it outstandingly productive by world standards.[12] This productivity, in turn, allowed most of the settled rural population in the US to escape from the position of social and economic inferiority and of cultural isolation in which almost everywhere, even in the late twentieth century, country-dwellers stood in relation to town-dwellers. McNeill rounds up the essay, however, by noting that this American success story is largely based on the lavish employment of gas- and diesel oil-fuelled engines and machines, and for the same reason it could be instantly jeopardized – to the disadvantage, of course, not just of the rural population but also that of the cities – if those fuels became unavailable or prohibitively expensive.

Finally, the natural capacities of human individuals became fixed into a stable biological template many thousands of years ago, whereas over the same span our power (in the sense of the term assumed so far) has accumulated enormously. As a result, there is often an increasingly poor correlation between, say, our basically unchanging perceptual and motor skills and that power build-up; the former can no longer reliably control and direct the latter. Consider the following trite example. Some forty years ago, a number of countries allowed individuals to drive without a licence motorcycles, scooters or mopeds whose engine displacement was no more than, say, 75 cubic centimetres; the reason was that at that date a two-wheeler with an engine below that capacity could not exceed a speed considered safe. Since that time, however, those small engines have been technically improved, and can now easily exceed such a speed. As a consequence, in countries where appropriate changes were not made in the rules, untrained, often very young drivers can legally put themselves in charge (but alas not necessarily in command!) of increasingly powerful and dangerous machines.

This example may be misleading, for sometimes the human capacity to learn new skills does, to a mystifying extent, keep up with new technology. For instance, people of my generation are baffled by the ease with which their grandchildren master the demanding motor and perceptual skills and the intellectual competences required, say, to handle electronic devices, from video recorders to computers and video games. For all that, the title of a book by Gehlen, *Urmensch und Spätkultur* (which I would translate somewhat freely as 'Immature man and overripe culture')[13] seems to me to convey a plausible (though not universally valid) intuition, which of course other authors have formulated otherwise. In the context of our argument, that intuition may perhaps be phrased, in the old-fashioned, 'sexist' way, as 'man empowered is man endangered'. (This, it occurs to me, may be the deeper message of an apparently shallow Italian proverb 'Uomo a cavallo, sepoltura aperta', that is, 'man on horse, grave agape'.)

Let us return to Rosinski, from whose argument the one above has to some extent distanced itself. According to him, the vagaries and pitfalls of the human species's inescapable recourse to power in dealing with nature bespeak a more general quandary. That is, power has a *subjective* aspect, represented by the extent to which it assists the effort of individuals to realize their interests, the most general and compelling of which is nothing less than their physical survival; but unavoidably it has also an *objective* aspect.

> The unique character of reality as the realisation of subjective powers of every kind is not its only aspect. . . . Reality – and power – also have another side. Reality at any given time is not simply the end product of a process of realisation. . . . In addition . . . power stands as realised, established, objectified power, ready to exert its own influence. . . . As a unique part of reality, [such an] 'established fact' exercises an influence. . . . [It] can offer resistance to any effort to dislodge it. . . . The things that man creates become objectified as established facts which thereupon begin to exercise a power of their own.[14]

Ordinarily, Rosinski suggests, this is an unintended process. 'In the overwhelming majority of cases, man simply creates the things he needs and desires without giving any thought to the objective power they are bound to exercise.'[15] In advanced industrial society, however, that objective power becomes overwhelming, due to the complexity of human products and arrangements and the extent to which these are saturated with energy. At this point it increasingly frustrates purposeful human activity, and comes to represent, from the human standpoint, not so much power as 'counterpower'. It may also begin to threaten the very survival of the human species. In the face of this development,

> [w]e cannot continue to increase our power blindly and still hope to escape, somehow, the inevitable consequences of our own blindness. We must come to recognise . . . that all creation of power must henceforth become a two-sided process . . . in which the responsible recognition and control of power goes hand in hand with its creation.[16]

Social power

This argument does not apply only to the particular manifestation of power constituted by the storage and deployment of natural energies by humans. In fact, as Rosinski formulates it, the argument also addresses another phenomenon with which this book is much more closely concerned – social power. This is power pertaining not to the relationship between human beings and nature, but to that between human beings: power implicated in the arrangements through which human groups constitute themselves, structure the relations between their constituent parts, deal with one another.

Why is there such a phenomenon as social power? Recall our preliminary understanding of power in the broadest sense, as the distinctive human ability to make a difference to natural circumstances of the species. In the light of that understanding, social power should be thought of as the ability to make a difference to the making of differences; were it not a poor pun, one might say that social power is power to the power of two. Luhmann phrases this point as follows, in a text where 'power' means what is meant here by 'social power': 'The person subject to power is envisaged as someone who selects his own action and to that extent is capable of self-determination. On this very account [someone else] employs against him means of power – threats, for instance – in order to control the choice he makes.'[17]

By the same token, those 'dilemmas and contradictions' of power we have considered previously (with some assistance from Rosinski's book) in our discussion of a primordial manifestation of it – power as accumulated and deployable natural energy – reappear compounded in any serious analysis of social power. In so far as power relations necessarily throw upon one another primary and secondary difference-makers (as it were), some tough problems unavoidably emerge: *who gets what?* whose interests are chiefly served by the power connection existing between the two parties? to what extent does the organizational machinery establishing that connection become an end in itself? Long ago Robert Michels's master-piece, *Political Parties*, demonstrated how serious these problems are, even (paradoxically) in voluntary organizations purportedly expressly con-structed to benefit their rank and file.[18]

We may rephrase these and related dilemmas by applying Rosinski's vocabulary to social power relations in general. Here, one party's 'subjec-tive' power becomes embodied and objectified in institutional arrangements allowing it to activate and control the other's activities. But this particular form of 'objective' power does not only display the same inherent danger-ousness and the same inertial qualities as *natural* power; it may also come to reflect the subjective strategies of the *other* party. For the latter may seek to resist too large an intrusion upon its own freedom of action and what appears to it an abuse of its own capacity for action and a neglect of its own interests. It may even attempt to subvert the power relationship to its own advantage: 'Ôte-toi que je m'y mette!'[19] What appears to one end of the relationship as the inertia of objective power may express the recalcitrance and cussedness of the other end, and thus represent for it a quantum of subjective power. This is perhaps an application to the realm of social power of the so-called 'double contingency' characterizing all social interaction according to Parsons. Max Weber's view that resistance is at least potentially inherent in power relations, according to a definition I shall recall later, may also point to that possibility.

A further complication of social power relations, present only marginally in the context of human power over nature, lies in the fact that such relations can be 'reflexively applied to themselves', to use Luhmann's formulation.[20] That is: if the social power holder is in the business of making a difference to the differences another party makes, then a further party yet may in turn make a difference to how the first party conducts its business, and so on. This happens in a particularly elaborate fashion within multilayered political and administrative systems, which for that very reason we often visualize as pyramidal in shape. Needless to say, this arrangement does not necessarily add to the quantity of power actually available in the system (however you measure that quantity); for it may also multiply the opportunities for power dispersion, resistance, even subversion.[21]

What most distinguishes social power from natural power, however, is the former's intrinsic artificiality, which engenders specific problems. Social power does not manifest itself with the same necessity as does power over nature. Above, we have construed power over nature as an unavoidable response to the poor correlation between the natural equipment of the human species and the requirements of its physical survival. To that extent, in spite of the hubris it betrays, the Cartesian view that 'l'homme est maître et possesseur de la nature' is a tenable (though contestable) contribution to philosophical anthropology. It constitutes a plausible elaboration of the apparent fact that man and nature do not lie on the same plane, for the former is structured differently from all other parts of nature, and can seemingly sustain his own existence only by 'mastering and possessing' those. But we would hardly consider it plausible for someone to define 'man' as 'maître et possesseur de l'homme'. True, on the face of it Hobbes's ghastly formula, 'Homo homini lupus' ('Man is a wolf to man'), may seem to come close to such a characterization. In fact, even that formula implies instead a primary equality between its referents – Person 1, as it were, and Person 2 are equal in constituting a deathly threat to one another. (Leave aside the fact that the formula is defamatory to the reputation of the wolf.)

Against the background of such equality, the emergence of social power becomes something of an ethical contradiction. In a social power relation, I have suggested, an individual avails himself of the ability that that individual possesses to make a difference *qua* human, in order to control the ability to make a difference that another individual possesses *qua* human. As Simmel says, the typical power holder does not want to suppress the power subject's subjectivity and freedom, but rather wants them to 'act back upon himself'.[22]

The well-known Jesuit and Prussian formulas according to which the superior demands the subordinate to obey 'like a cadaver' are both, on the face of them, nonsensical; you want the person subject to your power to be very much *unlike* a cadaver – to be a sentient, active human much like yourself. In other words, as Person 1 considers Person 2, Person 1 is bound to see in Person 2 first and foremost 'son semblable, son frère'; yet for that very reason Person 1 seeks to treat Person 2 as inferior. Thus, the establishment of a power relation between the two is tantamount to Person 1 excluding Person 2 from the reciprocity to which Person 2 is obviously entitled. While discussing political power, we shall consider some ways in which this ethical contradiction is confronted.

The grounding of social power in asymmetries

Let us return to the nature of social power. The characterization of it that I have suggested so far (power as someone's ability to make a difference to the differences others make) is excessively generic, for it can be achieved in too many different ways: for instance by sharing one's knowledge (or for that matter ignorance!) with others; by evoking their admiration; by performing feats that others will spontaneously imitate because they consider them exemplary; by exchanging the product of one's own autonomous activities for the product of the activities others carry out according to one's directions; and so forth.

According to a majority of the less generic conceptions of power, a social power relationship between two parties involves a particular asymmetry between them: one party has the upper hand, for it is able to make the other's resistance to its own directives too costly, and can thus dissuade the other from resistance or compel it to desist from it. In other terms, a social power relationship requires that one of the two parties be in a better position to punish and deprive the other – *if necessary.*

According to this last statement – 'if necessary' – relations of social power always entail an explicit or implicit 'or else . . .'; but optimally this clause has its effects on the party under power without the 'else' having actually to take place. The officers of the Holy Roman Inquisition, for instance, were not supposed to put the accused to the torture without previously threatening them, first by describing to them the nature of the torture in question (*territio verbalis*), then – if necessary – by showing them the relative instruments (*territio realis*). Other systems of power generally have more delicate ways of hinting at what risks the power subject incurs by persisting in his or her recalcitrance – among other reasons, perhaps, because on the whole the risks involved are not quite as extreme.

Specifying the nature of social power by reference to processes such as threats, dissuasion, the blocking or overcoming of resistance, and the like, narrows down considerably the broader meaning of the concept, and attunes it to some of the resonances it has in everyday talk. More clearly when we speak of 'power politics' between states, somewhat less clearly when we call someone 'power-mad' or suggest that someone is engaged in 'power games', the expression 'power' generally suggests a situation where characteristically one party is able and willing, if necessary, to hurt and deprive the other in order to have its way with it. Whether the other party, assuming that it finds the current situation irksome, seeks to modify it to its own advantage or indeed to subvert it, depends largely on how it assesses the present and future costs and benefits of it, on whether it has experienced or can plausibly project alternative circumstances, on what it expects to happen if it challenged the existing ones.

The common use of 'power' also implies an aspect of the phenomenon I have tried to convey by using frequently, above, the expression 'ability'. This aspect is conveyed particularly clearly in some Romance languages, where the expressions *potere* (Italian), *pouvoir* (French), *poder* (Spanish) refer both to a noun (meaning 'power') and to a verb (meaning 'to be able to'). What this correspondence suggests is that to *have* power is tantamount to *being in a position to* do something. As Coser writes: 'Power refers to the *capacity* to exercise control over others. The power of a superior in an organisation rests on his ability to hire and fire employees, even though he may not have done so over a long period of time.'[23] (This reminds me of a story concerning *Time* magazine. During one presidential election a number of liberal-minded journalists were beginning to oppose the pro-Republican line pushed by the chief editor, Henry Luce. The latter called a meeting at which he introduced himself as follows: 'I am Henry Luce. I hire and fire around here. Any questions?' There were none.)

We may express this point by speaking, as has been done, of power's intrinsic 'potentiality', an expression that in turn makes more explicit a noteworthy aspect of the phenomenon than the expression 'power' itself does. That is: power has to do with the future, with expectations, with hopes and fears. In this sense, too, it has 'anthropological' significance, at any rate if Hobbes was right in saying that humans alone, among animals, can feel tomorrow's hunger today. We can think of power (both power in general and social power in particular) as a way of confronting and controlling the inexorable sense of contingency and insecurity generated by our awareness of the future. This awareness – we have learned in the last few decades from scholarship on the social dimensions of time – is once more a generic property, which expresses itself in very varied forms from culture to culture. However, no matter how it expresses itself, it adds significance, as I have just suggested, to the potentiality intrinsic in the notion of power. One gains some purchase on the vagaries of unfolding time in so far as one is blessed *now* with the ability to do something in the *future*.

What the power holder can do, in turn, encompasses the issuing of credible threats toward its counterpart and if necessary the inflicting of pain or deprivation upon it, but normally does not limit itself to that. The playground bully who continually boasts about his ability to hurt other children does so in order to exact various acts of compliance from them: handing over their sweets, speaking respectfully to him, and so forth. The state's distinctive ability to have people gaoled or executed on its officials' say-so empowers it to do any manner of things, from imposing taxes to recruiting soldiers, monopolizing lucrative trades or establishing literary academies.

In any case, social power should not be thought of as a substance one has, but as a more abstract matter, a facility of which one can avail oneself. This view (which one may contrast both with Hobbes's definition of power as 'a man's present means to any future apparent good' or with Bertrand Russell's as 'the production of intended effects') is sometimes fancily expressed by categorizing power as 'a dispositional concept'. A concept of this kind, for instance 'combustibility', applies to an entity by virtue not of properties it continually exhibits but of contingent effects it can be expected to produce under certain circumstances. 'Keep your powder dry' suggests that if you do it will, when sparked, propel your bullet; if you do not, it will not cease to be powder, but it will very likely fizzle out. Both the potentiality of power, and the dispositional nature of its concept, suggest that power *has to do with the future.*

Max Weber's understanding of social power reaffirmed

The abstractness of the concept results also from the consideration that social power exists in so far as two parties stand in a certain relationship to one another; it is, indeed, an aspect of that relationship, not something that either party possesses (or is deprived of) in isolation from the other. Two famous, overlapping definitions of power formulated by Max Weber a few years apart both convey (in the passages below) this 'relational' nature of the phenomenon. Note, furthermore, that in both definitions the term 'chance', which I translate as 'probability', suggests its 'dispositional' nature:

> By 'power' we mean, quite generally, an individual's or a group's probability of realizing its will *in the context of collective activity* even against the resistance of others *involved in it.*

> Power is the probability, *within a social relationship*, of realizing one's own will even against resistance, regardless of the basis on which this probability rests.[24]

Both of Weber's definitions are somewhat bloody-minded, and on that account too narrow. From the standpoint of the power holder, 'others' appear exclusively in the capacity of potential resisters. It is not indicated (except somewhat implicitly in the expressions I have emphasized) that often their activities are expected positively to assist in the implementation of the power holder's will, rather than being relevant to it only as potential obstacles. Put otherwise, social power should be thought of as the capacity for one party to cause another to act in certain ways, which *include* abstaining or desisting from opposing the former party's preferences but may go beyond such abstaining and desisting. Weber himself, at one point, cursorily characterizes power as 'the possibility of imposing one's will upon the conduct of others'.[25] The bloody-minded tone remains, but there is implicit recognition that you may get others to do otherwise than 'ceasing and desisting' from opposing you.

On the other hand, even when it does occur that the second party positively assists in fulfilling the first party's preferences, this does not mean that the resultant action necessarily corresponds with the interests of *both* parties, much less that it corresponds with those interests *to the same extent*. As I have already indicated, even in well-established power relations 'who gets what', or to what extent the interests of both parties are served, is intrinsically an open issue, not to be settled by definition, as Parsons tried to settle it in a statement about power we shall consider later.

Whereas Parsons sought to improve on Weber's definition 'from the right', as it were, by de-emphasizing the asymmetry that the power phenomenon in my view necessarily involves, later writers have criticized it 'from the left'. By emphasizing the actual or potential clash between opposing preferences as the issue the resolution of which points up who is in power, Weber allegedly had neglected the extent to which power relations are embodied in apparently unproblematical, unchallengeable structures. Power works primarily through the muted, routine workings of such structures, which systematically favour the interests of one party, not by that party's assertion of its superiority in episodic confrontations. The other party's perceptions and understandings, its preferences themselves, are largely the products of such workings of power, and to that extent offer no grounds on which resistance may be realistically expected to arise. One may see a sophisticated variant of such a broad view of power in Michel Foucault's construction of it, which overlaps power widely with such phenomena as 'knowledge' and 'discourse', though it does not necessarily confuse it with either.

My chief objection to this critique of Weber and related definitions of power is that by detaching conceptually 'power' from 'agency', by merging the former into 'structure', it impoverishes the conceptual resources of social theory. Let me introduce a grammatical parallel. Ancient Greek had two very distinct forms of past tense: the perfect, referring to something that had happened in the past but which in a sense continued in the present; and the aorist, describing one-off actions which occurred in the past but broke its continuity. (Archimedes, on this account, must have forgotten his grammar in the excitement of his great discovery, for in announcing it he should have used the aoristic form *euron* rather than the perfective form *eureka*). Now, modern social theory has a deterministic bias which expresses itself through the preponderance of conceptual aids to description and explanation of a *perfective* nature – such as 'situation', 'structure', 'role', 'institution', 'norm'. Whatever the flaws of Weber's definitions, they present us with a concept of (social) power which has instead an *aoristic* bias; it focuses on the unblocking of situations and the constituting of new situations, rather than the unperturbed continuation of established arrangements. It thus suits my own preference, indicated from the beginning of this chapter, for seeing the making of differences as the core of the power phenomenon.

I shall close the chapter by reluctantly attempting a definition. Social power relations exist wherever some human subjects (individual or collective) are able to lay routine, enforceable boundaries upon the activities of other human subjects (individual or collective), in so far as that ability rests on the former subjects' control over resources allowing them, if they so choose, to deprive the latter subjects of salient human values. The chief among such values are bodily integrity; freedom from restraint, danger or pain; reliable access to nourishment, shelter or other primary material goods; the enjoyment of a degree of assurance of one's worth and significance.

The next chapter elaborates this last statement.

2

Power Forms

The power advantage

If it is conceived as suggested in the previous chapter, social power is definitely a good thing to have, *in so far as* those who do not have power over others are likely to be subjected to others' power over themselves – and that 'in so far as' clause is likely to obtain under nearly all conceivable conditions, no man being 'an Island entire of it self'. Unavoidably, individuals have to take each other into account, and reckon (among other things) with the numberless possibilities there are for them to cherish, support, please, succour, assist, disappoint, vex, frustrate, diminish, humiliate, hurt, torment and destroy one another. In view of this, it behoves individuals to seek to increase their own freedom of action and limit that of others, by establishing and gaining access to social power arrangements which vest in them the ability to lay boundaries on others' activities, and deny that ability to others.

In the light of this, it is not *only* the concept of power that is essentially contested; it is social power itself, which, by structuring asymmetrically the relations between individuals or groups, unavoidably poses the problem of which individuals or groups will be in power over which. I think Humpty Dumpty had it about right when he sourly instructed Alice that, even when it comes to the meaning of words, 'The question is ... which is to be master – that's all'.

There are of course other relevant questions concerning power; for instance how, once more or less stably vested, it is going to be exercised; or whether, once vested and exercised, power may assist the pursuit of interests common to both ends of the relationship, asymmetrically structured as it may be. Yet Humpty Dumpty raises, I think, a prior problem: how is social power acquired by some, and how are others excluded from it and indeed subjected to the power of the former?

I will turn again to Max Weber for what still is, I think, a conceptually valuable solution to that problem. First, let us reconsider a definition I introduced previously: 'Power is the probability, within a social relationship, of realizing one's own even against resistance, *regardless of the basis on which this probability rests*.' Here I am chiefly interested in the passage I emphasize, which suggests a few elementary considerations.

First, the probability in question is not assigned to actors at random, much less bestowed upon some of them for the asking. In order to acquire power and exercise it, some actors must avail themselves of some resources inaccessible to others. Second, these resources must be such that their possession would allow those actors, if confronted with the resistance of others, to override it. Third, although for the purposes of a general definition of power it is immaterial which specific resources are decisive, different ones may be decisive in different circumstances and for different purposes. As Lewis Coser writes:

> The resources that can be turned into power are varied. They may involve control over financial means or over means of coercion. They may consist in privileged access to knowledge or the monopoly of access to circles of persons possessing superior power. They may flow from privileged commerce with sacred beings or from magical abilities. They may stem from the ownership or control over means of production or over means of distribution.[1]

Finally, a consideration of those resources may allow us to differentiate the concept of social power, to distinguish the most significant forms of it.

This last point, admittedly, is not directly evinced from this text. But there are innumerable other texts that make it, in Weber's writings and in countless other sources. There is even a curious Neapolitan proverb, for which I have no source other than a recollection of my mother's quoting it: 'Chillo è putèntë: u' papa, u' re e chi nun tëne niente' – 'These are powerful: the pope, the king, and one who has nothing.' (I will not elaborate on the final, provoking insight, for alas it goes against the grain of arguments I seek to make later.)

Weber himself remarked on the 'amorphousness' of the power concept,[2] and on that account did not use it much. Instead, on the one hand he emphasized the related but considerably narrower concept of *Herrschaft*, generally translated as 'domination'; on the other he acknowledged the existence of distinct forms of social power, and wrote at length on how they emerged and how they interacted with one another. On this last account, his writings will constitute a major source for what I am trying to say in this book. But they do not contain as explicit and diffuse an account as one could wish of the specific conceptual problem I am raising here. That is: if we seek to differentiate forms of social power by referring to the different 'bases' of it, how many forms should we come up with?

Three basic power forms

A second quotation from Weber provides some key components of the answer I would like to develop here. It consists in the opening sentence of one of his most famous texts, 'Classes, status groups and parties'. The sentence states: 'Classes, status groups and parties are phenomena of the distribution of power within a collectivity.'[3]

This text has been put to much use in deriving from Weber, as one generally says, a *multi*-dimensional view of stratification, and contrasting it with Marx's *one*-dimensional view. Although not all renderings of this particular aspect of the hoary old 'Marx vs. Weber' question are equally valid and enlightening, that contrast is undeniable, as one sees instantly by comparing Weber's opening sentence quoted above with that of *The Communist Manifesto*, 'All history hitherto is the history of the class struggle.' However, usually discussions of 'Classes, status groups and parties' do not make much, if anything, of the fact that Weber's sentence treats those terms, each referring to a different kind of stratification unit, as aspects of 'the distribution of power within a collectivity'. Thus, the fact that Weber saw social power and stratification as very closely related, and indeed attributed to the former some conceptual priority over the latter (for he considers classes and so on as phenomena of the division of power rather than vice versa) has attracted little interest on the part of students of both phenomena.

What follows is not as a Weberological exercise intended to remedy such neglect, much less to revisit one aspect of the Marx vs. Weber issue. My sole concern here, as I have indicated, is seriously to absorb the content of Weber's first sentence in 'Classes, status groups and parties', and put it to use in a conceptual derivation of the chief forms of social power.

Let me begin, however, with a reference to a very different source, 'Some principles of stratification' by Davis and Moore. According to this famously controversial essay, the theory of stratification has as its object the distribution of rewards among actors within a social unit. Given the diversity between the positions making up a society's division of labour, and between the skills they require,

> it does make a great deal of difference who gets into which position. . . . Inevitably, then, a society must have, first, some kind of rewards that it can use as inducements, and, second, some way of distributing these rewards according to positions. The rewards and their distribution become a part of the social order, and thus give rise to stratification.[4]

Now, Weber's reference to social power in the first sentence of 'Classes, status groups and parties' suggests (to myself at any rate) that Davis and Moore have got it all wrong. For Weber the phenomenon of stratification, although of course it eventuates in the unequal distribution of *rewards*, has to do in the first place with the unequal distribution of *facilities*. These are resources significant primarily not because, like rewards, they can directly satisfy various human needs, but because of the use to which they can be put in *controlling* the distribution of rewards; or, to reintroduce an expression from my first chapter, because of their use in *making a difference* as to who gets what reward (if any). *Qua* 'phenomena of the distribution of power', classes, status groups and parties constitute themselves *upstream*, as it were, of the final destination of rewards; they control their *downstream* flow. Although some of Weber's own texts suggest otherwise, for him the differences between class, status group and party have to do not so much with what kinds of rewards each type of stratification unit primarily enjoys, as with the distinctive resources each type brings to bear on the distribution of *any* rewards; or, of course, with the distinctive resources each *lacks*.[5]

What are those distinctive resources, corresponding (if the current argument has any merit) with the different forms of social power? To answer this question we must go beyond Weber's argument, and consider three fundamentally different ways in which, within any society, rewards of any kind are allocated between individuals or groupings. A society's 'goods', or indeed its 'bads' (so to speak) can be allocated:

- through custom. That is, access to or exclusion from all or some of those 'goods' and 'bads' is bestowed or imposed on the basis of a diffuse, culturally prescribed understanding of what personal qualities and social positions a person embodies that *intrinsically deserve* to be so rewarded or punished. Put briefly, with custom allocation what one gets depends on what one *represents* for others;
- through exchange. In this case, the society's 'goods' and 'bads' circulate among its component units on the basis of what each unit, in dealing with others, can offer them from what it has (if anything) in return for what it lacks and desires. Put briefly, with exchange allocation what one gets depends on what one *has* or on what one can do *for* others;
- through command. In this case a society's 'goods' and 'bads' are shifted around on the say-so of a unit which can enforce its preferences on others by threatening them with punishment if they do not dispossess themselves of some of their goods or do not subject themselves to a disproportionate share of the society's 'bads'. Put briefly, with command allocation what one gets depends on what one can do *to* others.

Given each mode of allocation, the possession of or exclusion from a different kind of resource becomes critical, and grounds the emergence of a different kind of stratification unit. Where custom is the prevalent mode, we may call the critical resource 'status'. This consists in the extent to which given individuals possess intrinsically valuable attributes, those that the group's culture places at the very centre of its construction of reality, and which impart order and significance to it. A favoured 'status group' is constituted by those individuals who do possess such attributes, and a disfavoured one by those deprived of them, since the former have a prior claim to the society's rewards, and the latter must take at best second place. We may label as 'ideological / normative power' the form of social power at stake here, for ultimately it rests on shared understandings of what is true and proper.

Where exchange is the prevalent mode, we may call the critical resource 'wealth'. This is a store of possessions, of things at their disposal, on which individuals can draw in order to obtain from others, in return for them, things or services they desire but do not yet possess. Thus, exchange allocation favours those who have at their disposal a *large* store of things, and optimally one that is continually replenished through the activities of those deprived of wealth, and who on that account must work on behalf and to the advantage of the wealthy. We may call 'classes' the groupings formed by individuals who respectively do and do not have access to what in a given society constitutes the chief form of wealth. The possession of wealth constitutes the chief form of economic power, which expresses itself through a circuit of acts of exchange (typically, *market* transactions), and affects in the first place the production and reproduction of the society's material resources.

Where command is the prevalent form of allocation, we may call the critical resource 'rulership'. This is an individual's or a group's ability to make enforceable arrangements and issue orders as to who should have access to the society's goods or be deprived of them, or shoulder its burdens. Typically, the enforcement involves the threat or execution of severe punishments against those opposing the arrangements or evading the orders in question. We may call 'party' (in a very wide meaning of the term – wider perhaps than Weber's own meaning) the grouping constituted by those individuals who in a given society may to a more or less similar extent determine the content of those arrangements and orders and / or the making and execution of serious threats against others. Access to rulership (and through it to the determination of what counts as policy within the collectivity) is the principal stake of a third basic form of social power, 'political power'.

Thus understood, Weber's characterization of significant stratification units (status groups, classes, parties) reflects what he calls 'the multiplicity of power forms'.[6] Each kind of unit typically aligns individuals who share the possession of (or the lack of) a distinctive power form, centrally relevant in turn for the purposes of a different allocation process. This derivation of a basic trinity of social power forms (again: normative / ideological; economic; political) is confirmed, as I have already indicated, by numerous other tripartitions from very diverse sources, which of course vary (among other things) in their terminology. Some of these expressly anchor the power trinity in some other phenomenon (as *I* have tried to do with the allocation process).

For instance, the German sociologist Karl Otto Hondrich grounds his tripartition of political, economic and normative power on the distinction between different kinds of means to the satisfaction of human needs: physical, material and psychological means respectively.[7] (One may put to non-Marxist use a characteristically Marxian expression, and speak of 'means of production, persuasion and coercion'). Other authors, instead, *imply* a similar tripartition while expressly conceptualizing other ones. Heinrich Popitz, for instance, distinguishes three kinds of 'power actions' on the basis of the kind of damage they can inflict: 'They consist in actions which diminish others' social participation and social integrity, produce material disadvantage, or bodily damage. There can of course be overlaps (being branded with a hot iron, for instance, is both a form of bodily damage and a mark of social discrimination) but normally it is possible to identify one central aspect.'[8]

The tripartition of power forms is also imaginatively projected by the title of a recent book by Ernest Gellner, *Plough, Sword, and Book*.[9] Furthermore, one can derive it, somewhat indirectly, from a passage of *Die Religion innerhalb der Grenzen der blößen Vernunft*, where Kant discusses the 'hostile dispositions' men have towards one another, and names expressly three: *Herrschsucht, Habsucht* and *Neid*.[10] The correspondence between the first two (seeking to rule and seeking possessions) and political and economic power respectively is obvious; somewhat less so, but still plausible, is the correspondence between *Neid* (envy) and ideological / normative power, if by envy one means a passion for 'standing out', expressed negatively as the ill-feeling of those who do not stand out towards those who do. Finally, it has been suggested that three tragedies by Christopher Marlowe, *Tamburlaine, The Jew of Malta* and *Dr Faustus*, chiefly deal, respectively, with political, economic and ideological / normative power.

Other tripartitions, instead, concern themselves expressly with the power concept. For instance, the Italian legal and political theorist Norberto Bobbio writes (I translate somewhat freely):

> We may classify various forms of power by reference to the facilities the active subject employs in order to lay boundaries around the conduct of the passive subject. . . . We can then distinguish three main classes of power: economic, ideological and political. Economic power avails itself of the possession of certain goods, rare or held to be rare, in order to lead those not possessing them to adopt a certain conduct, which generally consists in carrying out a certain form of labour. . . . Ideological power is based upon the fact that ideas of a certain nature, put abroad in a certain manner, may also exert an influence upon the conduct of associated individuals. . . . Political power, on the other hand, is grounded on the possession of facilities (weapons of all kinds and degrees of potency) by means of which physical violence may be exerted. It is coercive power in the strict sense of the term.[11]

Two things should be noted about the tripartition in question, in Bobbio's formulation or in others. In the first place, of course, it is no more (and no less) than a conceptual distinction, claiming no more purchase on ultimate reality than any other such distinctions, particularly within the social sciences. Although above I have derived it from a conceptually prior distinction, that between allocation processes, one might well wonder how *that* distinction is itself grounded: why should there be three and only three such processes?

In the second place, the reader should be warned that while I am committed to the notion that the basic forms of social power are the three discussed above, the way this book is organized conveys my *pragmatic* agreement with (as against my *principled* disagreement from) Mann's recent argument for a quadripartition of social power, juxtaposing to its political, normative / ideological and economic forms the military form. The reasons for both agreement and disagreement will be given in the next chapter, dealing with political power.

Contests over power(s)

Let us return, at this point, to my argument so far. A trinity of power forms mediates between, on the one hand, the three kinds of allocation processes, and, on the other hand, the three kinds of stratification units – status groups, classes and 'parties'. As I have indicated, status, wealth and rulership are the resources critical for shaping and controlling the allocation process when it takes place chiefly through custom, exchange and command respectively.

In other words, the nature of the allocation process *selects* the forms of social power most significant under different circumstances. To this extent, that process is like a card game in which, with each hand, a different suit may become trumps. But the analogy should not be taken too far. Usually, in a game of this kind, *which* suit is trumps in any given hand would not depend on how previous ones have gone, but is determined at random, or by the application of some rule of rotation. In no case does it depend on the outcome of a contest over 'trump-ness', as it were, between the various suits. In the allocation game, however, which power form is preponderant in a given hand depends *both* on how previous hands have gone *and* on how the other suits react to their previous lack of success. The results of past hands, as it were, place a lien on the current one; but, as this one unfolds, the lien is sometimes lifted as a result of contentions between the suits.

Why such contentions? As I said at the beginning, having social power is a good thing; but since it means that *someone* can exercise a leverage on his or her future by making a difference to *someone else*'s activity – and thus, *nota bene*, to that person's future – people will quarrel with one another over who's going to be someone, and who's going to be someone else. Not all people, though. Those more likely to quarrel will not be all who have a stake in the final outcome of the allocation process, the distribution of rewards – everybody has a stake in that – but those who have some power, that is, those who have some chance of influencing that process. But since that chance rests on the possession of some resource, they will quarrel in the first instance in order to establish that the resource in question should have prior influence; that it should (to return to the card game metaphor) *trump* the others.

There is a neat example of a quarrel of this kind in an episode from William Golding's *Lord of the Flies*, where the boys lost on the desert island discuss how to organize themselves in order to survive and await rescue. Each boy and each group of boys, it turns out, has an argument that justifies his or its demand for a maximum share of whatever there is to go around, based on the specific resources the boy or the group has.

Note that this is an example of a fairly civilized quarrel: at any rate for the time being, the contenders are *talking* over priorities, however narrowly the content of their arguments may be determined by the nature of their respective material resources. Sometimes, however, there is no public forum whose rules compel contenders to leave their resources at the door. Rather, the contenders slug it out: they bring to bear, as it were, the sheer cash value of their resources, and do not entrust their success in their quarrel to their ability to reason out a case for the greater significance of those resources.

This notion of a contest raging over 'what's trumps' may appear very abstract. Yet one may use the distinction between custom, command and command allocation, and the related one between status, wealth and rulership, in order to characterize concrete, and sometimes massive, social phenomena. The Australian sovietologist Harry Rigby, for instance, developed a sophisticated variant of the first distinction to conceptualize nothing less than the contrast between what used to be called the First and the Second World – a contrast around which much of twentieth-century history was played out.[12] In Rigby's argument, in the First World the chief mechanism that shaped society at large was the market – the prevalent locus, in our terminology, of exchange allocations – and the key premise of that mechanism was the existence of a plurality of individuals and organizations. These interacted with one another autonomously, each on its own behalf; and did so chiefly to guard and increase the respective accumulations of wealth. There was no such plurality of autonomous units in the societies characteristic of the Second World. These, instead, were each constituted as *one* gigantic organization, at the top of which one enormous accumulation of rulership power sought to steer the whole social process in its totality through innumerable acts of (in our terminology) command allocation.

While this example shows how the tripartite distinction might bear considerable weight, for certain purposes it must be elaborated further, by articulating its components into conceptual units at a lower level. Weber, for instance, does not only differ from Marx in juxtaposing status groups and parties to classes as the primary collective units of stratification. On the one hand, he agreed with Marx that 'class' is the appropriate concept to apply to inequalities of economic power, and that in the course of modernization the alignment of individuals into classes has become more significant than their alignment into status groups.

On the other hand, Weber proposed a concept of class at considerable variance from Marx's own (since it emphasized the relations individuals establish in the market rather than within the process of production), and one that suggested not only a dichotomous confrontation between owners and non-owners of the means but the existence of different *kinds* of classes, including those based on the possession (and possibly the monopoly) of valuable skills, and those (particularly significant in classical antiquity) constituted respectively by creditors and debtors. Furthermore, he emphasized the historical significance of the difference between the ownership of land and the ownership of commercial or industrial assets as the key economic resources – and the significance of the related conflicts. It is as if, to return to the metaphor of the card game, once it is settled which suit is trumps, the issue becomes which of the various *cards* of that suit could in turn trump the other cards. There can be, in other terms, power games within power games.

For another reason why the phenomenon of social power is inherently conflict-laden, reconsider the three resources on which the components of our tripartition are based. One should not only expect conflict *between* status, wealth and rulership over which of them should play the critical role in shaping society; but also conflict *around* each resource. Status pertains to a given individual or group to the extent that it is seen to lie at or near the centre of the culturally approved map of society. But this means that status is inherently invidious, that even groups equally committed to the critical significance of status will struggle with one another to position themselves toward the centre of that map, to increase the saliency of the values they identify with, the virtues they typically cultivate. Or – as with the so-called 'trickling-down of status symbols', a phenomenon studied primarily in the context of caste society – they will try to imitate the practices by which the more established status groups signal and assert their own advantage.

In the same way, wealth is bound to become the object of conflict not just because (as we have just seen) there are various kinds of wealth, each 'promoted', as it were, by a group in possession of it, but also because possessions are inherently scarce. In whatever specific class of possessions wealth may be embodied (this will change from situation to situation), people will struggle to increase their holdings of it at each other's expense. For instance, landed nobles will seek to outdo one another in seeking to increase their estates through conquest or through their marriage strategies; industrialists will do so by competing with one another; craftspeople by monopolizing skills and seeking to forbid the introduction of new productive techniques which may devalue those skills.

Relations of political power, as I shall emphasize below, make particularly irksome the asymmetry inherent in all power relations, for they often place very many individuals under the thumb of a very few, and find expression in particularly visible instruments and symbols – for instance the executioner's axe, the banner around which a nobleman expects his dependants to rally in battle, or the final notice from a state agency in charge of collecting taxes. Thus, rulership is particularly likely to be resented by those who have no hope of contesting it, and resisted or challenged by those who have accumulated some political resources of their own. Alternatively, these will seek to manage those resources more and

more autonomously, or at least to employ them in order to affect the
rulers' decisions that impinge on their own interests, to influence their
policies. Finally, distinct political power centres may contend with one
another about their territorial reach or over other significant stakes. The
folk view that 'history is all about kings and battles' is of course wrong-
headed; but it does point up the peculiarly visible and dramatic nature of
the political dimension of the power struggle.

The competitive building-up of distinctive power sources is not the only
kind of power conflict other than what we have called the struggle over
'trump-ness'. A further kind develops as each power form tries not so much
to eliminate or subordinate the others, as to complement itself with them,
to absorb them. It is as if the multiplicity of power forms were perceived
by each of them as an irksome and disturbing phenomenon, as a persistent
threat of disorder.

In response to this perception, a contest goes on between power forms
not so much over priority as, somewhat paradoxically, over the possibility
of transcending their diversity and their actual or potential contrast. In
principle, each power form is attracted by the prospect of itself doing the
unifying, on its own terms. But if it seeks to realize that prospect it may
have to confront the fact that, lo and behold, the very same thought had
occurred to another party, which also pursues it, but on *its own terms*.
Neither of the power forms involved seeks to suppress or sharply to
downgrade the other; it may be willing, indeed prefer, for it to survive and
prosper – as long as, of course, it does so as an aspect and an instrumentality of its own recognized superiority, within a unitary framework constructed around it. (As a sociological joke has it, 'Let's have some division
of labour around here! – *I* divide, *you* labour.') As we shall see later, for
centuries in the history of Christendom, conflicts of this nature marked the
relationship between church and empire or state.

What makes conflicts of this and other kinds more complex in their
structure, and more open-ended in their outcomes, is the fact that they may
involve more than two power forms at a time (or more than two power
centres within each form). The presence of actual or potential third parties
to a bilateral conflict encourages the formation of alliances between them.
These alter and sometimes subvert the power relations previously existing
between any two parties, and open up for one of them strategies it would
not have otherwise undertaken *vis-à-vis* the other one. For instance (at any
rate according to some conventional interpretations) the expropriation of
monasteries in England was the intended outcome of an implicit alliance
between royal power and the land-greedy economic power of the gentry, at
the expense of ecclesiastical power.

Furthermore – as observers of international conflict have long known –
alliances, like promises and piecrusts, are made to be broken; the very
shifts in the power balance an alliance produces may remove its *raison
d'être* and cause it to be abandoned, sometimes quickly and brazenly. The
complexities produced by such possibilities constitute one reason among

others why I shall not try, in what follows, to discuss systematically
triangular relationships between power forms. However, I will occasionally
remind the reader that the dealings of one form of them with another may
be affected by the presence of a third one.

What about the powerless?

Complex and varied as they are, these relations between forms (or
subforms) of social power do not exhaust the theme of power-related
conflict. While again this book will not systematically consider it, another
kind of conflict barely glimpsed so far plays a significant role. It concerns
not so much the contrasting interests of the holders of power in its various
forms, as the tensions arising from an obvious point, mentioned at the
beginning of this chapter: power means that *someone* can make a difference
to *someone else's* activity.

At any rate, in by far the majority of human societies it has been the case
that most of the population – let us call them 'the common people' – have
found themselves in the position of being *someone else* to all power holders.
This plain fact has two contrasting effects on the relations between the
holders of different power forms.

On the one hand, it constitutes a key reason for their rivalry: in most
circumstances, all forms revolve around the control of the activities of *the
same people*. The holders of ideological / normative, economic and / or
political power in the end all tap into the energies, the capacity for
submission, compliance, loyalty, commitment and forbearance, of the same
common people. This is potentially a cause for friction between the diverse
power holders, in terms both of quantity and of quality. First, those
energies and capacities can be variously increased and stretched, but in the
end they are necessarily limited: if one power overdraws on them, the other
must go short. Second, the content of the demands placed by the various
powers on the energies of those submitted to them, the nature of the
boundaries placed upon their conduct, may differ qualitatively to the point
of being incompatible. For instance, priests and monks may extol tradition
as the best guide to the common people's conduct, while military com-
manders and political leaders would like to induce them to undertake new
forms of activity. On both counts, different power forms may be placed at
loggerheads: the holders of each form feel that the holders of another are
overburdening the common people and pulling and pushing them in the
wrong direction.

On the other hand, even those condemned by their circumstances to
being and remaining *someone else* – even the common people – may gnaw
away at those circumstances one way or another,[13] and even try to subvert
them. They will manage the latter only *very* rarely;[14] but the possibility of
their even trying to do so occasionally, and the much greater likelihood of
their marginally reducing their submission and their impotence, make them

a kind of hidden but potentially troublesome party to the relations between powers of all kinds.

As a result, the holders of such powers, no matter how quarrelsome their relations, may share a sense of how frightful it would be if the common people – the *classes dangereuses*, the damned of the earth, the great unwashed, the mob, the masses, the lower orders, *them* – made an undiscriminating attack on *all* their diverse betters, as in that socialist song which looked forward to hanging the last capitalist boss with the entrails of the last priest. However, some power holders are often tempted to associate themselves with, or even to encourage and to lead, the onslaught of the lower orders against their own rivals; they assume that even a partial success in their attack will satisfy the lower orders' aspirations, exhaust their energies, spend their momentum. The balance between these different strategies will vary with the circumstances; but even the second one implicitly acknowledges the danger of a generalized attempt at subversion, although it discounts its probability.

In any case, however it impinges on our chief concern here – which we may envisage as the *horizontal* relations between different power forms – the tensions revolving around the *vertical* relations between any power holders and (so to speak) 'their' power-less are a noteworthy aspect of our general theme, if only to the extent that, when push comes to shove, it induces a kind of presumptive solidarity between power holders of all kinds.

Other considerations may point to further, more subtle restraints on rivalry between different power forms (and subforms). The presumptive solidarity between power holders I have just mentioned operates (if it does) via their perceptions and the resulting strategies. In the context where they are competing for control, suddenly the petty and lowly social element looms very large and threatening in the eyes of the powerful, who become aware of shared interests. On that account, a mechanism of *social* integration may come into play between different and potentially conflicting sets of people.

But there may also be in operation a different kind of integration (or for that matter conflict) which we may call *systemic*. This concerns not exclusively or directly the concrete human groups which at any given time control and manage, as it were, a given form of power, but the objective mutual bearing of the related processes. For example, there may be more to the relationship between religion and politics than the relation between church and state. Whatever the rivalry or the accommodation between the latter two, considered as distinctive sets of institutions, one may consider, for instance, whether the ways in which the religious experience is conceived and routinized in a given society are compatible or incompatible with the ways political experience is conceived and routinized. One may even ask: under what religious conditions is politics possible? – and vice versa.

I suggest that, in the systemic perspective, restraints upon power conflict come to the fore first, because the broadest hypothesis one can formulate from that perspective is the following: economic, ideological / normative and political power are differentiated expressions of one primordial phenomenon – let us call it power-at-large. The building up of each power form takes the form of its increasingly separate institutionalization, and this entails also the possibility of conflict between them; but, *for all that*, the process of institutionalization they separately undergo increases the total amount of power-at-large available in society as a whole.

This increase, as Rosinski suggests, may pose problems for that society; but it also means that, behind the backs of the conscious and self-conscious power actors, with their potential or actual contrasts, a kind of muted conspiracy exists. For instance, at least in some historical situations the development of money took place at the hands of the holders of economic power (traders in particular), without any assistance from the political authorities, and indeed as a way of circumventing those authorities' heavy-handed interference with landed wealth.[15] Yet, once money had emerged as a routine medium of economic operations, it assisted the building up of political power itself: by rationalizing the economic process and making it more productive, it made it possible for the political power holders to rationalize the political process in turn. It allowed rulers, for instance, to control their administrative officials from above by means of budgetary allocations and of monetary emoluments conditional upon those officials' efficient performance of their duties. It improved the provisioning of political agencies with resources by allowing those resources to be extracted from the society's economy in the form of money.

The upshot of this line of thinking, as far as our theme is concerned, is that there may be a tendency for power forms to enhance one another, and together to enhance society's power-at-large, irrespective of the conscious competitive *or* solidarity policies of the respective power holders. It is not part of the same line of thinking to assume that this process cannot go into reverse. In the above example, it may occur that for whatever reason (say, the exhaustion of the reserves of metal suitable for coinage) the position held within the economy by the money medium shrinks almost to nothing. In this case the system of rule in turn will have to forego the advantages it derived from extracting and allocating resources in that same medium.

However, this line of thinking often does overemphasize the spontaneity of the tendency it depicts – the tendency of various power forms to sustain each other, as well as the advantages society as a whole derives from the resulting enhancement of its power-at-large. In the next chapter, while dealing with political power, we shall consider some objections to that emphasis. In any case, a sustained consideration of the mutual effects of differentiated power forms not mediated through the consciousness of actors and their deliberate policies need not assume that those effects tend to be positive. On the contrary, in some phases and aspects of his work Marx made the point (not phrased, it must be noted, in terms of power) that between the various spheres of a differentiated society there may develop basic 'contradictions', which only that society's revolutionary transformation may overcome.

In any case, throughout most of this book I will emphasize those aspects of its theme that arise from the express confrontation and accommodation between the holders of various forms of social power. Thus, most of what follows concerns the policies of more or less well-established elites, whose dealings with one another engender shifting patterns of social integration or social conflict.

3

Political Power

Command

This book takes a particular, limited approach to its theme, the relations between different forms of social power. It gives political power alone the status of a constant point of reference in its argument: that is, it discusses on the one hand political power *and* on the other (successively) ideological / normative, economic and military power. This is one justification for beginning our discussion of the several power forms with political power; in this book, it is meant to play the *protagonist's* role, in the etymological sense of being the chief character in a drama.

Another justification is that, in a sense, political power is power *par excellence*; it presents a number of features of the power phenomenon, including some of its dilemmas and contradictions, in a uniquely intensive and sharply profiled manner. In fact, in much sociological and public discussion, when one says 'power' one really *means* political power – a fact which sometimes causes misunderstandings.

Why is political power so distinctively central to the broader phenomenon of social power that sometimes the latter tends to collapse conceptually into the former? Consider an elementary, exemplary manifestation of institutionalized political power (what Weber calls *Herrschaft*, domination or rule) which we derive from an unlikely source, the so-called 'centurion episode' in the Gospel according to Luke. The centurion, a minor Roman official, asks Jesus to heal a servant of his. Jesus offers to come and heal him, but the centurion replies: 'Do not trouble further, sir; it is not for me to have you under my roof, . . . say the word and my servant will be cured. I know, for . . . I am myself under orders, with soldiers under me. I say to one, "Go", and he goes; to another, "Come here", and he comes; and to my servant, "Do this", and he does it' (Luke 7: 6–8). What we have here is a superior issuing a command to a subordinate, who complies with that command. This is straightforward enough, and we can easily sense its psychological resonance for the superior; according to Bertrand de Jouvenel, it amounts to 'an incomparable pleasure', for 'a man feels himself more of a man when he is imposing his will and making others the instruments of his will'.[1]

Observing in passing that Jouvenel does not bother to suggest what the experience feels like from the other end, let us look again at this apparently straightforward command / obedience relation. To begin with, as the centurion himself describes it, the relationship typically involves *one* subject at one end, and a *plurality* of subjects at the other. But this raises the problem inimitably phrased by Hume: 'Nothing appears more surprizing to those, who consider human affairs with a philosophical eye, than the easiness with which the many are governed by the few.'[2] In fact, perhaps Hume is being disingenuous (implausible as this may sound), when he claims to see as problematical the *governing* of the many by the few. What is really provoking is that the many allow the few not just to govern them, but to take advantage of them. As they obey commands, the many engage in ventures into which the few have no intention to lead them; they abstain from undertakings that would benefit them; they allow goods and services to be exacted from them to the benefit of the few; they subject themselves, at the few's behest, to humiliating, hurtful, cruel forms of oppression and exploitation. *This* is really puzzling.

To address the puzzle, consider first an aspect of the centurion episode which the centurion leaves discreetly unspoken. To epitomize the phenomenon of political power, the things the centurion says to his servants must constitute proper, enforceable commands. That is: in the first place, a superior's 'sayings' do not simply express his wishes, leaving his subordinates at liberty to act or not to act upon them; they contain an implicit (sometimes an explicit) 'or else' clause, that is, they imply (sometimes they state) that the subordinate's eventual non-compliance will have negative consequences for him or her. In the second place, these potential consequences will be of a particularly stringent nature: typically, they will consist in a punishment inflicted upon the subordinate by means of overwhelming physical force or constraint.

In other terms, any particular command / obedience interaction instantiates something more permanent, less *ad hoc* – a relationship between subjects asymmetric enough, in terms of power, to allow one subject routinely and bindingly to commit or to block the energies of the other, to make a difference to what the other does, forebears to do, or allows to happen to her- or himself. What qualifies the power in question as *political* is the fact that it rests ultimately upon, and intrinsically (though often not expressly) refers to, the superior's ability to sanction coercively the subordinate's failure to comply with commands.

Fear and politics

This grounding of political experience, when all is said and done, in the harsh reality of physical coercion may be a further reason (or at least a constant background possibility) why political power looms so large as a form of the power phenomenon. For political power is unique in directly putting at stake something as basic as the sheer integrity and safety from harm and hurt of the individual's bodily self, and thus it actually or potentially awakens emotions of which all humans are capable *qua* sentient creatures, *qua* animal beings. The most potent and general such emotion is fear – fear of pain, physical violation, forceful restraint or death at the hands of the Other. The German sociologist Heinrich Popitz emphasizes the centrality of this phenomenon: 'The ability to inflict physical damage on others, and the vulnerability to physical damage from others are essential components of the social process. The concern, fear, anxiety, we experience in face of one another constitute an ineliminable aspect of social experience. To exist together always means also to have fear for oneself and to protect oneself.'[3] A similar view is expressed by Guglielmo Ferrero's reflections on the political significance of fear. Although this is an emotion humans share with other animals,

> man is the being that experiences and provokes most fear, as the only living being aware of, obsessed and frightened by, the dark abyss towards which incessantly rushes the stream of his existence – death. He alone knows how to contrive life-destroying instruments. . . . But on that very account he is even more afflicted with fear . . . for those very weapons could be used to hurt him, too. . . . Because of his very ability to frighten others he is frightened of himself.[4]

The relation between fear and political power is a complex one. Political power arises as a remedy to fear, but works by awakening fear. As Hobbes made apparent long ago, on the one hand their fear of one another motivates individual actors to overcome the excessive dangerousness of the state of nature, by consenting to erect an overpowering artificial being, the Sovereign, who deprives them of the ability to threaten one another. On the other hand, the Sovereign operates in turn by evoking a kind of second-degree fear, for it threatens to visit its overwhelming, punitive displeasure on individuals who exercise force (or practise deceit) on one another, or otherwise fail to obey its commands. Thus, political power arises as a remedy to fear, but works by awakening fear. As Ferrero puts it: 'Power is the supreme manifestation of the fear man awakens in himself, for all his efforts to overcome it.'[5]

Bobbio's definition of political power quoted earlier, with its emphasis on 'weapons of all kinds and degrees of potency', Ferrero's reflections on it, Lenin's crude saying, 'What is the state? Bodies of armed men' – all these texts remind us of the harsh material basis of primordial political experience, and of the elemental nature of the emotions it addresses and evokes.

The justification of political inequality

But there is another side to political power. In fact, in the centurion episode neither fear nor weaponry is in evidence at all, and it is only our surmise that the centurion's commands to his servants somehow imply an 'or else' clause. Making such surmises, making explicit the implicit, are critical tasks of social theorizing; but they should not overshadow entirely the 'face value' of phenomena. In that episode, the asymmetrical nature of the interactions between the centurion and his servants is fully evident; but so is the fact that the interactions are intersubjective ones. The individual at the top end of the asymmetry treats the individuals at the bottom end as capable of understanding and acting upon verbal messages, assumes that they share with him a language, as well as all manner of knowledge relevant to the business to be transacted via the execution of commands. Considered in this way, political relationships are peculiar ways of shaping and biasing communicative processes between subjects who in principle acknowledge one another as equal, as each the other's *semblable et frère*.

Note that assuming a kind of commonality between the parties to a political relationship is not a consideration extraneous to the harsh realities we have mentioned before. According to Ferrero, we fear others because we know them to be like ourselves. For Hobbes, in the state of nature all individuals are equal, none of them is ten feet tall, and none may entrust his security to his natural ability to subdue and oppress the others. For this very reason, those individuals can only escape their shared insecurity by jointly contriving an artificial sovereign endowed with overpowering majesty and awesomeness. The inquisitor knows what emotions he can awaken in the defendant through the *territio verbalis et realis* because he can easily echo them within himself.

Thus, in political relationships there is an inherent tension between the sharpness of the inequality they normally posit and assert between the parties, and the potential equality they assume between them. The first aspect normally plays the role of 'figure', the other of 'background', and a remote, dim background at that. But both are present, and this poses an abiding problem for political relationships: how to justify that inequality.

An indirect indication of the seriousness of this problem is supplied by the so-called *Überlagerungstheorie*, a cluster of arguments, mostly formulated by sociologists and anthropologists writing in German, concerning the origins of political power. According to these writers, such power could not develop spontaneously in socially and culturally homogeneous societies, but originated (in various parts of the earth, at various times) from the forcible subjugation of settled, agricultural populations of a certain ethnic stock by a nomadic, warring population of different stock, which 'superimposed' itself on the former. This theory implicitly acknowledges the inherent tension asserted above, for it assumes that strongly egalitarian social conditions inhibit the spontaneous development of power relations.

Perhaps a further reason why political power appears as social power *par excellence* is exactly that it must confront in a particularly explicit fashion the problem of the incompatibility of power relations with an *assumed* equality, a problem that in principle affects social power in all its forms. Being constructed and managed largely through communication, political relationships must also, to a greater or lesser extent, *communicate* about themselves, and most particularly, I suggest, about why they are intrinsically unequal.

Let us reformulate the root problem: the parties to political relationships – let us name them again Person 1 and Person 2 – are equal in nature. The problem's solution may then consist in obscuring, circumventing or moderating that equality. Let us consider some different (though not mutually incompatible) strategies to this effect.

If we take literally the view that Person 1 and Person 2 are equal *in* nature, then an obvious solution to that problem consists in conceiving one party as standing, instead, *outside* nature. One way of doing this is to suggest that Person 1 is in fact *not just* human, but possesses supernatural qualities which place him somehow above the realm of nature to which Person 2, instead, entirely belongs. Alternatively, the often very apparent inequality between the two parties is, so to speak, sublimated, for one party's superiority is seen as reflecting the unchallengeable supremacy of an entity that stands over and above both parties, but chooses to see itself represented and embodied by the superior party. We shall consider in a later chapter some ideological constructions and institutional arrangements in which this solution can be embodied.

A similar though obverse solution consists in suggesting instead that Person 2, in turn, is *not quite* human, but an *Untermensch*, or a being 'like unto a beast of the fields', or a 'work-tool endowed with speech' (a cute way Roman lawyers used to characterize slaves). Louis de Rouvroy, duc de Saint-Simon, recounts in his *Mémoires* a striking anecdote conveying, in less crude form, Person 1's presumption that Person 2 belongs to an inferior order of nature or to a lower realm of reality. An aristocratic lady at the court of Louis XIV, on being shown her servant's newborn child, was amazed to see that she had exactly the same number of fingers as her own children. In the same spirit, it is recounted, a young woman from the English gentry of old, having been initiated by a lover in the delights of sex, was dismayed to learn that the lower orders also *did it*, and enjoyed it; it seemed to her 'rather too good for *them*'.

A very different strategy consists in accepting that nature encompasses both Person 1 and Person 2, while pointing out that in nature there exist plenty of relationships whose components on a number of counts belong together, but where nonetheless sharp inequalities of power also exist. For instance, in classical China the ruler was often depicted as 'mother and father of the people'; in many cultures, political inequalities are represented as paralleling those existing between different animal species. The lion and the eagle, of course, feature particularly frequently in the iconography associated with this solution.

Alternatively, one may try to de-emphasize the gradient of inequality between the parties, rendering it less obvious and invidious. For instance, the liabilities and disadvantages of political superiority may be stressed, as in 'uneasy lies the head that wears a crown'. Shakespeare's Henry V, in his

monologue on the night before the battle of Agincourt, discusses at length
the advantages the commoner has over the king:

> What infinite heart's ease
> Must kings neglect, that private men enjoy!
> And what have kings that privates have not too,
> Save ceremony, save general ceremony?
> And what art thou, thou idol Ceremony? . . .
> O Ceremony, show me but thy worth!

And so on – there is no advantage, apparently, in being a king.

Or it may be argued that that superiority is deceptive, in that it obscures
significant services performed on behalf of the subordinates by their betters.
The characterization of the pope as *servus servorum Dei*, 'the servant of
the servants of God', well conveys this strategy. It is widely echoed in
secular constructions of *service* as the essence of and the justification for
rulership – as in the motto of the Hohenzollerns and the princes of Wales,
'Ich dien', or for that matter in the British notion of 'civil servant'.

Even when the superiority of the powerful party expresses itself harshly
and punitively, that party may find ways of suggesting that 'it hurts me
more than it hurts you, son'. Or the superiors may hold forth on the long-
term benefits, especially moral ones, that the subordinates may derive from
the dutiful acceptance of their inferiority. The Italian proverb 'Il lavoro
nobilita l'uomo' ('Work ennobles man') has all the appearances of having
been fashioned for the usage of their inferiors by noble people who did not
believe a word of it; this is suggested by the existence of a mock version of
it, 'Il lavoro nobilita l'uomo – e lo rende simile alla bestia' ('Work ennobles
man – and makes him like unto a beast').

A further way of neutralizing the tension between the inherent asymmetry of the political relationship and the presumption of equality between its
two parties consists in reducing or masking the sharpness of that asymmetry, or tempering it with forms of equality. Rulers can sometimes develop a
personal style suggesting modesty and approachability, and project an
image of themselves as 'just regular guys'. In times of crisis they can
credibly suggest that what is at stake is not simply their personal advantages, but the welfare of a broad circle of associates, for the sake of whom
they are willing to suffer not just the burdens of office and the tedium and
constraint of ceremony, but danger and deprivation. If such a condition is
shared with the subjects, as it is in war, it creates a commonality between
the two parties: see again Shakespeare's Henry V addressing his soldiers
and himself as 'We few, we happy few, we band of brothers'.

Occasionally, the powerful make use, self-consciously or otherwise, of
situations that display their human weakness and vulnerability, in order to
bestow on their inferiors the rare luxury of expressing sympathy and
solidarity towards their betters. A situation of this kind (admittedly, not in
an explicitly political context) is described in Thomas Mann's *Joseph in*

Egypt. Potiphar's wife, once more frustrated by Joseph's refusal to lie with her, revenges herself by proclaiming in front of her many household servants that Joseph had tried to rape her and invoking their solidarity. Mann depicts ironically the effect her surprising appeal has on her audience:

> 'Egyptians!' she called. 'Children of Keme! Sons of the river and of the black earth!' What was going on? They were ordinary people, those she was turning to, and furthermore at that very moment almost all a bit drunk. Their legitimate status as children of the Chapi – in so far as they were at all, for among them were also Moors from Kusch and people with Chaldean names – was a natural distinction they had done nothing to acquire, and no use to them when something went wrong with their services in the household: their backs would then be powerfully beaten until large weals formed on them, never mind how distinguished their birth. Now all of a sudden they were being made aware of it – although normally nothing was made of it and it was of no practical use to any of them – in an emphatic and flattering fashion, because one could make use of their sense of honour, their puffed up communal pride, against someone whom one wanted to bring down. That appeal struck them as odd, but it did not fail to work its effect on them, particularly as the spirit of the barley beer was making them receptive.
> 'Egyptian brothers!' (Brothers, yet! This was a real hit with them, they liked it very much). 'You see me, your lady and mother, Potiphar's first and rightful wife? You see me on the threshold of the house and we well know one another, you and I?' – 'We', and 'one another'! This suited them fine, it was a good day for little people.[6]

We see here the occasional recognition by the political superior of a kind of largely symbolic commonality with the politically inferior, the affirmation, however perfunctory, of a sense of fellowship, which bespeaks the presumptive equality – 'for a'that, and a'that' – of the parties to a political relationship. The Mediterranean institution of Godfather-hood works to this effect by encouraging powerful personages to enter into quasi-familial relations with powerless characters, including in many circumstances their dependants.

The most common strategy, however, is probably to strike a kind of compromise between asymmetry and equality by *layering* the political relationship. The centurion himself exemplifies this when, before enumerating some ways in which he exercises authority *over* his servants, he refers to himself as 'a man *under* authority'. Essentially, in this strategy those who are subordinates in one direct political relationship are in turn superiors in a relationship downward from it, and so forth; *and* the amount of inequality between parties to each direct relationship is reduced. In this way, given the appropriate number of layers, a huge power discrepancy can exist between the top and the bottom of the system, while on each given layer those who stand in a proximate political, command–obedience relationship are not *so* sharply unequal, and deal with one another to some extent on the basis of mutual respect.

The key effect of this strategy, which associates power differences with broader differences in rank or social standing, is to stabilize the overarching political structure by diminishing the friction within each layer of it. In the Christian West, it embodied itself in complex institutions regulating the interactions between members of the aristocracy, such as the use of heraldic symbols, nobility titles or chivalric ritual: for example, the occasional practice of the 'round table', which on the one hand levels the differences between personages sitting at it, but on the other acknowledges, through the seating arrangements, their greater or lesser proximity to one personage they all recognize as dominant.

Again, Shakespeare witnesses *a contrario* to the intended stabilizing effect of layering when he laments (in *Troilus and Cressida*) the effects of disturbing relationships of rank ('degree'): 'Take but degree away, untune that string / And hark! what discord follows . . .'. The musical metaphor is striking: what produces harmony is degree, tuning, that is, recognition of and respect for natural differences between individual sounds; these, how-ever, implicitly refer to one another, and to that extent belong together.

A final strategy is nearly as common as layering. It consists in building some aspects of exchange, of *quid pro quo*, into intrinsically asymmetrical relationships, where normally the subordinate's compliance with the superior's wishes need not be directly paid for or expressly rewarded. The very widespread phenomenon of 'clientele' can be interpreted in this sense. Here, the sharp power difference between two parties is fully acknow-ledged, yet the subordinate party is allowed to make his or her remaining within the relationship depend upon occasional evidence of the superior's favour by means of some material advantages bestowed on the subordinate, for instance a degree of immunity from public exactions or of privileged access to public authorities. The loyalty and the subjection demanded of the subordinate can be very wide, but to some extent are understood to be conditional. It is the strength of the clientele institution that it combines into a given relationship, sometimes in a very complex manner, apparently contradictory aspects. Generally speaking, the chief effect of the combi-nation is to strengthen the relationship's core feature, which remains the substantial power inequality between the parties.

I have dwelled at some length on strategies of justification of political power differentials between actors in the more or less direct presence of one another, for two rather different reasons. In the first place, to suggest the validity of Max Weber's sustained concern with 'legitimacy' (or legiti-mation), which he treated as the key organizing principle of his typology of domination. In the second place, the problem itself of justification arises, at any rate conceptually, from something I am keen to emphasize – the tension between the inequality which political power relations emphasize and dramatize, and the potentially subversive import of their intersubjective nature. Basically, I repeat, we are dealing with an ethical paradox.

However, one should not overstate the significance ethical concerns have for political relationships, or the need of the powerful to justify their superiority and the advantages they derive from it. The asymmetry can be so strong that subordinates become utterly invisible from the superior's vantage point, and ethical concerns simply evaporate. Consider for instance a passage from *Fontamara*, a novel by Ignazio Silone written in 1933. A visitor to the possessions of the greatest Italian latifundia owner of our century, Prince Torlonia, asks what position the prince holds with respect to his ultimate dependants, the landless rustics (*cafoni* – an expression loaded with contempt in Italian parlance):

> Michael patiently told the stranger how it looks to us: 'On top of everything there is God, the master of heaven. Everybody knows this.
> Then comes Prince Torlonia, the master of the land.
> > Then come the Prince's guards.
> > Then come the dogs of the Prince's guards.
> > Then, nothing.
> > Then, again, nothing.
> > Then, again, nothing.
> > Then come the *cafoni.*'

Violence

At this point, to emphasize further the distinctiveness of the political dimension, I shall return to the question of violence, making considerable use of Popitz's treatment of this theme. Although what is prima facie distinctive about violence is its stark factuality, its significance as a medium of social control is enhanced by two overlapping aspects. First, recourse to violence can be very carefully and subtly graduated, both when it is used as a means of punishment and when it is deployed in the context of warfare (see the notion of escalation). Second, the sheer physicality of even the most obvious and brutal forms of violence is always associated with varying emotional resonances which are culturally grounded; think of the difference between hitting someone about the body and striking someone in the face, between beating up a woman and raping her. Again, to some extent this applies also in the military context, as suggested by an ancient Greek text where the poet–soldier Archilocus remarks ironically how many of his companions are boasting about the fact that 'we have killed seven enemies, and those by kicking them'. (A comical high-school episode in Fellini's *Amarcord* recalls this text.)

Archilocus points up the emotional resonances at the active end of the exercise of violence. They are mostly even stronger at the passive end. In particular, according to Popitz, physical punishment deeply affects the victim's sense of self:

> In the end the person may loosen itself from the social attachments which are denied to it; it may maintain a sense of self independent of the material possessions taken away from it – but it cannot separate itself from its body. . . .
> The sufferings inflicted on us by another are never something 'merely physical',

for in dealing with another person we cannot withdraw from our body. On this account whoever is subjected to physical punishment perceives his or her power inferiority as a condition not of partial but of general, existential subjugation.[7]

A further aspect of violence is its potential boundlessness, which has several aspects. In the first place, the human capacity to exercise violence, like other distinctive capacities of the species, is not tightly programmed by nature. It is not the case, for example, that all human violence is triggered by aggressiveness, or hostility motivated by an instinctual attachment of individuals and groups to a 'territory'. Violence ranges, and rages, over an open-ended variety of circumstances, pursues multiple designs. To quote another striking passage from Popitz:

> Man never *needs to*, but always *can* act violently; never *has to*, but always *can* kill: singly or collectively; with everybody taking part in a joint deed, or through a division of labour; in all manner of situations, in battle or while feasting; in different states of feeling, with or without anger, with or without pleasure, while screaming or in silence; for any conceivable purpose – everybody can.[8]

In the second place, the boundlessness of the violent act is compounded by that of the violent imagination:

> For man, violence *is* not only that which occurs or has occurred and is being remembered; but also what could occur: the violence feared from the stranger, the fond wish of one's own triumphant violence. This horizon of the possible . . . widely surpasses anything one can realistically project. Images of possible violence flash deceptively within all manner of day-dreams and nightmares. . . . This imaginative activity has an un-bounding effect because it is not tied to experience, so that the purely imagined is even more restraint-less than our actual deeds. The power of the imagination can think up anything. Images of violence can force themselves upon our consciousness anytime, in response to no visible external stimulus. . . . Finally, the imagination of one's own violence is boundless – dangerously so – exactly because it can dispense with any sense of risk . . . and represent itself as enormously successful.[9]

Finally, the boundlessness of violence rests on the possibility of continually increasing its actual effects through technology, which multiplies (eventually *ad infinitum*) the original capacity of humans for hurting and killing one another.[10] The technology can be both material – 'weapons of all kinds and degrees of potency' as Bobbio says – and social – means of organizing the collective production and use of weapons and other means of violence, as, for instance, in prisons.

Popitz's focus on violence as the core of political power and his sustained emphasis on the boundlessness of violence accord well with Max Weber's views on the same topics, and particularly with the following three points.

1 'The nature of political organisation can only be specified by referring
   to a *means* which may not be exclusive to it, but which is specific to it
   and intrinsic to its essence (and which occasionally becomes an end to
   itself) – namely, violence.'

2 As a consequence,

> it is not possible to characterise a political organisation ... by reference
> to the *ends* to which it orients its activity. On the one hand there is no
> end, be it the provision of food or the protection of the arts, which has
> not been pursued, albeit occasionally, by some political organisation. On
> the other hand, there is no end, be it the safeguarding of the individual's
> security or the enforcement of laws, which has been pursued by all political
> organisations.[11]

3 Exactly because violence constitutes a means to so many ends, the
   possibility of exercising it becomes the target of multiple, competing
   ambitions on the part of individuals and groups. These contend with
   one another not just *by means of* violence means, but also *over* violence
   itself, and particularly over the control of the dominant material and
   social technology of organized violence. These contentions are not
   necessarily themselves violent (remember Thurber's uncle's lonesome,
   dangerous experiments with explosives in his attic?) but they tend to
   engender confrontations. The outcome of these is necessarily highly
   contingent, for it depends, when all is said and done, on the parties'
   sheer ability to prevail on the ground, an ability each party may have
   to demonstrate either by fighting it out or by conveying in unmistakable
   terms its own unchallengeable superiority. On this account, the grounding of political power in violence induces the irreducible contingency of
   political experience – an aspect of it Machiavelli theorized as *fortuna*,
   and which in more modern language we might label its intrinsic
   irrationality.

The reasoning that suggests this is clear and compelling. A power centre
constructed by accumulating and managing a potential for violence may
always have its viability challenged by another such power centre. If so
challenged, it can only prove that viability by demonstrating the superiority
of *its own* potential for violence. That demonstration may have to take the
form of a trial of strength; and the outcome of this, much as it may appear
predetermined when examined retrospectively, is necessarily a contingent
matter, to be settled on the ground. (After all, no wars would be fought if
it were possible to determine which is the stronger party by other means
than fighting them, and letting the chips fall where they may.) The same
implication of irrationality attaches also to the undeniable tendency for
political actors to accumulate power entirely for its own sake. (Consider
Hobbes: 'I put for a general inclination of all mankind, a perpetuall and
restlesse desire of Power after power, that ceaseth onely in death.')[12]

Restrictions on violence

Yet, the emphasis I have laid in the last few paragraphs on two aspects of the phenomenon of violence – what I have called, following Popitz, its boundlessness, and its irrationality – may produce an excessively bloody-minded view of the nature of political power. Max Weber himself, who did not mind being bloody-minded on these matters, speaks of violence as the distinctive *means* of politics, not as its very essence.

Suppose we reconsider a statement made earlier – 'Political power arises as a remedy to fear, but works by awakening fear' – and say instead 'Political power works by awakening fear, but does so as a remedy to fear'. This new statement (also) throws light on the nature of politics. To a greater or lesser extent, political power typically works to reduce the boundless-ness of violence and its irrationality, even if it does so by building up its own potential for violence and occasionally by exhibiting it harshly and destructively.

Let us see how this may occur. As I have indicated, various actors, individual and collective, contend over and through the control over the potential for violence; and although this contention is contingent in its outcomes, and may be frequently renewed, generally it sorts out, within a field of contestants, 'the men from the boys'. That is, it tends to simplify that field, to mark out some contenders as more significant, that is, more powerful than others. More significant political actors differentiate themselves, for longer or shorter stretches of time, from less significant ones.

Now, a significant political actor often seeks to restrict the violence on which it ultimately rests by adopting one or more of a few basic approaches. Its first preoccupation is not so much to limit the volume of the violence that occurs in the world, but to reduce its pervasiveness, its tendency to occur *all over the place*. To this end a political actor generally stakes out a field on which his or her own capacity for violence can be given free rein, while other political entities have to hold off theirs. In this way, no matter what happens within the *system*, as far as violence is concerned, much of the violence in the world is kept out of it, in its *environment*, and this renders the system itself relatively indifferent to it.

The field within which a political actor's violence is given exclusive sway – the boundaries of the system, in other words – can be variously determined; but generally political actors seek to determine that field in territorial terms, by locating themselves in a given portion of the earth, large or small. Alternatively, but less frequently, they may refer instead to an ethnically distinctive population, in turn more or less territorially settled. Within this field, it is possible in turn to distinguish a centre and a periphery, and the periphery itself at a certain point reaches an outer perimeter, which normally bounds on (though sometimes it overlaps with, as in the case of 'frontier regions') the periphery of another political formation. In this approach to the reduction of violence, it is essential that the perimeter should in fact keep violence that occurs in the environment from spilling over into the system. To this effect, each system will tend to build up *its own* potential for violence at the perimeter or in its proximity.

A second approach is complementary to the first. Once violence outside its perimeter is somehow made irrelevant, a political formation can further reduce the amount of relevant violence by broadening that perimeter, in other terms by becoming larger. This operation, too, bears the promise of reducing violence, since its success would correspondingly abridge the system's environment, and distance its centre from the turbulence occurring in that environment. However, the pursuit of this policy, if contested (as it is likely to be) by other political formations, may have the paradoxical result of raising the probability that violence will occur over the location of the perimeter itself.

Third, the political centre may (and normally will) take steps to reduce the frequency and possibly the intensity of the violence occurring within the system itself. It is in its interest to do so, for two reasons: first, each part of the system that engages in violence on its own behalf disperses some of the total potential for violence which the system can use for keeping at bay violence originating from outside it, for securing its perimeter; second, each such part may be tempted to challenge the centre itself, and potentially to imperil it. Once more, the short-term effect of this approach may be to increase the occurrence of violence within the system, since the various parts will resist the centre's attempt to reduce their autonomy, and more than one of them may claim the privilege of defining itself as the centre.

The imagery I have adopted so far in detailing reasons why political power is likely to seek to control violence has primarily to do with *space*: I have spoken of delimiting systems, of centres securing peripheries and reducing the violence practised in various parts, and so on. But an imagery emphasizing *time* is at least as relevant to our problem. If you think of the problem as the *occurrence* rather than the *location* of violence, of violence itself as an incident in the calendar rather than as a spot on a map, then another solution suggests itself: lengthening the intervals between episodes of violence, at any rate those occurring within the system.

The basic idea is to make *situations* (understood as durable conditions of things) widely prevail, in the flow of time, over *events*; or, more precisely, to have most of the time taken by countless, repetitive, predictable, non-violent events rather than by occasional, unpredictable, violent ones. This need not mean forgoing the possibility of violence, but rather assigning it to the background of social existence, while disengaging it from the foreground. In these circumstances, the background may be held by a multitude of muted, uneventful activities: a myriad enactments of custom, the periodic unfolding of rituals, the spontaneous traffic between exchange partners, the diffuse process of communication, negotiation and mutual sanctioning through which individuals assume and perform roles.

From its background position, political power can significantly help these ongoing processes to become and to remain orderly. It can do so either by placing its own unique facility for sanctioning the conduct of individuals (the exercise of violence) at the service of otherwise established institutions, or by itself fashioning institutions. By one means or another it can foster the continuity of social existence, which finds its most significant expression in the succession of generations within a population. To this extent, political power plays a role in binding and transcending time, in making its flow confirm and enhance the population's awareness of a shared past, its sense of its own continuing sameness, instead of eroding and negating them.

But it is not only time that can be bound and transcended by the activities of political power; space, too, can be. That power's endeavour to establish and secure a territorial base provides for the population a context that fosters its sense of identity. The ineluctable severalness of individuals as occupants each of a different place, the resultant distances between them, are vaulted over, so to speak, by political activities and political symbols which treat one place and the next (and the next, and the next) as nonetheless constituting together a *single* space, and as a result a 'home' for the whole population, no matter how large, dispersed and diverse.

Political power institutionalized

In so far as political power operates in these ways – that is, in so far as it shifts the prevailing locus of violence (including, if necessary, its own violence) to the environment, and within the system makes violence (including its own) an exceptional occurrence, while keeping itself ready to exercise it – its key role with respect to the social process at large becomes that of an order-keeper or a guardian. As cultural diversity increases within it, and the division of labour advances, a population may derive a sense, however tenuous, of its distinctiveness and of its historical continuity only from the continuing guardianship exercised upon it by political power.

In this respect, political power may appear to perform a valuable moral service, although some moral doctrines object to the fact that it hangs on to its potential for violence, no matter how selectively and infrequently it exercises it. If political power is to act as guardian of the social order, however, it is not only necessary that the use of violence be circumscribed and made more selective and discreet. More generally, the solidity, the visibility, the effectiveness of the existent political arrangements must increase; the precariousness and volatility which they continue to derive from their grounding in violence (for violence can always be challenged and checked) must be placed under control. This may be achieved through a process that Popitz calls 'institutionalization of political power'.

According to Popitz, the process in question has three main aspects. The first he calls the *depersonalization* of power relationships: 'Power no longer stands or falls with one particular person who happens to have the decisive say at a particular time. Rather, it comes to be connected with determinate functions and positions which are super-personal in character.' The second is the *formalization* of power relationships. That is, 'the exercise of power becomes more and more clearly oriented to rules, procedural arrangements, rituals'. Finally, those relationships become increasingly *integrated* into a broader, encompassing order: 'Power becomes geared into the 'going arrangements''. It connects with and becomes absorbed into a social whole, which it supports and which supports it.'[13]

As this last point suggests, 'institutionalization' is not necessarily, for the politically powerful, a matter of surrendering or limiting their privileges, recognizing that some values transcend their own interests. By becoming depersonalized, formalized and integrated, power relationships are made more secure, and their sway over the social process may become greater.

Of course, although for example 'the formalization of the exercise of power responds to the power holder's own interest', when it takes the form of laying down norms for the conduct of the subordinates, 'also the powerful must pay a price. In situations for which he has formulated norms for the subordinates, he cannot from any moment to the next [*alle naselang*] demand something entirely different. He must subject also his own will to a given arrangement, if only because otherwise the subordinates cannot learn the conduct expected of them.'[14] However, there is a difference between exercising power through the imposition of norms, and imposing norms on the exercise of power itself, such that the deviation from norms on the part of the power holders themselves exposes them to sanctions. This development presupposes, but is much more infrequent than, the institutionalization of political power. For example, one approach that seems immediately to suggest itself – dispersing the ability to exercise violence to a plurality of power centres which would thus become capable of sanctioning one another – entails a great risk of multiplying strife and de-institutionalizing political power in general, rendering it both brutal and unstable. For that very reason, it could hardly go on practising its guardianship of the social order.

According to Popitz himself: 'Only rarely, in the history of society, has it been possible even just to pose purposefully and consequentially the question of how to limit institutionalized violence. Basically, this has only happened in the Greek *polis*, in republican Rome, in a few other city states, and in the history of the modern constitutional state.'[15] We are not going to retrace the historical trajectory suggested by Popitz, but consider only its first and its last moments: the Greek experience of politics, and that characteristic of the modern constitutional state.

For the Greeks, political power emphatically maintained its grounding in violence. Typically, full membership in the Greek *polis* was the prerogative of all free, adult males who served in the army or the navy; and the glory and splendour of Athens in its heyday was based on the size and efficiency of its navy, which allowed it to extract tribute from militarily subjugated outside communities. Yet there was another aspect to political experience – let us call it 'politics' – which, it has been authoritatively argued, the Greeks *invented*.[16] In the context of politics, the inhabitants of the Greek *polis* (or rather, again, the adult, free, militarily active males among them) were not simply a population 'guarded' by political power, but were the *constituency* of that power, which belonged to them although it guided and disciplined their conduct.

Politics was the process whereby, through complex and sophisticated arrangements, the town members became collectively involved in deliberating *which* mode of life the town would adopt as its own, which values the citizens should share, which rules they were to follow in their social intercourse. To this end, politics took place in a space of its own, distinct from those exclusive to the single households – the public space of the square and of a variety of buildings and facilities intended for collective uses (worship, entertainment, gymnastic exercise, commercial traffic, adjudication, military exercises) – and developed as a specific form of discourse.

Ideally, such discourse, conducted within appropriately regulated public settings, evoked rational assent by appealing to the town's distinctive moral commitments, its shared past, and by discussing the circumstances the town confronted, the advantages and disadvantages of alternative ways of dealing with them. In principle everybody could take part in it; according to a myth recounted (according to Plato) by Protagoras, in order to assist the Greeks in organizing town life, Jupiter had endowed all townsmen, to the same extent, with two distinctive virtues: *dyke* ('justice', more or less) and *aidos* (commonly translated as 'shame', but implying also the ability of individuals to recognize each other as human).

Although townsmen were expected to form views of their own and to seek to persuade one another through argument, a body of rules allowed the contrast between arguments to be settled by appealing (typically) to the vote of the majority of the members of a constituted body. In this manner, *politics* could produce *policy*; that is, at some point the question 'what is to be done?' would cease to be an object of public argument, and a determinate, express answer to that question would become a set of valid, enforceable directives for action by public authorities – including, of course, the threat or the use of violence.[17]

There is something paradoxical about the Greeks' 'invention of politics'. On the one hand, political power sets itself imperiously in the middle of the social process in the *polis*, undertaking to shape it, and ceasing to be merely its guardian; on the other hand, it opens itself up to impulses freely emerging from the population, acknowledging the capacity for autonomous judgement of its parts and even the legitimacy of contrasts between the resulting options. In principle, it is possible for these two aspects not to develop jointly; in particular, the hold of political power on society may increase, assisted perhaps by society's decreased capacity for self-regulation, yet *without* a parallel development in the public sphere, which would allow divergent views and interests to express themselves, to confront one another, and to determine policy through the orderly resolution of their contrasts.

This would be a fearsome development, giving a negative response to the question 'Is it possible for political power not just to reduce and control the interference of violence in social life but *to bind itself?*' Such a negative answer is suggested by innumerable episodes within the political history of humanity. In the twentieth century, in particular, within both Fascist and Communist party states, the ruling party systematically uncoupled the exercise of its power from any spontaneous process of formation and expression of political preferences on the part of the population. It made its business to monitor, control and direct all manner of social business through a range of techniques, including systematic ideological indoctrination, large-scale use of spies and informants, and the massive recourse to unrestrained violence. In this way political power, far from guarding the social order, wilfully assailed it and sought to undo and redo it at will.

Disturbingly, also in democratic polities the twentieth century saw an attenuation of politics, a degree of uncoupling of the exercise of political power from the free expression and confrontation in the public sphere of the views and preferences of its constituency. As political power took a more and more conspicuous and commanding position at the centre of the social process through an enlarged range of activities, there was no proportionate increase in the opportunities for the citizenry at large to keep itself politically informed and involved.

Fortunately, this did not cause the total unbinding of political power in those systems. On the one hand the mechanism of political representation and the workings of the party system, on the other the expansion of literacy and the growth of the media, allowed some amount of continuous monitoring and criticism of political agencies on the part of the public, as well as periodic opportunities for the authoritative expression of approval or disapproval of the political leadership by the electorate. Furthermore, in its medieval and modern phases, the history of Western political arrangements had seen the development of new strategies for the containment of political power which remain valid, in principle, for the modern constitutional state. Two such strategies deserve mention.

The first strategy comprises the division of powers. This rests largely on two aspects of the institutionalization of political power mentioned by Popitz: its integration into the larger social order, and its depersonalization. As the social order becomes more complex, political power can only become and remain integrated into it if it attends purposefully and systematically to distinctive, discrete aspects of it. In the process, political power itself becomes internally differentiated, since it engages in diverse activities, including some whose relationship to violence is increasingly indirect and remote. Through depersonalization, these activities become the concern no longer of single individuals, but of distinct sets of roles, specialized components of a comprehensive machine for the performance of political tasks.

This machine, in turn, can be so designed that those components (a) are operated by people with different competences and interests; (b) function according to different rules; (c) can operate autonomously for certain purposes; and (d) require the co-operation of other components for other purposes. If these conditions are fulfilled, on the one hand the machine as a whole will be capable of performing a variety of different tasks in a sophisticated and competent manner, on the other it is not likely to become single-mindedly committed to increasing indefinitely its own power at the cost of disrupting the social process. Its sheer complexity will slow it down, the diverse interests and dispositions built into it will constitute (in a famous phrase) 'checks and balances' upon one another.

There are two classical forms of the division of powers, which we may label respectively vertical and horizontal. Federalism distinguishes *vertically*, within a large political unit, those interests and concerns pertaining to it as a whole, from those pertaining to its several parts, and allows the latter to be pursued autonomously by corresponding political subunits. *Horizontally*, one distinguishes instead between various political activities (typically: legislation, adjudication, administration), assigning each primarily to a distinct organ. (In federal polities, this distinction can be replicated at each level.)

Somehow, the prominence of these two kinds of division of powers in the analyses of political theorists and jurists has obscured the relevance of another kind – the increasing specialization of the political activities directly involving violence, and their progressive 'segregation', so to speak, from the others. There is a clumsy but useful expression characterizing this process – the 'civilianization' of government. This has gone so far that a civics class or a course in constitutional law can discuss legislation, adjudication and administration at some length, without being forced to consider systematically those aspects of each activity directly involved with the dirty work of political power, without confronting directly those 'bodies of armed men' who according to Lenin *are* the state.

Yet legislation includes budgeting for the army; and, when the lawyers and judges have done their job in the adjudicating process, the uniformed, armed police and the prison guards, or perhaps the sheriff or the bailiff, take over; and the armed forces constitute everywhere one of the largest (and often *the* most expensive) components of the state's administrative machinery.

> Even in the politely operated societies of modern democracies the ultimate argument is violence. No state can exist without a police force or its equivalent in armed might. This ultimate violence may not be used frequently. There may be innumerable steps in its application, in the way of warnings and reprimands, but if all the warnings are disregarded, even in so slight a matter as paying a traffic ticket, the last thing that will happen is that a couple of cops show up at the door with handcuffs and a Black Maria.[18]

A further strategy consists in laying explicit legal boundaries upon the activity of political agencies, and making the validity of their operations (including those involving the exercise of violence) depend on the observance of those boundaries.

There are two overlapping ways to achieve this effect. First, political agencies are forbidden to interfere with the enjoyment by citizens of certain rights, and / or ordered to assist citizens in securing and enjoying such rights. Speaking metaphorically, political activity becomes like a body of water which, however fast and powerfully it floods over a stretch of land, never covers all of it, for it cannot surmount some heights and ramparts within the land which at worst, when the flood is at its highest, make it look like an archipelago.

The rights to practise one's own chosen calling, to acquire, own and dispose of property, to hire and fire employees, to express and propagate one's religious beliefs, to associate oneself with others in commercial or other partnerships without undue interference from the authorities, are particularly important because they constitute the legal ground on which may emerge forms of social power other than political, whose existence necessarily limits the freedom of action of political power itself. In this book, such non-political power forms constitute the chief interlocutors of political power itself.

The second critical instrument is constituted by a body of law which expressly establishes political agencies, assigns to them certain resources, faculties and responsibilities, and to a greater or lesser extent prescribes the ways in which they are to operate. The presumption here is that if an agency engages in activities outside its assigned competences, improperly funds them, or carries them out without observing the appropriate rules, such activities, being *ultra vires*, will fail to attain their expected result, and be declared null and void by a court or legitimately disregarded by citizens.

Through such arrangements modern Western polities (recently imitated in this by some non-Western ones) have sought 'to pose purposefully and consequentially the question of how to limit institutionalized violence', to quote Popitz again. This does not mean, of course, that they have always successfully answered that question. After all, one-party systems of the Fascist variety appeared first in political contexts where some of the arrangements mentioned above had apparently been institutionalized for some time – and they expressly declared that question irrelevant, and more or less openly displaced or circumvented those arrangements. Their story points to the persistent tendency of political power (but also of other power forms!) indefinitely to increase its sway and override and displace all constraints; to position itself at the centre of the social process while seeking to abolish the autonomy of social forces (including, again, other power forms) actually or potentially resistant to its own urgent claim for supremacy.

Strategies of justification, ancient and modern

Still, that tendency has been checked long enough, in enough countries, to support Popitz's positive appraisal of the modern constitutional state. This has developed, among other things, its own distinctive solutions to the problem I would call one of justification. That is, how can one account for the persistent (and, in some cases, growing) asymmetry between the two ends of the political relationship in spite of their presumptive equality *qua* human subjects?

There are two closely related strategies of justification. The first emphasizes the notion, which I have previously associated with the Greek view of politics, that within a system of political power the population over which the system rules is also its *constituency*. The system claims to derive its legitimacy from the population, often conceived as a single political subject, 'the people'. In the people is originally vested all political power, and (whatever the appearances to the contrary) it continues to be exercised on behalf of and at the behest of the people.

In the Greek *polis*, the design itself of the central public space, the *agora*, imparted a kind of prima facie plausibility to such a way of justifying political inequality. As Hartog writes, the *agora* was 'a circular, centred space, organized by notions of symmetry, parity, and reversibility – the citizen was in turn one who commands and one who is commanded'.[19] In such a public setting, one could reasonably argue that although the political relationship was asymmetrical, the subjects at the top end of it and those at the bottom end were the same. But the plausibility of that argument rested on the small size of the Greek *polis*, which allowed politics to be based on *participation* and a considerable amount of political business actually to be transacted in the *agora*.

In the modern constitutional state, instead, the essential mechanism for activating the citizenry politically is *representation*, and most political business is handled in a variety of dispersed settings, many of them not publicly accessible. Empirically, political power is exercised by individuals in control of numerous political agencies where that power, in its diverse aspects, is routinely and irreversibly vested. This is justified by pointing at various mechanisms of delegation and at various devices by which delegates can formally be held accountable to the citizenry – no matter that such mechanisms and devices generally do not work to the purported effect.

A second, closely related strategy of justification emphasizes that those individuals actually exercising political power only do so *qua* holders of constituted offices, established and financed through public arrangements, whose operations are mandated and directed by 'the law' in its various components, from the constitution to the tax collector's final notice to pay or a court's sentence. The subordination of citizens at large to the law, which those offices are supposed to respect and implement in their activities, is seen as compatible with their being fundamentally equal to the office-holders, for the latter, too, are subordinated to the law. Within democratic polities, furthermore, through the mechanism of political representation the citizens can determine the content of the law itself; they can also, by following the appropriate recruitment procedures, seek to be appointed to public offices of various kinds. In any case, the subsumption of rulership under the law depersonalizes its exercise and, so to speak, dulls the inegalitarian edge of relationships of command and subordination.

A final strategy of justification of power inequality in modern constitutional polities consists in emphasizing the material benefits that the population at large derives from the existence of more or less sharply asymmetrical structures of command and subordination, even when (as must be the case for the majority of the population) one finds oneself at the wrong end of such structures. One may bear that fate with equanimity – so the justification goes – because in more or less visible ways those structures benefit everybody. The institutionalization of sharply profiled political inequalities assists the state in shaping and executing policy directed *also* towards industrial development, the conquest of foreign markets by domestic industries, full employment, economic planning, the expansion of the welfare state, or 'structural adjustment' (a late twentieth-century technical expression meaning 'forget planning and full employment; go easy on the welfare state'). The pursuit of such goals (or of some of them) is a complex, sophisticated operation, requiring the unimpeded operation of the appropriate political structures. If sizeable sections of the populace seriously challenge their own disadvantage in the name of (of all things) political equality, this would dangerously interfere with the pursuit of those goals.

The slightly ironic tone I found myself imparting to these last few remarks should not suggest that I consider this and other forms of justification of political inequality to be wholly 'bunk'. I believe, in fact, both that any single-minded attempt to institutionalize political equality would seriously damage, and perhaps destroy, political power, and that this in turn would irreparably damage society as we know it. I still insist that a serious ethical tension between the phenomenon of political power itself and a claim to some form and extent of equality between the parties is inherent in political relationships by their very nature – or, rather, inherent in political relationships because they are *not natural*, but are artificially established between parties who necessarily recognize each other as equal, otherwise one of them could not command and the other obey.

What one may call 'strategies of justification' are in fact theories intended to mask, or to moderate, or to accommodate this inherent political tension, *but* they do not all succeed in doing so (or fail to do so) to the same extent. In particular, taken as a class, modern, constitutional polities succeed in doing so to a greater extent than other types of political arrangements – and precisely to that extent they are not 'bunk'. I dissent, in this, from Vilfredo Pareto, who in his *Trattato di sociologia*, after mentioning *lo Stato di diritto* (*Rechtsstaat*, constitutional state) writes ironically: 'The reader will excuse me if I do not provide a definition of this wondrous entity, but it has totally eluded all my inquiries into it, and I would as soon define the Chimera.' My own sense of irony does not reach that far.

An alternative view of political power

To conclude this chapter, I will consider briefly a view of social power, authoritatively proposed in the 1950s by the American social theorist

Talcott Parsons and later elaborated by the German social theorist Niklas
Luhmann. I discuss it at this point because (particularly in its early version
by Parsons) it concerns in fact not social power in general, as it claims to
do, but *political* power. It was expressly put forward as a critique of
conceptions of political power that were overly concerned with the question
of *who has the power* in a given society, and disregarded the purportedly
much more significant question of *how much power there is* in that society.
Parsons complained that:

> the dominant tendency in the literature . . . is to maintain explicitly or
> implicitly that power is a zero-sum phenomenon, which is to say that there is
> a 'fixed quantity' of power in any relational system and hence any gain of
> power on the part of *a* must by definition occur by diminishing the power at
> the disposal of other units, *b, c, d* . . .[20]

Of course, Parsons acknowledges, (political) power relations are asymmetrical, and this does raise the question of who is at the top and who at
the bottom of them. By the same token, however, the very existence of
power asymmetries, and especially their institutionalization, confers on a
part of society the ability to commit and if necessary constrain *other parts*
to act (or forbear to act) in a certain fashion, and this ability constitutes a
resource for the *whole* society. It benefits the whole society if arrangements
are in place to enforce its norms, patrol its physical boundaries, to deal
effectively with the threats and opportunities emerging in its natural and
social environment, to make sure its collective interests are embodied in
and served by express, binding policies, and to entrust the formation and
implementation of such policy to specialized structures.

These structures, furthermore, are typically endowed with legitimacy,
that is, they are supported by the society's shared values and beliefs,
underwritten by moral consensus. Furthermore, at any rate in modern
society, they operate chiefly with reference to a valid legal system. True,
their operations presuppose the possibility that violence may be brought to
bear in order to effect policy, and, true, now and then violence is actually
visited on particularly recalcitrant members of the society. However, such
events are much less frequent and significant than is presumed by students
with a radical, bloody-minded attitude:

> While undoubtedly sociology can and should take cognizance of the phenom-
> enon of a brutal and self-interested use of power . . . one should not deny . . .
> that such a phenomenon is surpassed in its significance for society by the
> institutionalization of binding legitimate power. A society's day-to-day exist-
> ence is affected to a much larger extent by reference to power normalized by
> means of law than by the brutal and self-interested exercise of power.[21]

Besides (and this is a view already presented by Durkheim) even punitive
and cruel visitations of violence on errant members of society have largely
symbolic significance; they reaffirm threatened values and, when they take

particularly spectacular forms, allow the majority of members to renew their own sense of moral commitment. In sum, in this perspective, according to Parsons:

> power is a generalised facility or resource in the society. It has to be divided or allocated, but it has also to be produced, and it has collective as well as distributive functions. It is the capacity to mobilise the resources of the society for the attainment of goals for which a general 'public' commitment has been made, or may be made.[22]

The emergence of political power has, for societal evolution, a significance comparable to that of money. In fact money and power have much in common, for both render societies more capable of handling rationally and selectively (respectively) their relationship with nature and their articulation and pursuit of collective goals, including those relating to the existence of a plurality of societies. Again, radical views ignore that significance. They also ignore the fact that just as one society's monetary system can differ from another's both in its technical sophistication and in the extent to which it is employed to mediate social relations, so can a society's system of political relations differ from another's. They differ chiefly in the extent to which they manage to institutionalize their political arrangements, vest them with cultural significance, standardize their operations by means of law or otherwise, inspire in society at large a sense of confident commitment to themselves, and can be put to effective use in guarding and occasionally modifying the social order.

It is in this sense that societies differ in the amount of power they possess and manage collectively. This difference, and not the relatively trivial fact that within societies power must be allocated unequally between its parts, should be the main concern of a sophisticated theory of political power. In other words, such a theory should not conceive of political power primarily, much less exclusively, as power *over* somebody, but rather it should articulate a sense that, at bottom, all power is power given *to* sombody in order to allow the collectivity as a whole to attain its goods.

To assess this view, we must in the first place acknowledge as valid the insight that the institutionalization of political relations may, as it were, *empower* society as a whole. The American political scientist Samuel Huntington made this point, as I interpret it, in a very different context – a critique of conventional approaches to the comparative study of government systems, which according to him overstressed the question of the *distribution* of political power (the reader should disregard the fact that some of the statements in the following long quotation sound somewhat odd today):

> The most important distinction between countries concerns not their form of government but their degree of government. The differences between democracy and dictatorship are less than the differences between those countries

whose politics embody consensus, community, legitimation, stability, and those countries whose politics is deficient in those qualities. . . .

The United States, Great Britain, and the Soviet Union have different forms of government, but in all three the government governs. . . . All three countries have strong, adaptable, coherent political institutions: effective bureaucracies, well-organised political parties, a high degree of popular participation in public affairs, working systems of civilian control over the military, extensive activity by the government in the economy, and reasonably effective procedures for regulating succession and controlling political conflict. These governments command the loyalties of their citizens and thus have the capacity to conscript manpower, and to innovate and execute policy. If the Politburo, the cabinet, or the President makes a decision, the probability is high that it will be implemented through the government machinery.[23]

Huntington goes on to compare unfavourably the governmental arrangements of Third World countries with those of the US, Britain or the Soviet Union. In other words, he considers the *empowering* effect of different degrees of institutionalization of political relations between societies that coexist in time.

Some critics of the Parsons–Luhmann view of power have acknowledged the same effect in the context of comparisons between societies located at different points along a continuum of societal evolution: 'In evolutionary terms there is good support for the thesis that the emergence of organised domination was a necessary condition for developments that go beyond the most elementary division of labor built on differences of age and sex. . . . In the emergence of more complex social structures . . . power plays a role similar to that of monetary market exchange.'[24]

Finally, one may also concede that, as Luhmann suggests, compared to the unrestrained recourse to it 'the interference of legitimate coercion is greater; think it away, and all of normal societal existence is perturbed and transformed'.[25] Granted all this, and acknowledging therefore its theoretical significance, this view of political power inappropriately settles by conceptual fiat an intrinsically empirical question: how far in given circumstances is power actually put to use in serving collective interests, as against those of the part of society that directly manages it?

One cannot deny that two sets of potentially contrasting interests are at stake, even if one assumes, as Jouvenel does in the following quotation, that society at large may be served by the development and institutionalization of power: 'society, in setting up an apparatus for its service, has brought to birth a small society which differs from itself and has, inevitably, its own sentiments, interests, and personal wills'.

Jouvenel quotes a telling reflection by Viscount Henry Bolingbroke, an important eighteenth-century English statesman:

I am afraid that we came to court in the same disposition that all parties have done; that the principal spring of our actions was to have the government of the state in our own hands; that our principal views were the conservation of this power, great employments to ourselves, and great opportunity of reward-ing those who had helped to raise us, and of hurting those who stood in opposition to us.[26]

Given this point (which constitutes the main theme, among other things, of one of the masterpieces of political sociology, Roberto Michels's *Political Parties*),[27] it makes little sense to assume, once and for all, that the question of the whole society's *power to* overrides one part of society's *power over* the other parts.

Furthermore, while probably in the majority of settled social circum-stances the political system's superior capacity to use violence as a means of enforcement is assumed and kept in the background by institutionaliza-tion rather than being wantonly and brutally displayed, such settled social circumstances are in turn the product of wanton and brutal violence, however occasionally exercised. Jouvenel, for whom power in its pure form consists in enforceable commands, criticizes the notion that 'a formation in which command is set up had needs and feelings in common – was in fact a community. Whereas, as history shows, communities of any size owe their existence to one thing only – to the imposition of one and the same force, and one and the same command, on divergent groups. . . . Beyond all question, power came first.'[28] If so, then the role that violence plays within political arrangements *in statu nascendi* – through military subjuga-tion, regime changes, the suppression of opposition, should not be declared to be theoretically less significant just because such arrangements, once in place, may endure with a less lavish and visible expenditure of violence.

A final point: as we have seen, the Parsons–Luhmann view of (political) power attacks an alternative view (largely inspired by Weber) that allegedly overemphasizes the distribution of power within a system, assuming it to be a *zero-sum* game; that view focuses instead on the variable quantity of power at the disposal of the system as a whole. In other words, the Parsons–Luhmann view considers *power over* as significant chiefly in so far as it increases or decreases (through the extent and manner of its institu-tionalization) *power to*. However, if one asks oneself how the amount of 'power to' available to a system can be measured, one is forced back, in my view, to the question of 'power over'. How would one decide whether system A possesses a greater or lesser quantity of the collective resource 'power' than system B other than through a mental or factual experiment in which one tries to prevail over the other, either through a direct confrontation or in competing for some goal they both aspire to but which they cannot attain to the same extent?

Differentiation as the master process

In my view, the necessity of resorting to such an experiment suggests that *power over* is conceptually prior to *power to*. By claiming the opposite, Parsons and Luhmann fashion a view of political power that excessively

resembles what I called earlier a strategy of justification, however sophisticated. If that claim is disregarded, however, the view becomes theoretically
significant in three related senses.

First, it counteracts an excessively bloody-minded view of the power
phenomenon. Second, as I have already stressed, it poses a number of
empirically important questions: for example, to what extent are which
collective interests served by a society's political system (or, rather, by
specific policies it undertakes)? to what extent is the recourse to violence
by that system effectively moderated and reduced by, say, its legal system?
to what extent is the political system supported by the hold upon the
population of which views of its legitimacy and appropriateness?

Finally, the Parsons–Luhmann view may be seen as a somewhat over-
sanguine, overconfident theoretical rendering of a very significant historical
phenomenon: the development of the modern state, particularly in its
liberal-democratic forms. It captures something unique about that development in that, in the course of it, political power both extended its
presence in the general social process *and* became relatively moderated in
its exercise, through a series of devices mentioned above (for example, the
division of powers, civilianization, the counterbalancing presence of other
forms of social power).

That view also entails a valuable hypothesis on how it has been possible
to reconcile these two apparently contrasting developments, the expansion
and the moderation of political power. It sees them as instantiating,
together, a very broad process which we can label institutional differentiation. That is: all societies have to confront a persistent set of basic problems
(such as how to extract natural resources, how to settle internal conflicts,
how to socialize the new generations, how to secure their physical boundaries, and so on); but some societies (modern ones in particular) increasingly assign such problems to institutionally distinct social practices, and
such practices increasingly follow different rules, deploy different resources,
control the activities of individuals through different roles. Thus each
institution can function according to the specific requirements of its
assigned problem, on the assumption that the others are being attended to
in the same specialized manner by other institutions. Their distinctive
activities can be brought to bear on one another by the means, once again,
of differentiated media, such as money and power.

Given this, the specific import of differentiation (or of the social division
of labour, another expression for the same process) is that, on the one
hand, each institution, not just those relating to political power, perfects its
own activities and makes them more rational, and, on the other, all
institutions assume, and adjust to, the presence of one another, since they
depend on each other's outputs for their own inputs, and vice versa.

Whatever the general merits and weaknesses of the notion of institutional
differentiation, it is difficult to see why Parsons and Luhmann used it to
enlighten us as to the nature of political power – or, indeed, of power – in
general. In doing so they overextended what is at best a sociological

interpretation of the course of Western modernization and of *its* political aspect, the development of the modern state. Apart from this, their emphasis on the notion itself of differentiation has its own uses for the rest of the argument in this book. As I have already indicated, after outlining its *protagonist*, political power, we shall now bring in the other forms of social power, considering them chiefly as interlocutors and contenders *vis-à-vis* political power itself.

This way of organizing the argument, however, only makes sense within a historical framework where both political power and the other forms are in fact, to a greater or lesser extent, institutionally differentiated. Each is assumed to inhabit a relatively distinct social sphere, to pursue relatively different social interests through different sets of practices, at the behest of (to some extent at least) different bodies of personnel. It is this that makes it possible and (hopefully) useful to entertain the question of *how* each of the other forms of social power relates to political power (though not, within *this* argument, with one another).

However, I shall emphatically not adopt, in my argument, an assumption commonly associated with the notion of institutional differentiation – that all differentiated institutions tend to co-operate with one another within a broad division of social labour producing the greater and greater efficiency of the parts and thus the superior harmony and rationality of the whole. On the contrary, I shall largely be interested in tensions and contrasts between the various forms of power and the relative elites.

These do not exclude either forms of explicit accommodation between those elites, or less visible forms of systemic collaboration, or, for that matter, systemic conflict between the respective power forms. The institutional configuration of each, after all, tends to lay constraints on that of the others: you cannot have a highly bureaucratized polity without a money economy for instance; yet there may be such a thing as a 'fiscal crisis of the state', or the way of pursuing political goals may choke a money economy and cause it to revert in the direction of a natural one.[29] In other terms, it is not the case that at the elite level we find both co-operation and conflict and at the systemic level only a relatively harmonic division of labour: here, too, the requirements of the system's diverse parts may conflict with one another.

The modern state

In any case the counterpart to each of the non-political forms of social power discussed by this book is largely the modern state. This is a set of co-ordinated institutions more or less expressly designed to perform all, and only, the *political* tasks pertaining to a bounded territory, within which it claims a monopoly of the legitimate use of violence. What tasks are defined as 'political' varies from situation to situation, but in spite of such variation it is assumed that there are realms of social activity with respect to which the state operates, if at all, exclusively in the role of guardian.

The monopoly of legitimate violence applies, so to speak, both on the inside slope of the territory – that is, in the enforcement of law and order – and on the outside slope – that is, in the deployment by a state of military force in defence of its own territory against encroachments from outside powers. In so far as the claim to such monopoly is a credible one – that is, if necessary it can assert itself factually, by prevailing against any who would challenge it – the state can be said to possess sovereignty. Each sovereign state confronts a plurality of other such states, all delimited by acknowledged boundaries. But from time to time boundaries may be 'up for grabs'; two adjacent states may contend over territory, or one of them cross over a previously acknowledged boundary in order to wage war on the enemy's territory rather than on its own. To be in 'the states' business' a polity must be recognized by other states as an entity of the same kind as themselves – that is, as a sovereign, territorial, political entity – and deal with other states on a footing of equality.

The dealings between states with one another in peace and war are most eminently a matter of relations between powers, since each state, as I am suggesting, is but one particular aggregation of political power, characterized by its relation to a given territory, by its sovereignty, and so on. Not for nothing, when one speaks of *Machtpolitik* ('power politics'), is the chief and sometimes the sole referent of the expression the relations between states. But, as I may need to remind the reader, this is not part of our theme here; we are not dealing with the relations between different collective embodiments of the same form of power, but with those between different power forms, as each manifests itself within a given state's territory, and to that extent somehow subject to its jurisdiction.

One final point: at the beginning of the modern era, when European polities begin to reconstitute themselves as states, the military dimension of political experience, and thus the phenomenon of violence in its most acute form, plays an absolutely central role. Whether it is a matter of enlarging the territorial holdings of a royal dynasty, or of preventing regional and religious conflicts from tearing apart the population within a given territory, those who want to stay in the political game must first and foremost increase their armed might and be willing to use it. Advances in the material and social technology of killing require such parties to mobilize greater and greater resources; thus for a long time, in most polities, the nucleus of the civilian apparatus of rule itself, the fiscal administration, is chiefly concerned with financing the armed forces, and lavishly deploys violence itself against the domestic population itself in order to extract those resources.

Subsequently, however, through complicated processes we cannot examine here, in many European polities the military dimension begins to lose visibility. It remains an essential part of the political business, but one that engages directly one specialized part of the apparatus of rule, within which other specialized parts multiply and begin to absorb a greater share of the public resources. Furthermore, the apparatus for exercising violence on the domestic front becomes progressively differentiated from the military proper, and is increasingly controlled by civilian authorities. In sum, political power undergoes the process I have already named 'civilianization'; those institutions more continuously and visibly involved in building it up and managing it are less and less directly involved in preparing for, threatening and practising violence.

This process goes further than anywhere else in the contemporary liberal-democratic polities. Here, as I have written in a previous work:

> [M]ost aspects of . . . political experience have become distinctly 'civilianised', and make little direct use of or reference to the ultimate sanction of violence. Those who normally act as the state's agents, in most aspects of its political and administrative activity, are conventionally attired, conventionally-mannered people, who operate in a most un-military fashion. Formal laws and explicit terms of appointment, together with well-established conventions, compel them to use highly stylised forms of speech in their activities, to refer to shared information, quote authorities, formulate rationales, cite precedents, acknowledge rules, avoid contradictions and *non sequiturs* and make a case for the action they are taking or intend to take.[30]

But if this is to happen without the renunciation by the state of its indispensable grounding in violence, there must exist, side by side with state institutions that operate in this fashion (and, *ideally*, under their control), others that continue, at the very least, to prepare for war. The expression 'ideally' above is intended to suggest that this relationship, whereby a thoroughly civilianized system of political authority remains throughout the arbiter of where, when, by whom, under what circumstances and at what cost for the larger society war should be prepared for or waged, is in fact often difficult to establish and to maintain. On this account, committed as I am to the notion that violence, including military violence, belongs to the essence itself of political power, I feel that my primary reference to more or less civilianized systems of political power authorizes me to treat their relationship to *their* armed forces as somewhat analogous to their relationship to other forms of social power. I shall do so in the last chapter of this book.

4

Ideological/Normative Power

Is there such a thing?

In this chapter, I intend to discuss chiefly the nature of religious power, which I consider as the primary instance, though not the only one, of what I call ideological/normative power. Before doing so, however, I should like to deal with two objections one might pose to the view that a power form exists to which one might reasonably apply that name, and which deserves separate consideration within a discussion of the broader phenomenon of social power.

According to the first objection, there is something doubtful about the notion itself of such a power form, for the coupling of 'ideological' with 'normative' yields an unstable, and indeed a contradictory, compound. The notion of 'ideology', if traced back to its precedents in the Enlightenment notion of 'prejudice', suggests a critical and indeed perhaps a 'debunking' view of cultural products and processes. In this view values, beliefs and norms appear as epiphenomena, that is as superficial representations (and concealments!) of underlying material structures of power and domination; and the people primarily involved in elaborating such representations, broadcasting them and inculcating them into others – priests, lawyers, philosophers, writers, academics – figure chiefly (whether they realize it or not) as the more or less useful servants of the powers that be. The notion of 'normative' has (as far as I know) a much shorter pedigree in the social sciences, but writers who make much use of it (for instance Talcott Parsons) or who do not use it but who inspire others' use of it (in particular Émile Durkheim) tend to take 'the *normative*' very seriously; value commitments, shared beliefs and values, are for them utterly central to the social process, and at any rate not secondary to any other components of it.

In other words, the point of the notion of 'ideology' is that one *should not* take ideas too seriously; the point of the notion of 'normative' is that ideas *cannot* be taken too seriously. According to this objection, the very contrast between its two components reveals the instability of the resulting conceptual compound. However, this instability does not much bother me, given what I consider the key advantage of that juxtaposition – to point up the complexity of the phenomenon in question. The two expressions have indeed rather different semantic burdens: in Durkheimian vocabulary, 'ideological' points more to *manières de penser*, 'normative' more to *manières d'agir*; that is to say, one suggests the importance of 'images *of*', the other the importance of 'images *for*'. But exactly because there is a significant difference between them, both can be usefully yoked and employed together.

The second objection can be formulated as follows. A recognition of the significance of the power phenomenon, and even more so an emphasis on it, are generally associated with a *tough-minded* view of social existence. Within such a view, the intellectual and moral aspects of that existence are considered derivative and subordinate with respect to those that constitute the material circumstances of groups, such as the demographic structure of a population, the pattern of its settlement over the territory, the level of development of technological resources, the distribution of property and control over those resources, the occupational structure, the networks of organizational linkages between individuals, the nature of arrangements for determining and enforcing public policy. Conversely, a *tender-minded* view of social existence emphasizes its dependency on collective definitions of what is true and proper, and the constraints non-material culture exercises upon the ways in which individuals deal with one another, form groups and solve collective problems. Here, even gross differentials between groups in the access to economic resources or in control over political decision-making processes may be treated chiefly as expressing distinctive value preferences which individuals acquire chiefly through early socialization and which are subsequently reinforced as they enact their roles in everyday interaction with partners. In this perspective, in other terms, the power phenomenon itself tends to be devalued if not overlooked. If the key visual metaphor for society associated with an emphasis on the power phenomenon, and thus with a tough-minded perspective, is the pyramid, or at any rate a configuration of parts structured chiefly by a strong vertical, up-and-down gradient, and held together by the pressure which the 'up' parts place on the 'down' ones; in a tender-minded perspective society is often visualized as a circle. There may be an up and a down to a circle, but what characterizes it is the equidistance of its parts from a central point; a social entity conceived of as a circle is supposed to be held together by the fact that all parts address their attention and their commitment to the same central beliefs and values.

In sum – the second objection goes – the expression 'ideological / normative power' contains a *contradictio in adjecto*, for both adjectives (whatever the tensions between them) belong chiefly in a universe of discourse associated with a tender-minded view of society, while an emphasis on the phenomenon expressed by the noun 'power' is generally associated with a tough-minded view.

To my favourite reply to objections of this nature – 'I contradict myself? Very well, I contradict myself' – I would add that in this case I am in particularly good company. Consider in the first place the so-called 'classics' of sociology. Karl Marx, for instance, certainly had a tough-minded view of society, and he expressly formulated a theory of ideological products as epiphenomena, grounded on and subservient to class inequalities arising in the first instance from the relations within which the material conditions of life are produced and reproduced; *yet* he devoted most of his immense theoretical labours to the task of disproving a particular set of ideological views, those concerning the nature of capitalism. More generally, Marx never thought that the derivative nature of ideological phenomena made them any less significant.

Vilfredo Pareto, for another example, was as tough-minded a social theorist as any; yet he chiefly theorized the hold upon the human mind of a diverse set of views and understandings, none of which he subscribed to but which he expected nonetheless to continue to inspire the actions of multitudes. (There are problems with the English translation of his *Trattato di sociologia generale*, but the title given to it by the translators, *The Mind and Society*,[1] accurately describes its theme.)

Among contemporary writers, Michael Mann, who can safely be said to hold a tough-minded view of society, has expressly committed himself to the view that there *is* a form of social power that one can legitimately label 'ideological'. Better yet, Mann has persuasively argued *why* there is; and in order to confront this question in turn, I will outline his own argument,[2] which identifies as many as three roots of the phenomenon.

In the first place, says Mann, 'we cannot understand (and thus act upon) the world merely by direct sense perception. We require concepts and categories of meaning imposed upon sense perception.' Hence, he argues, within any society a group (if any) which manages to elaborate a more or less coherent set of such concepts and categories, to 'sell' it to the rest of society, and to continue to validate it, if only by excluding alternative sets from a hearing, on the one hand empowers the society itself, on the other empowers itself over the rest of society.

In the second place, 'norms', that is 'shared understandings of how people should act morally in relation to one another', promote 'efficient social co-operation' and solidarity. Again, a group that can persuasively produce such understandings and ensure that they will be sanctioned by society thereby raises its 'mutual trust and collective morale' and can be the prime beneficiary of the resulting advantages.

Finally, a society is empowered by the extent to which certain forms within it of non-instrumental activity, embodied in ritual speech and motion and in visual and auditory artefacts, are seen as intrinsically appropriate, as symbolizing in a distinctively compelling manner particularly significant sentiments and intuitions, especially those relating to extraordinary, awesome and transcendent experiences. By the same token, a group can be said to possess power within such a society in so far as it is able to establish as uniquely valid and life-enhancing its own ritual and aesthetic 'symbolling' practices.

Mann summarizes as follows this construction of 'ideological' power: 'When meaning, norms, and aesthetic and ritual practices are monopolised by a distinctive group, it may possess considerable . . . power.' Note the symmetry between this construction and the way we have construed social power in general: what is decisive is a group's ability not just to possess itself of certain resources but to exclude others from them. Mann, however, does not make clear what is at stake in this power form as concerns the individuals subject to it. If, at bottom, what is at stake in the case of political power is the mortality and the susceptibility to pain, constraint and mutilation of the individual's bodily self, and in the case of economic power their need to have access to means of production if they are not to starve, what further generic human vulnerability is addressed (and exploited, and catered to) by ideological / normative power?

The answer is, in my view, best expressed in the Gospel's 'Man shall not live by bread alone'. Humans in general have indeed a complex and delicate need for psychical and moral well-being, not *just* for bodily integrity and for a full belly. They constitutionally bear the peculiar burden of artificially shaping their own existence in the absence of precise directives from nature and in the presence of and with the (often unforthcoming or unreliable) co-operation of one another. This – together with their aware-ness of their own finitude, fragility and mortality – potentially exposes them to an unbearably high degree of contingency and insecurity. They can counter this circumstance only by developing a sense of trust – trust in one another, trust in the solidity and validity of an intrinsically artificial, optional mode of existence, trust in the significance and continuity of their own identity.

In other words, individuals need to feel that the world makes sense, that they make sense to others, that others make sense to themselves. But they must protect themselves from the frightening awareness that the sense the world makes, others make, they make, is always an imputed, artificial, arbitrary sense. They live, so to speak, by writing meaning *onto* the world, but they must deceive themselves that they read meaning *off* the world. Or, to adopt Clifford Geertz's simile, they are like spiders hanging from webs of meaning *which they themselves spin*.

To protect themselves from the dizzying awareness of this condition, individuals must see themselves as parts of an overriding, comprehensive whole, to which are seemingly anchored the webs of meaning from which they are suspended.[3] Nothing less depends from their ability to relate themselves to this whole than their sense of personal identity and of worth. Only a socially validated complex of understandings into which they are socialized and which is authoritatively broadcast and coherently sanctioned by social practice can fashion and sustain such a context. Naturally its perceived significance varies to an extent from individual to individual, and for each individual according to the contingencies of his or her existence. However, to *some* extent each of us assumes all the time that our life unfolds within a larger whole, an 'order'.

Perhaps the coexistence in the expression 'order' of two contrasting yet mutually referring meanings conveys the complexities of what is involved here. In English as well as in other languages, 'order' suggests on the one hand a condition of given reality, a patterned, stable *arrangement of things* – as when we say 'everything is in order'. On the other hand, in its meaning of 'command', 'order' conveys an imperious, wilful, contingent *act of arranging* – as when we say '. . . and that is an order'. To take up again an analogy from Greek grammar I employed in chapter 1, 'order' has both a perfective and an aoristic meaning. This duality of meanings perhaps points to the fact that *states of order* depend on *acts of ordering* – yet in turn such acts produce their ordering effects only when somehow authorized by another layer of order.

The contours of the order we need to feel part of are – to begin with – mapped by our language. This is itself, of course, an artificial product, but we acquire it, and normally we employ it, as a *natural* medium of our relation to an intrinsically ordered reality, assuming once more as natural its capacity to represent that reality and to share that representation with others. In turn, language allows us to form, in communication with others, a more or less elaborate picture of the world, as well as a set of expectations concerning our relations with other subjects. As we have learned from G. H. Mead's theorizing about the formation of selfhood, it is ultimately from the stability and (again) the orderliness of those relations (particularly those with *significant* others) that we sustain our sense of personal identity. It is against the standard set by their moral expectations, in particular, that we measure our own standing as responsible, accountable agents. Once more, the content of the expectations themselves is at bottom arbitrary (remember Pascal's remark about acts which are meritorious on one side of the Pyrenees and criminal on the other side), but they can act as such a standard only if they are perceived as intrinsically valid and as compellingly binding, that is as themselves parts of an ultimate order of things.

In sum, the first two components of Mann's argument for the existence of such a thing as (in his terminology) an 'ideological' form of power – the necessity of a set of meaningful frameworks for the apprehension of reality and of a set of moral constraints on social conduct – turn out to have a decisive bearing not only on the ordering of social affairs, but also on the individual's need to feel assured of the meaningfulness of his or her own personal existence. To protect themselves from the destabilizing effect that the awareness of their arbitrariness would produce, both sets need to be perceived as part of a higher order of things: the categories of meaning as articulating ultimate Truth, the normative prescriptions as entailments of the ultimate Good. This may amount to saying that humans need to deceive themselves as to the origin and nature of some very significant aspects of their view of the world, particularly concerning the highest order of being. As Mary Douglas puts it: 'Delusion is necessary. For unless the sacred beings are credited with autonomous existence, their coercive power is weakened and with it the fragile agreement which gave them being. A good part of the human predicament is always to be unaware of the mind's own generative powers and to be limited by concepts of the mind's own fashioning.'[4]

This twofold reference to an ultimate, transcendent level of reality engenders the problem of how beings bound by time and space can experience it, represent it to themselves, address it; the third component of Mann's argument deals with this problem, since it concerns ways of symbolizing the ultimate, of evoking emotions focused on extraordinary experiences. This component, too, operates also at the individual level, affording the person a socially validated way of expressing an awareness of and a commitment to transcendent forces, amd thus securing the individual against the experience of cosmic loneliness and moral insignificance. (Again, Pascal has a passage where he recommends that the Christian beset by doubts about his faith should not suspend his practices of piety, but should go on enacting them regardless of those doubts, for at length, paradoxically, those practices themselves will regenerate within him that condition of self-confident belief from which normally they flow.)

The power of religion

I have argued so far that one may tenably regard ideological / normative power as a distinctive form of social power, resting on the extent to which certain constructions of reality affect the individual's capacity to locate mentally his or her own existence within an encompassing reality endowed with some moral purpose. Much of the argument will have suggested to the reader that the primordial institutional embodiment of ideological / normative power is constituted by religion, broadly understood (following Durkheim) as a complex of socially prescribed beliefs and practices relating to a realm of reality conceived as sacred.

In what sense, and to what extent, is it appropriate to think of religion as *having to do with* social power? I would argue that the connection between these two phenomena is very profound, and indeed belongs to the essence of each. To begin with, religion has generally been the original medium for confronting the first two problems characterized by Michael Mann. Time and again, a sustained confrontation of individuals and groups with the sacred has engendered sets of ideas and practices which in turn have served as primary vehicles for:

1   An understanding of the nature, origin and purpose of reality at large. Most mythologies – sets of narratives of primordial events inaccessible to human recollection and empirical account, and generally involving the actions and passions of sacred beings – provide, one might say, both a chart of and a charter for reality. More elaborate forms of religious thought, for instance holy scriptures and theologies, do this in a more self-conscious and more or less systematic manner, sometimes by distinguishing sharply between the realm of reality which is their primary concern and other realms, which are thus theorized, so to

speak, through difference. One way or another, religious thought is always concerned to make a statement about the world, and particularly to locate within it both human beings and higher beings.

2 An authoritative set of normative, sanctioned prescriptions dictating how human beings ought to conduct themselves with respect both to one another and to higher beings. Such prescriptions, which originally structured most of social conduct at large, may again be vehicled through myth or articulated in theological arguments. They may be embodied also in patterns of specifically cultic conduct, such as ritual; but ritual originally invested most fields of action, not just those expressly relating human to higher beings. This connection between religious practice and the normative shaping of social conduct is not only detectable in the context of preliterate and prehistoric societies. Fustel de Coulanges, a great student of the institutions of antiquity, saw that connection at the very core of the historical experience of ancient Greece and Rome. In both, originally, 'The city is, so to speak, a church; the town is a temple; statutes and the law are a religion; the magistrates are priests.'[5]

With some exaggeration, one may say indeed that the primordial form of prescribed collective conduct has everywhere been ritual, while the primordial form of collectively entertained belief has everywhere been myth. The connection of religion with the third problem mentioned by Mann, that of articulating an appropriate form of aesthetic expression, seems less clear – until one reflects on the role played here, again, by religious ritual. Much ritual consists in patterns of movement (including of course speech and chant, body ornament, posture, attire) styled in such a way as to express in a distinctly appropriate fashion, and to evoke in others, sentiments of awe, devotion and commitment with respect to higher beings, chiefly in order to placate, propitiate and celebrate them. But this connection between on the one hand externally perceivable behaviour (and/or artefacts and other objects) and on the other hand given emotional states – in particular, exalting or otherwise intensely significant states – which the behaviour seeks to express and/or to induce is the essence of aesthetic experience. And in fact that experience appears to have had its primordial forms, at any rate on a collective basis, in ritual behaviour. Dance, song and the production of visual artefacts, from masks to sculpture, poetry and theatrical representation, were probably everywhere, at first, components or adjuncts of cult and religious ceremony. Durkheim makes this point as follows in a broad-ranging statement: 'It is from myths and legends that science and poetry have separated; it is from religious ornamentation and cult ceremonies that the plastic arts have come, law and morality were born from ritual practices.'[6]

On these counts, it seems, religion, at any rate in the early phases of societal development, has taken charge of the three problems specified by Mann as the roots of the phenomenon of ideological / normative power. Its ability to do so rests in the very nature of its core concern as an institution – to define, project, preserve, *manage* the 'sacred'. Above, while specifying, as I phrased it, what is at stake for the individual in the emergence and workings of such power, I pointed up a basic social quandary: how to make what is artificial appear natural, and what is contingent and arbitrary, absolute and intrinsically valid. Solving that quandary is what sacredness is all about; its essence, according to an argument by Durkheim I consider still valid, lies in asserting and protecting the unique significance of certain aspects of reality (certain places, objects, words, persons, gestures, descriptions and prescriptions) by sharply separating them from all other aspects. The basic way of doing so, echoed in a brief passage from the *Aeneid* – 'Procul, o procul este profani' – consists in vetoing any profane, that is any casual, matter-of-fact approach to or handling of the privileged aspects. By implication, actors are forbidden to place alternative ways of thinking and acting on the same level as those aspects, forbidden to tinker with the latter, to replace them with the former in the light of mundane considerations of efficiency.

Thus, sacralization constitutes the primordial way of stabilizing what is intrinsically unstable, and to this extent is the manner *par excellence* of dealing with the above quandary. One symptom of this among many others is the fact that even Marx, committed as he was to the notion of secularization, and convinced that in modern society alienation no longer took chiefly religious form, recurrently fell back into religious imagery in criticizing the dominant modern forms: consider his notion of 'fetishism of commodities', the fake religious commandment 'Accumulate, accumulate: This is the law and all the prophets', the mock pious last words of his *Critique of the Gotha Program*, 'Dixi, et salvavi animam meam' ('I have spoken, and have saved my soul').

As I interpret it, religion's specific vocation for investing with extraordinary significance aspects of experience which are by their nature ordinary – being human products, aspects of the cultural process – assigns it, so to speak, a favoured starting position among all institutions in the race towards ideological / normative power and by the same token puts it, to change the metaphor, in the business of social power at large. One may detect other mutual implications between these phenomena, arguing for instance that the very concept of power as a unitary force affecting and ordaining reality has religious overtones, and finds an early formulation in such notions as 'mana' or 'the numinous'; or that the core aspect of political power, the ability to make a difference to reality by uttering commands, transfers to the secular plane a prime religious experience, the wondrous efficacy of the Word ('In the beginning was the Word').

In some of his posthumously published writings, Weber uses the religiously laden expression 'charisma' – gift of grace – as a generic noun designating a primordial, power-laden reality, and qualifies it with *two* adjectives lying on the same conceptual plane as one another – 'political' and 'magical'. A key sentence from those writings, 'the contrast between political and magical charisma is primaeval',[7] both implies the deep affinity between the two phenomena I am trying to point up here, and suggests their tendency to oppose one another, which I will stress later.

Significant as it may be, the mutual implication between religion and power does not indicate how religion, rather than simply referring to the power phenomenon, may itself become vested with a distinctive form of it. Even assuming a human need for certainty, under what conditions do those who address that need in others, by formulating certain ideas, teaching and leading certain practices, acquire a specific kind of power over those whose need is being addressed? A preliminary answer to this question, as I have already suggested, is implied by Mann's statements to the effect that in order to acquire such power a group must monopolize, so to speak, the *supply* of cognitive meaning, of moral regulation, of compelling aesthetic expression. Such a monopoly is more easily established when many individuals share the same existential needs, and these remain the same across time. Tocqueville develops a sophisticated argument to the effect that this is indeed likely to happen, in a passage from the second part of *Democracy in America* which deserves quoting at length:

> There is hardly any human activity, no matter how particular one considers it, which does not originate in a very general idea that men have conceived of God, of his relationship with humankind, of the nature of their soul and of their duties toward their fellow men. Nothing can prevent such ideas from being the source from which all the rest derives. Men, therefore, are immensely interested in acquiring fixed ideas about God, their souls, their general duties toward their creators and their fellow human beings; for doubt upon these primary points would deliver all action to chance and condemn it somehow to disorder and impotence. . . .
>
> Unhappily, this is also the matter on which it is more difficult for everyone, left to himself, and through the sole effort of reason, to acquire fixed ideas. . . .
>
> Fixed ideas about God and human nature are indispensable to the daily practice of their lives, and this practice itself prevents them from acquiring them. . . .
>
> [On this account] general ideas concerning God and human nature are, of all ideas, those which it is best to withdraw from the habitual activity of individual reason, and concerning which there is most to gain and least to lose in acknowledging an authority. The first object, and one of the main advantages, of religions, is to supply on each on these primordial themes a solution which is clear, precise, intelligible to the populace [*la foule*], and highly durable.[8]

Creating insecurity

In our current terms, Tocqueville's 'principle of authority' entails that within a given social group one source of such ideas tends to establish a *monopoly* in producing and broadcasting them. Often, this is not a matter solely of excluding from a hearing alternative sources of ideas of the same nature, but also of belittling the significance of ideas of a different nature, such as empirical ideas about mundane reality. Typically, it is asserted that such ideas are contradictory or delusory or, more radically, that their object – mundane reality itself – is insignificant, *not worth* knowing about.

Such cognitive 'devaluations of the world' are probably most outspoken in Eastern religions (Buddhism in particular), but can also be found in Christianity. A twelfth-century poem by the English monk Serlo of Wilton, for instance, emphasizes the transiency of human experience and the world's perishability:

> The world passes away as fast as time, as the river, as the breeze
> . . . The world passes. Quickly passes the name, and the world with the name
> But faster than the world's name, the world itself vanishes.
> Nothing exists in the world except the world that passes.
> The world passes; throw away what passes; and the world itself does. . . .
> The world passes; but Christ does not. Thus, worship what does not pass away.[9]

Characteristically, as this last line of verse suggests, religion, and particularly Christianity, not only asserts the ultimate insignificance of secular experience and condemns it, but holds forth a promise of release from that experience. Following the lead of previous critics of religion, in a famous sentence – 'Religion . . . is the opium of the people' – Marx argued that such promise is intrinsically deceptive, that religion affords only imaginary relief from the real evils of human existence. He might have made a further critical point: institutional religion often goes out of its way to generate the miseries that it then claims or seeks (effectively or otherwise) to remedy; the monopolistic suppliers of unworldly hope, as it were, *create* (do not just *meet*) the demand for their commodity by fostering fear and trembling. This mechanism is at work, for instance, in medieval Christianity's obsessive harping on death – as in the text of a fourteenth-century *Dance of Death*:

> You'll be a vile cadaver. Why don't you fear sin? You'll be a vile cadaver. Why do you swell with pride? You'll be a vile cadaver. Why are you greedy for riches? You'll be a vile cadaver. Why do you dress ostentatiously? You'll be a vile cadaver. Why do you hanker after honours? . . . You'll be a vile cadaver. Why don't you confess and repent?[10]

I would like to emphasize the complexities of the relationship between ideological / normative power (religious power, in this case) and those human vulnerabilities that, I have argued, it addresses. Ultimately, religious power rests on the individual's need for a feeling of moral security, a sense of personal worth. But such need cannot be assumed as a constant quantity; although it is rooted in the inescapable artificiality of the condition of the human species, it may remain unperceived by given members of it. This may happen, in fact, under very different circumstances. On the one hand, sheer material deprivation and brutish personal subjection may desensitize particularly wretched individuals to such need. On the other hand, particularly fortunate individuals may take utterly for granted their advantageous condition, consider themselves entirely deserving of it, and feel complacently assured of its stability; even when they know full well that 'stable, it ain't', they manage wilfully to suppress the resulting anxiety – though this is a difficult feat, as Horace acknowledges in his ode *Tu ne quesieris*. In both these contrasting circumstances, religious institutions may have to awaken a need for reassurance, before they can cater to it. Because the circumstances in question are so different, the need-inducing practices and beliefs of many religions tend to vault over that difference, as it were, by focusing on undeniable and inescapably universal human failings and liabilities. This may be one reason for their concern with death.

In any case, religious institutions often delicately juxtapose within the same context anxiety-arousing and anxiety-assuaging moments. For instance, in the Catholic mass for the dead – as I recall it from pre-Vatican Council II days – the celebrant's ceremonial clothing and the surrounding decor are in mournful black, and the text of the ritual is at first dominated by a disquieting dirge, the *Dies irae*; but increasingly, as the ritual progresses, reassuring and comforting words are spoken (for example, 'Vita mutatur, non tollitur' – 'Life is transformed, not taken away'), and the ceremony immediately preceding the burial culminates in a ringing 'Proficiscere, anima christiana' – 'Depart, Christian soul'.

Yet, if at some point relief from need is offered, this cannot happen without making sure that the need itself continues to be felt. A similar mechanism, incidentally, is at work in other forms of social power (and indeed extends to some practices that do not immediately appear to be in the power game, as Karl Krauss suggested in a biting aphorism, 'Psychoanalysis is the disease of which it claims to be the cure'). The mechanism is most clearly in operation in the primordial forms of the 'protection racket'. The racketeer first convinces potential protégés of how vulnerable they are to various kinds of damage, for instance by brutally disrupting their traffic, then steps forward to offer them 'protection' from further damage. In a manner more or less corrected by folk tradition, legal custom or religious values, the same mechanism appears in some embodiments of political power; for instance, in feudalism.

The mechanism, basically, fosters the continuing dependency of the power subjects on whatever the power holder can supply. In the case of religion, this consists in the assurance of one's good standing in the face of potentially punitive spiritual forces; and the beauty of the mechanism lies in the fact that such assurance, once acquired, can always be undermined, and the perceived need for it reproduced, by raising the criteria against which that standing is assessed. For even the just every day commit seven times seven sins; and even an individual who is openly irreproachable as concerns the grosser violations of religious obligation and moral duty can always be pointed to higher standards by which that individual cannot, so to speak, fail to fail, and can thus be urged ever anew to strenuous moral effort in order to protect his or her moral standing.[11] As Dante says of a soul in Purgatory, 'O dignitosa coscienza e netta / come t'è picciol fallo amaro morso'. In any case, it behoves everybody to take on board the sheer fact that at any time all humans can find themselves inexorably confronted with the *four last things* – Death, Judgement, Hell, Heaven.

Furthermore, apart from the failings of any single individual, human nature itself is often construed as constitutionally *at fault* in the sight of God – for instance, by the doctrine of original sin. Finally, a deeply felt self-abasement, a keen awareness of one's sinfulness, may be defined as itself an indispensable requirement of one's repentance and redemption. In the Gospel, Jesus condemns the self-righteousness of the Pharisee, who proudly compares himself to the publican. In Catholic moral theology 'the presumption of saving oneself without merit' is seen as itself a damning sin. In all these ways, to evoke again Marx's metaphor, the need for religious opiates may become a self-sustaining addiction; and on the supply for them – once more: if monopolized – can be grounded a distinctive form of social power.

Although, according to the argument so far, the colloquial expression 'putting the fear of God into people' characterizes what is perhaps the essential component of the power of religious institutions, that power may have other, different components. Besides inducing – and then assuaging – fear, religion may foster in believers a positive, energetic sense of moral well-being, of privileged fellowship, of assured, fulfilling destiny, of spiritual election, of personal significance in the sight of the deity. Such feelings may also sustain the believers' commitment to the religious institution and increase its capacity to make a difference to their conduct – which capacity, may I remind the reader, is the core of the social power phenomenon in all its forms. Consider the tremendous sense of heartfelt gratitude, of confident abandon, of trustful affiliation with God that Mary, pregnant with Jesus, voices in the *Magnificat*: 'My soul doth magnify the Lord, and my spirit hath rejoiced in God my Saviour'.

The hierarchical ordering of religious institutions

Religions vary in the manner in which they mix 'fear and trembling' (and the reassurance that counters them) with these positive motivations to belong to religious institutions and to comply with their requirements. The mixture also varies, within institutions, with levels and kinds of membership and leadership. This variation is one aspect of a broad tendency of religious institutions to acknowledge and to generate internal differences among believers. These, while sharing a generic membership, are 'layered' by the different extent of their religious qualifications and commitments, and by the different nature and significance of the related institutional roles. Weber emphasizes this differentiation:

> The empirical fact that men are *differently qualified* in religious terms stands at the beginning of the history of religion. . . . The sacred values that have

been more cherished – the ecstatic and visionary capacity of shamans, sorcer-
ers, ascetics, pneumatics of all sorts – could not be attained by everyone . . . It
follows from this that all intensive religiosity has a tendency toward a sort of
status stratification in accordance with differences in charismatic qualifications. 'Heroic' or 'virtuoso' religiosity is opposed to mass religiosity.[12]

Such differences do not necessarily translate into differentials in the extent
to which individuals come to possess and exercise power within religious
institutions. Jesus, for instance, contrasts Mary with Martha simply by
saying that the latter 'has chosen the better part', but does not assign her a
hierarchically higher position within the following to which they both
belong. (Neither sister qualified for admission to the strictly male circle of
Jesus's disciples.) In highly developed religious institutions, however,
Weber's 'differences in charismatic qualifications' tend to become corre-
lated with different locations within their hierarchical structure.

This correlation, however, may underplay the strictly personal nature of
those differences and treat them as attributes of the roles within that
structure. In Catholic theology, for instance, the efficacy of sacraments in
imparting or restoring grace to the soul does not depend on their being
administered by individuals not themselves in a state of sin, much less on
their personal saintliness or on what Weber would call their 'charismatic
virtuosity'. Rather, it depends on whether such individuals legitimately
occupy specific offices in the hierarchy (for instance, the office of ordained
priest for the sacrament of penance, the office of bishop for the sacraments
of confirmation and ordination) and duly perform the appropriate ritual
acts. The custodians and administrators of saving grace do not have to be
themselves, as it were, 'full of grace', but rather function as conduits
through which grace passes *ex opere operato*, by virtue of what they do (if
they do it properly) rather than by virtue of their personal qualities. In
Weberian terms, 'charisma' has been institutionalized.

In fact, the Catholic church has mostly looked with suspicion at those
spontaneous movements of religious feeling and thought that have periodically developed within it around unauthorized, self-appointed 'holy men'
and 'holy women'. The hierarchy has given recognition to such movements,
and made use of their capacity to revitalize the religious experience of the
masses, only to the extent that it could somehow pigeon-hole them within,
or next to, the church's own authority structure. Popes and bishops have
consistently claimed as their prerogative to vet and charter the internal
statutes of those movements, to monitor periodically their activities, to
make sure that the movements acquired, in turn, a firm organizational
structure, which could then be co-ordinated with (and subordinated to)
that of the church at large.

Such practices confirm that the monopolizing of resources remains a
critical strategy in the power game in all its forms. Once more, the Catholic
church on the one hand traditionally proclaims that 'extra ecclesia nulla
salus' – 'there is no salvation outside the church'; on the other hand, as we

have just seen, it assigns the control over the means of salvation to a structure wherein all significant authority, ultimately, flows from a summit occupied by a single individual.

But the relationship between these two aspects of the monopolizing strategy is complex. In the medieval context the whole Christian West acknowledged the bishop of Rome's supremacy and the church was truly Catholic, that is, it embraced the universality of people (with very few exceptions); thus the principle 'extra ecclesia nulla salus' had great prima facie plausibility. Yet at this stage in its history the church had a more loosely articulated internal structure than it acquired subsequently; it allowed greater autonomy to bishops and abbots, as well as greater heterogeneity in the religious beliefs entertained by clergy and laity and in their religious practices. Among other things, according to some historians,[13] this looser structure allowed the church, during the early modern period, to play host to new and daring intellectual and artistic developments associated with the Renaissance, to reconcile itself with, or indeed to promote, the humanistic 'new learning', and so forth.

Subsequently, by breaking up the religious unity of the West, the Reformation challenged the 'extra ecclesia' principle, transforming it from an assumption apparently in keeping with factual conditions into the stubborn claim of a now embattled church. At length, in the Council of Trent, the church responded to the challenge by producing its own internal reformation; that is, it structured itself much more hierarchically, and began to develop a much more elaborate body of binding belief and practice, which it imposed intolerantly wherever possible. The less realistic the *extra ecclesia* principle became, so to speak, externally – that is, the more it was denied by the actual religious condition of European society at large – the more imperiously did the hierarchy insist on its internal monopoly over truth and grace.

There are, in any case, other approaches to monopoly-building, characteristic of religious institutions whose structure, for one reason or another, does not have the sharp hierarchical slope of the Catholic structure. For instance, in Christian sects that expressly deny their ministers an exclusive role in forming the members' beliefs and in administering grace, and proclaim 'the priesthood of all believers', the ministers are sometimes expected to monitor each other's compliance with a strict code of religious and moral practice; and they often cultivate a jealous sense of spiritual exclusiveness and righteousness. Other religious groups, and particularly those often designated as 'cults', do not acknowledge ministers in any capacity – but the resulting, apparently 'flat', organizational structure is in fact built around the unchallengeable supremacy of one charismatic leader who has exclusive control over all religious resources of the group (and sometimes all material resources, including the monopoly of sexual access to the group's women).

Normally, in any case, religious power (as a prime and indeed primordial manifestation of ideological / normative power) emerges to the extent that a body of especially qualified personnel can routinely extend a sense of moral assurance and worth, a prospect of salvation, to less qualified individuals – and from now on, for the sake of simplicity, let us label the former personnel 'clergy' and the others 'the faithful'. The clergy's practices are likely to be especially in demand when the faithful encounter existential crises and transitions; they may serve either to celebrate the significance of some such occasions (as in the case of a child's birth, or of the attaining of puberty, or marriage) or to neutralize the sense of dread and the threat of meaninglessness that attend others (as in the case of death and bereavement).

A power mechanism is in operation in so far as the performance of these and other practices becomes an occasion to confirm and perhaps reinforce the asymmetry between those performing them and those on whose behalf they are performed. In administering the sacrament of penance, for instance, the Catholic priest recites the words 'in quantum possum, et tu indiges' – 'for *I* am empowered [to impart absolution], and *you* are needful of it'. This asymmetry is persistently confirmed and reinforced, since typically the faithful perform their own religious activities under the more or less direct guidance of their religious betters, and in the process of doing this ritually acknowledge their own inferiority. Their part in the clergy's religious activities, if any, is a subordinate one, and expresses in various ways (through posture, attire, demeanour, through obligatory rites of preparation) their submission and dependency.

Furthermore, the faithful's spiritual well-being is made to depend not only on their dutiful participation in such and other rituals but also on their learning and professing appropriate beliefs, acknowledging the weakness and vulnerability of their standing with God, orienting their own consciences to God's command. The clergy stand as an indispensable means to all these spiritual attainments: they elaborate and teach the beliefs, they assist the faithful in gaining insight into their moral failings and remedying them.

The inequality of religious standing between these two broad classes of institutional participants does not exclude some form of reciprocity on the spiritual plane. As they perform their services the clergy may not just bestow religious benefits on the faithful (assisting them through moral crises, informing their views of the world and of themselves) but may themselves gain moral assurance and spiritual merit from the sheer fact of 'doing their job', which is often characterized as a *service* to the faithful. To that extent, the clergy's spiritual welfare itself depends on that of the faithful, on their willingness to seek the clergy's services and duly perform their own religious role. According to Catholic doctrine, the church constitutes a kind of mystical depository of saving grace, continually replenished and augmented by the spiritual merits of all its members, clergy *and* faithful, although it is the prime responsibility of the former to see to it that the depository is duly drawn upon and to set the standards by which spiritual merit can be acquired.

In spite of these elements of reciprocity, whose significance varies from religion to religion, the workings of all highly institutionalized religions typically allow the clergy to make a greater difference to the faithful's ways of thinking and acting than the faithful can make to the clergy's. The flow of spiritual benefits is mainly one-way, from the clergy to the faithful, and this asymmetry may have to be compensated by a counter-flow of different benefits. Thus the clergy exact from the faithful various status and material advantages: they expect to be respected and deferred to, and they expect to be supported. But optimally this counter-flow is not perceived as of a wholly different nature from the flow to which it corresponds; paying respect to the clergy and supporting it economically, in whatever way (from almsgiving to tithe-paying or paying a fee for rituals performed), are construed as themselves meritorious acts, acts of piety, integral aspects of the individual faithful's spiritual redemption and progress.

This mutual implication of the spiritual and of other aspects of the clergy–faithful relationship is neatly indicated, I think, in a minor religious custom still practised in the countryside of the highly Catholic region of Venetia when I was growing up. The custom was charmingly called *el porzéo dele áneme*, literally 'the pig of the souls'. Each year, some peasant household would donate to the parish one runt from its own sow's litter. Over the following several months the piglet would be raised collectively by the parishioners, through a simple device: each peasant family, in succession, would feed the growing pig for a week or two at a time together with those belonging to itself, before passing it on to another family. In due course the pig, now fully grown, would be slaughtered and auctioned or sold at market value. Over the following year, the proceeds of the sale would be expended in paying the priest (on the usual 'fee for service' basis) for celebrating a number of indulgence masses – masses, that is, intended to afford spiritual relief to the souls (presumed to be in purgatory) of recently deceased parishioners.

One can see here some similarity with the late medieval practice of 'coins for indulgences' (which so outraged a young Augustinian monk, Martin Luther). In my view, however, the *porzéo dele áneme* custom bespeaks an intricate interlacing of economic interests, moral pressures, beliefs, willing attitudes and dispositions. It points up to what extent, even in its material aspects, religious power rests on the hold upon people's minds of engaging, compelling ideas. When this hold is loosened, religious power largely dissolves; or, to maintain itself, it must seek to summon to its side other power forms, and particularly the state. This possibility points up our next theme: the relationships between religious and political power.

5

Religious Power and the State

A variable, but always significant relationship

Let us assume that in a given society (to quote again Mann's perhaps overly concise formulation) 'meaning, norms, and aesthetic and ritual practices are monopolized by a distinctive group'. We have argued that this monopoly – however it is acquired and exercised – confers on the group in question a significant form of power. In so far as the group's activities are predicated on the existence of a sacred realm of reality and focused on the related human needs and emotions, we may label that form 'religious power'. That is, we assume that the group will routinely make use of its monopoly over 'meaning, norms, and aesthetic and ritual practices' to make a difference to the existence of the individuals active in that society.

It is of course a variable matter *which* aspects of that existence will be so affected. As we have seen, even such a mundane deed as handing over money or produce to other people may be treated as an obligatory or a meritorious religious activity when the beneficiaries are priests or monks. Furthermore, even activities where no such personages are involved, but which people perform on their own—for instance, sowing their fields or harvesting their garden produce—may be of some religious significance in so far as they are ritually regulated; that is, if people are expected to perform them *just so*, in a respectful and awe-filled frame of mind, on the assumption that a different way of going about such activities may offend the gods and bring misfortune.

All the same, Mann's expression 'distinctive group' suggests that normally the people who have acquired the monopoly in question operate in an institutionally differentiated context. That is, typically they do not seek to make a difference (or to make a difference *to the same extent*) to all social activities, but leave people to attend to some of them in a different frame of mind, in keeping with different rules and understandings, under guidance and control from *other* 'distinctive groups'. This will be true no matter how wide the scope of 'the sacred', and how widespread a reverent concern with it. To paraphrase Lincoln, some people will attend to sacred things all the time, and all people some of the time; but it cannot be the case that all the people attend to such things all the time. This raises the question of how the arrangements presiding over the people's dealings with the sacred relate to other arrangements. If we further assume that the latter also have a power dimension – that is, that there are 'distinctive groups' who routinely lay them down and make them binding for others – that question becomes: how does religious power relate to other power forms? However, as the reader will remember, our present remit is constituted *only* by its relations to political power.

This is in fact a very large theme, variations on which constitute a vital aspect of the institutional identity of both powers. As I have already suggested, their relations must be seen, to begin with, as expressing something like a common origin, or at any rate a primordial condition in which the political and the religious aspects of the power phenomenon were barely differentiated, if at all. Commonly, the holders of early forms of political leadership – tribal chieftains, for instance – have laid claim to an investiture from higher beings; they have grounded on mythical accounts of those beings' doings and sufferings the collective identity of those they led, the nature and the extent of their powers as chieftains. They have exercised these in highly ritualized forms, made use of sentiments of awe and fear appropriate to dealings with higher beings as motivations for complying with their commands.

Conversely, understandings of reality primarily concerned with ultimate things (typically, the nature and significance of the individual's death) have supplied the primary charter of many arrangements dealing with mundane matters, including who should hold political power, and committed such power in the first place to celebrating and upholding the folk ways derived from myth and echoed in ritual. In other terms, primeval leadership has cosmic origins and cosmic responsibilities; it is construed as an expression and a prop of an order of things centred upon the imperiousness and the overriding significance of the sacred. In a previous chapter, I have suggested that this tight overlap between the religious and the political also meets the leaders' need to hide from themselves and from those they lead the extent to which these two parties to the political relationship share a common blood, language, destiny. Once you *colour him sacred*, as it were, a leader appears to transcend these and other mundane commonalities, rendering them insignificant in comparison with the majesty he derives from such colouring.

The overlap is bound to become somewhat less extensive as political units become larger, for typically they do so by conquering, or by otherwise encompassing, a number of dispersed, diverse local communities. *These* typically constitute the referent of the primeval myths, the site of the chthonian divinities, the context of customs obtaining from time immemorial; all such warrants and charters of the primeval leaders' power must be either surrendered or complemented by new ones as those leaders transform, say, their chieftainship over a tribe or clan into rule over a plurality of peoples. But also the new warrants and charters tend to have a largely religious content, though often, to our minds, one too tainted by its fulsome celebration of sheer military might, conquest and the bloody extermination of enemies and rivals.

In any case, in the largest political units known to history – the great empires of Near Eastern and oriental antiquity – the whole institutional edifice always had massive, elaborate religious underpinnings. Of course it is difficult to establish what significance these may have had, in founding and managing those empires, in comparison with their more visible, material structures – for instance the ruler's standing army, the irrigation system he arranged to have built and maintained, or the networks of patrimonial officials who assisted him (well or badly) in extending the reach of his rule over larger and larger territories. The persistent overlap between religious and political aspects in particular arrangements for rule makes it difficult to assess the relative significance of either aspect.

For instance, consider writing – a formidable institutional device, whose early development is itself largely associated with those empires. Some of the earliest written documents that have come down to us from the ancient Near East, for instance, are inventories of possessions which scribes apparently prepared for the uses of administrators, to assist them in assessing and reporting the empire's material resources. Yet, in some cases at least, the local unit to which those possessions (and the scribes themselves) immediately belong is the *temple* – a place where fiscal, military and economic activities are routinely carried out, but (for all that) a place primarily characterized as a site of worship and cult, and guarded by (in Weberian terms) 'charismatically qualified' personnel. Besides, at least in some cases, writing itself was originally perceived as a sacred activity, as an embodied expression of the magical powers of the Word, and long remained the prerogative of individuals with priestly or semi-priestly qualifications.

This well-nigh inextricable entanglement between religious and political aspects in the ancient empires (present, incidentally, also in some of the later African empires, which, however, were constructed and managed without the aid of writing) is witnessed by a much later intellectual development. When some writers from the era of the European Enlightenment began to apply the concept of despotism to those empires and to their contemporary inheritors – the Ottoman and the Chinese empires – they chiefly intended to characterize a distinctive form of political rule, yet they emphasized that it had distinctive and significant *religious* components. In their view, echoed in later treatments of the concept, we are not dealing with despotism unless the ruler is surrounded by a sacred halo, his or her rule justified and supported by sacred ritual and myth.[1]

The Western version(s)

A closer look at this statement, however, raises a problem. Most early analyses of despotism were written by authors committed to the view that the phenomenon itself was an unenviable peculiarity of antiquity and of the

Orient, from which Western Christendom had been blessedly exempted. Yet some of those authors were writing in countries whose ruler was himself (herself, in a few cases) – as I have written above – surrounded by a sacred halo, his rule justified by sacred ritual and myth. A few of them may have stated, or suggested, that by the same token those Western countries were themselves tainted with despotism; but most of the others had a keen sense that, on the contrary, the involvement of religion in the construction and management of Western systems of rule, conspicuous as it may have been, *differed critically* from its political role in ancient and modern despotism.

Where did that critical difference lie? Essentially, in despotism the phenomenon of rule was itself the key source and the key referent of a distinctive set of cosmological beliefs and cultic practices; rulers did not simply make use for their own purposes of a self-standing religious system, but stood at the very centre of one specifically concerned with rule.[2] This did not necessarily mean that they suppressed other forms of religious thought and practice; often, they left those alone, for their scope was essentially local, and as such it did not necessarily interfere with their own concern – to build and manage a *trans*-local system of rule.

In the latter context, however, rulers typically claimed an autonomous, original religious position, not one bestowed on them by an outside religious authority, not one incidental to a religious system primarily preoccupied with matters other than political. For instance, at the beginning of the Christian era the Roman political system detached itself from the institutional form it had assumed under Augustus – often referred to as the Principate – and began to assume a more imperial form. In the process, the Roman emperor was increasingly considered divine, and relevant forms of cult were developed. Nothing, in this development, directly threatened local religions – which had, themselves, nothing to do with the empire – as long as their followers did not mind occasionally giving religious expression to their imperial allegiance by conducting the appropriate cults *on the side*, as it were. As it happens, Jews and Christians *did* mind, and thereby caused the empire (and themselves) no end of trouble.

In turn, the political environment in which the Enlightenment analysis of despotism was carried out presented two features that distinguished it sharply from despotism itself. In the first place, the political system of western Europe was not an imperial one, but had consisted for some time in a plurality of self-standing states, each controlling a sharply delimited territory and claiming the monopoly of the exercise of legitimate violence over it, all abstractly equal in their sovereignty and in their unchallengeable entitlement to define and assert (if necessary by waging war) their own interests.

In the second place, the European political system of the Enlightenment era inherited certain aspects of an earlier relationship with religious power which had reached its maturity in the Middle Ages. Here, all individuals and agencies involved in political business had had to come to terms with the existence of the Christian church – a self-standing, relatively well-organized and widespread system of religious power claiming to pursue a universal mission directly entrusted to it by God. This mission was of a distinctly spiritual nature, for it consisted in securing through time (*in saeculo*) the redemption of human souls from eternal damnation, and its significance transcended all worldly concerns, including political ones. The church could empower and recognize rulers and even assist them in their tasks, but only in so far as they, in turn, assisted the pursuit of the church's superior mission. Thus, rulers did not have, in the eyes of the church, any self-standing religious legitimacy and their activities had no absolute, but only contingent, significance in God's design – a design that the church, and the church alone, could directly interpret and safeguard, because again it had to do with spiritual redemption.

In other words, even the medieval political environment had been marked by dualism – for the political authorities saw themselves confronted by a self-confident universal, autocratically controlled church – and by the relative weakness of properly political institutions. That dualism had strong scriptural backing, and not just in Jesus's express commandment to 'Render . . . unto Caesar the things which are Caesar's', but in a number of other statements which counterposed his own mission of spiritual salvation to all worldly concerns. See for instance his provoking questions to people returning from having seen John the Baptist – '. . . what did you go out to see? A man dressed in silks and satins? Surely you must look in palaces for grand clothes and luxury. But what did you go out to see? A prophet? Yes indeed, and far more than a prophet' (Luke 7: 25–6) – or, most shockingly, his response to a disciple who before joining his following asked for time to bury his own father, 'Follow me, and leave the dead to bury their dead' (Matthew 8: 22).

For rulers, Christian dualism meant they had to come to terms, theoretically if not always pragmatically, with the existence of an autonomous religious power that they could not control. In fact, *it* sought to control *them*, by asserting the prior significance of its own mission, and this priority temporal rulers could not openly challenge. A maximum of accord and co-ordination between political and spiritual power was agreed to be the optimal condition; but each of the two powers had its own notion of *who* should frame the main parts of the accord and co-ordinate the other power with itself. In any case, even when the accord was at its greatest, and the related strains minimal, dualism was a persistent feature of the Christian West. One realizes this by comparing Christianity (and Western Christianity in particular) with Islam. Here political authority does not confront a specifically religious form of power at all autonomous of itself (there is no 'church' in Islam), but is itself directly and exclusively grounded on the Koran, and invested chiefly with religious responsibilities (the foremost among these being the propagation and defence of the faith). The imagery of the negotiation, which I am about to adopt to characterize the relationship between Western churches and Western states, does not at all fit this situation.

From the late Middle Ages, the West's inherent institutional dualism was made more visible by two processes of fragmentation. First, the semi-imperial framework of the *sacra Romana respublica* was challenged and increasingly weakened by the formation of a plurality of ever more independent centres of political rule, presaging the eventual division of Europe into a relatively large number of nation states, some of which would pursue in vain imperial designs of their own. Second, the religious unity of Western Christendom was broken by the Reformation. This second development variously interacted with the first. In some circumstances, rulers claimed sovereign, exclusive, paramount powers as a necessary means of protecting the political unity of their territory from the divisive effects of religious strife.[3] In different circumstances, rulers radicalized the political–religious dualism by committing themselves exclusively to the pursuit of specifically political interests, and declaring themselves indifferent to religious concerns and affiliations.

However, for the whole duration of the *ancien régime*, Western rulers never – well, hardly ever – sought to fashion anew or to re-establish forms of religious belief and practice expressly and exclusively concerned with political rule; they did not challenge the Christian assumption that religion has essentially to do with promoting spiritual salvation and should not be imperiously made to focus primarily on political concerns. When they distanced themselves from institutional religion, they sought distinctly secular new forms of legitimation: for instance, the promotion of the welfare of their country's population through police activities and the governmental sponsorship of progress.

Only the French Revolution, in one phase of its course, did not content itself with disestablishing the Catholic church but expressly attempted to impose a newly fashioned form of religious creed and ritual, non-Christian, and strictly oriented to this-worldly, collective, political concerns. The attempt did not take root; and from that point on Western political regimes have generally varied, in their attitude toward religious power, *only* on a spectrum that goes from a solicitous support of a single church to a sustained hostility toward some or all churches, but excludes any thorough attempt to resacralize the political domain.

Although this generalization will have to be qualified below, it is in my view valid enough to justify asking oneself why it is so. One may suggest two rather different hypotheses. First: Christianity represents a substantial, irreversible advance in the evolution of religion,[4] for it addresses primarily concerns defined as spiritual, shared by *all* individual human beings *as such*, since for each of them the Son of God was incarnate, died and was resurrected. No matter how weak the institutional and cultural presence of Christianity may have become (see the second hypothesis, below), this critical aspect of it prevents the West from taking on board with any degree of seriousness religious conceptions that would reverse that advance. A state embracing such a conception in the attempt to secure and strengthen itself would be on a hiding to nothing.

Second hypothesis: The cultural and institutional environment of modernity is the product of (among other things) a powerful process of secularization. Religion itself has been affected by it, in ways to be specified later. As to the state, its historical development in the West since the late Middle Ages has been a significant component of the secularization process; indeed it has to a considerable extent driven it. The very success of the process entails that there is nothing much the state can gain from entering, as it were, the religion business for itself.

The two hypotheses *converge* in suggesting that the state would have little to gain by redefining itself as also a religious institution, fostering a new (but, in fact, an archaic) conception of the sacred centred around its own distinctive institutional concerns – the organization of legitimate violence, the pursuit of power, or whatever. They *differ* in that, according to the first hypothesis, there is still enough Christianity around, so to speak, to make trouble for any state attempting such an operation; according to the second, in a thoroughly secularized society a religious redefinition of the state would ring hollow, and gain little or no additional leverage for the state upon that society.

Church and state

The previous few pages will have to suffice as a narrative backdrop, however minimal, to the task with which this chapter is mainly concerned – a conceptual discussion of the relations between religious and political power. To make the discussion more concrete, let us think of each power form as organizationally embodied in a distinctive institution, for which we shall use the conventional terms (respectively) 'church' and 'state'. These terms are by no means appropriate to *all* major embodiments of those powers; using them restricts the discussion to post-medieval, Western Christendom, and does not exhaust the variety of institutional forms of religion that existed in that context – but such a referent is wide enough for our purposes.

Church and state in principle constitute two autonomous entities, each seeking to exercise, by means of the distinctive power it possesses, the largest possible leverage over the current circumstances and the future development of the society in which they *both* exist. They thus operate in the presence of one another; and – here is the rub – neither feels it can make anything like the difference it would like to make to the environing society in the pursuit of its own institutional mission, without making some difference *to the other*, laying some constraints upon the way *it* operates. On a number of counts, each may find attractive the vision of a society where it exists alone (as in Henry II's plea during his conflict with Archbishop Thomas Becket, 'Will no one revenge me of the injuries I have sustained from one turbulent priest?'). Yet they are stuck with one another; their mutual strategies are generally *not* directed towards the elimination of each other. Each seeks, rather, to adapt to the other's presence, to minimize its interference, to ensure at worst a kind of constrained compatibility between the other's policies and its own, at best a degree of willing, express co-operation. But even that optimal situation would produce strains between the two, chiefly over *which* of the co-operators calls the tune and / or gains most from the co-operation.

A further complication is that some of the things each power wants from (and *for*) the society, some of the constraints it seeks to impose upon it, can only be made possible by the other power, and have to be mediated through it. To give a rough example, an ancient Christian prayer beseeches God to liberate its people 'a peste, fame et bello', 'from plague, famine and war'. While here God is considered as the sole *ultimate* source of protection against such scourges, *proximately* at least two of the obverse conditions (availability of foodstuffs, and a condition of peace) clearly depend on worldly activities, and the successful performance of these is the implicit object of the prayer.

To this extent, one power may not be merely compelled to assume the other's existence, but may *depend*, for its own sake, on its doing its job. Actually, things are somewhat more complex; in the short run, at any rate, one power may have something to gain from the other's defaulting its duty or shirking in its performance. At the end of the Franco-Prussian War of 1870–1, Bismarck observed that, as the German armies rolled into the French countryside, all structures of civil authority seemed to have crumbled – and 'the only people we found on their feet were the *curés*', the parish priests. And Gerald Brennan observes that in certain cases, during the conditions of heightened social and political disorders of the Spanish Civil War of 1936–9, the Spanish church seemed to have regained some of the moral stature it had lost in the previous decades.[5]

The upshot of these considerations is, I suggest, that church and state are best thought of as involved in *negotiating* with one another. That is, each party tends to confront the other with claims – claims for freedom from the other's interference, for assistance, for support, for co-operation – but also with the offer of counterpart performances. Each may challenge and threaten the other, but must also present itself as a potentially credible collaborator, able to deliver some useful goods. One party may even argue that it needs some satisfaction of its claims in order to *remain* able to deliver those goods; that, in sum, it is in the other party's interest to accommodate to its own interest. While sometimes one party may seek to do as much damage as it can to the other, normally what one finds between church and state is a *process* of mutual accommodation.

I emphasize 'process', because the complexity itself of the relationship will subject it to frequent strain and change. Besides, the terms of the accommodation may shift as a result of changes not directly and exclusively in the two parties' bargaining position, but in the environing societal circumstances. For example, cultural secularization and the advent of the market economy have deeply affected, *from outside* as it were, the content of church–state relations.

What the church can offer the state

In what follows I shall assume the standpoint of a thoroughly organized, self-confident religious institution – a Christian church, essentially, with the Catholic church providing as usual most of the examples. What can such an institution offer the state in the negotiation process?

Essentially, its ability to *consecrate*, to *hallow* social arrangements, to make them appear uniquely valid, significant and compelling. To political arrangements, in particular, the church can impart *religious legitimacy* – that is, it can induce the faithful to consider existent political institutions as a necessary, indeed a beneficient, component of a God-willed ordering of human affairs, entitled to dutiful submission on the part of those they control.

For political institutions, legitimacy means they can assume, in their routine operations, that subjects or citizens will comply with the orders of political authorities on the basis not only of unreflecting habit or of fear of punishment, but also of a willing disposition to obey, motivated by a sense of obligation and of moral self-respect. This condition greatly facilitates the workings of political institutions, relieving them to an extent from the burden of having continually to monitor the conduct of subjects or citizens, to frighten them or cajole into submission. Legitimacy need not be religiously grounded, but in an environment where a church enjoys much moral credit its offer to expend some of it on behalf of the state is not one the state can lightly refuse. One reason for this is that Christian churches have a particular ability to solemnize, to charge with symbolic significance, all manner of rites of passage, including those connected with the system of rule: the crowning and enthronement of a new ruler, the burial of the fallen warriors, the laying of the cornerstone of a new monument or a new official building, sometimes the public punishment of miscreants. The *oath* is (not only in Christianity, of course) a religious ritual which features within both such 'liminal' circumstances (for instance, the oath taken by newly inducted soldiers) and more humdrum ones (for instance, the oath taken by a witness in the course of a trial). In both cases, the state expects that ritual to endow the occasion with great emotional potency, making it easier for military authorities to send young men to be killed in war and for judicial authorities to settle a pending dispute.

A further, complementary reason is that a well-ordained Christian church is a complex, sophisticated organization, differentiated into various components, which is routinely present in all localities, addresses all social strata, and easily adopts the idiom and responds to the preoccupations of each – *yet* operates in a coherent, predictable manner, thanks to a more or less sharply hierarchical structure and to the prolonged process of socialization of ecclesiastical personnel. Being so constituted, Christian churches were able for centuries to make themselves particularly useful to political rulers who had not yet established an apparatus comparable with the churches' own in extensiveness, coherence and reliability. The services a church could offer were not exclusively connected with legitimacy, but sometimes assumed that legitimacy and addressed the more mundane needs of the political order (the communication of directives, the collection of information, the monitoring of compliance). The overlap in the English expression 'parish' between its properly ecclesiastical meaning as the seat of the local church and its meaning as an administrative unit is a reminder of the resulting situation.

Whatever its variants, the most significant benefit the church could normally offer the state in its negotiation has been its ability to legitimate the political system and thus (to use Weber's expression) to 'domesticate' its subjects,[6] making them more amenable to political control and discipline – indeed, to oppression. In the liturgy of the Russian Orthodox Church, for instance, the inculcation of obedience and indeed devotion to the tsar was *the* central message, incessantly broadcast to the faithful.

I have suggested above that this particular service to rulers involves the most generic property of the sacred, its ability to 'stereotype' conduct (another of Weber's expressions) by generating a respectful, 'hands-off' attitude toward existent arrangements, concealing their contingent origins. More peculiar to Christianity (though by no means exclusive to it) is the fact that religion acknowledges suffering, justifies a sense that things are not right in the world, yet largely shifts towards the hereafter the aspiration to set them to rights. Suffering itself, *if* borne in the appropriate manner – that is, in an attitude of hopeful resignation – is considered the safest avenue to salvation. Martin Luther, on being asked by a peasant girl how she should seek happiness, exclaimed that Christianity had nothing to do with happiness, everything to do with 'Leiden, Leiden! Das Kreuz, das Kreuz!' ('Suffering, suffering! The cross, the cross!'). And Marx ironically remarks somewhere that in nineteenth-century France the mortgage landlords held on peasants' holdings was secured by the mortgage the peasants held on heavenly holdings – if they behaved as proper Christians.

Closely related to the virtue of patience, as the willingness to experience suffering without anger, rebellion, or impatience, is a moral disposition to de-emphasize the significance for one's own existence of earthly goods and enjoyments – a disposition that according to Tocqueville constitutes religion's great antidote to the materialistic temper characteristic of modern times.[7] This disposition does not only have the *negative* political significance of curbing the corrosive influence of greed, but also the *positive* one of encouraging solidarity between individuals, for it allows them to focus their minds on values that they share as against things the competitive pursuit of which divides them.

Tocqueville's insight on this point indicates a further potential 'offering' to political power from religious power as embodied in a church. Under certain conditions shared religious affiliations may constitute the primary ground of collective identities, which potential rulers find, as it were, ready-made in the social environment and in the cultural heritage of a region, and which they can mobilize toward political ends much more easily than they could fashion them out of whole cloth. Within the compass of Christianity, one may consider Ireland and Poland as plausible exemplars of this phenomenon. In both cases a powerful collective identity was fostered at length by the Catholic church, under circumstances that forbade it to express itself politically, until it became possible for it to define *also* a political constituency. That identity had strong religious overtones; in both cases it was largely grounded on the peculiar status of Catholicism as the religion of the great majority of the population, and at the same time as a relatively underprivileged religion, with a stake in the amelioration and possibly the subversion of the political *status quo*. Religious symbols (St Patrick, the Polish Black Madonna of Czestochowa) supplied oppositional political leaders with highly effective, universally recognized ways of signalling their commitment to the preservation and reassertion of national values.

In essence, then, the church can chiefly make itself useful to political power when the latter on the one hand seeks to institutionalize itself – that is, wants to rely less and less openly and frequently on violence in order to exact compliance with its own commands – but on the other cannot, by itself, evoke enough willing, morally motivated compliance. The state is of course a highly institutionalized form of political power, which typically has made considerable advances towards an autonomous, strictly political justification of its own existence and of its activities. It appeals to the nation as its constituency, proclaims as its mission that of pursuing power in the international context or of fostering public welfare, commits itself to the rule of law and the political safeguard of civil society. All these strategies of justification have their own costs and their own limits, and probably cannot be as efficacious in 'domesticating' the population as a diffuse, implicit sense of moral obligation to obey the laws, pay taxes, support and cherish the rulers, willingly kill and be killed in war. But such a sense can be probably best inculcated (if at all) by religious power, thanks to its command (to quote Mann again) over 'meaning, norms, and aesthetic and ritual practices'. This is where the church comes in, offering to place that command at the state's service.

What the church expects of the state

For a consideration, of course. Indeed, what we have considered so far is only one side of a bargain – the other side concerns what the church expects of the state in return for what it offers it. Typically, the expected return consists in some form of public recognition of the church's existence and public support for its mission. This expectation arises from the fact that, under modern conditions, the state takes charge of a number of social activities with a direct or indirect bearing on the church's ability to preach the gospel and to guide individuals to salvation, and which in any case the church has traditionally considered legitimate concerns of its own. In particular, the state lays down to the public juridically sanctioned frameworks within which individuals are expected to encounter the great thresh-old experiences of the moral life – birth, copulation and death, as T. S. Eliot might say. Questions concerning sexuality, marriage, filiation, social-ization of the new generations, the appropriate treatment of the ill, the wretched, the deviant, the extent of the responsibility of the fortunate towards the unfortunate, the protection of the young from exposure to the brutalities of existence, the public treatment of ways to deal with these matters *in*consistent with the Christian heritage – all these questions, according to the churches, put the state in the business of morality in so far as it deals with them (and deal with them it *must*).

This raises a problem – from what source of moral authority will the state derive its answers to those questions, what values will such answers embody, which will they disregard or violate. The church considers itself the depository and the interpreter of ultimately appropriate answers to all those questions; but since *it* cannot publicly validate those answers, or give them the status of sanctioned, binding directives for moral experience, it expects *the state* to do so. The state cannot be morally neutral with respect to those questions, shun its duty to address them in an authoritative, binding fashion, or fashion itself as a self-standing source of moral inspira-tion. The state is, itself, a worldly reality through and through, therefore it should show its awareness that the church has, instead, a mission tran-scending the world. However, it cannot pursue that mission if none of the structures of worldly existence, and in particular those ordained through the state's commands, respect and reflect its own teachings. At bottom, the church would like the state to treat (at any rate some) *sins* as *crimes*.

This is, then, the other side of the bargain. The state, legitimated by the church – and thus allowed to benefit, while pursuing its own ends, from the church's unique ability to *colour sacred* certain human activities and institutions – is expected in turn to impart the unique authority of its own arrangements (ultimately, of its own monopoly of legitimate violence) to the church's moral vision, embodying it in binding public frameworks compatible with, and as far as possible inspired by, that vision. It may do so selectively and cautiously, respecting the equality of citizens before the law, protecting the rights of religious (or anti-religious) minorities, not going as far as conferring on any church established status or committing public funds to any expressly religious activities. But it cannot, as far as the church is concerned, turn its back on the necessity of (ultimately) taking a stand on matters of morality, both private and public, or ignore the fact that the church considers itself the judge of the validity of such stands.

These are minimal demands, advanced for instance by most American churches. These respect the heavy restraints that the US Constitution places on actions by the federal state expressly favouring (or disfavouring) any religious body, and on that account American churches mostly articulate their claims by appealing to such 'unofficial' grounds as the nation's Christian (or Judaeo-Christian) heritage, or the moral conscience of the American people, of which they consider themselves the guardians.

Churches operating under different circumstances are not so shy; they seek more forthcoming forms of support and recognition from the state, and sometimes expect these to be embodied not only in a state's current policies, but also in its constitution. The Italian constitution of 1948, for instance, explicitly referred to the Concordat of 1929, stipulated between the Holy See and the Italian state (then controlled by the Fascist party), as regulating the relationships between the recently constituted democratic Italian Republic and the Catholic church. This had gained through that Concordat very considerable public privileges which it had no intention of surrendering just because the Fascist regime had recently come to a sticky end.

In that case, and in many others, the public privileges conferred on the church concern in the first place two aspects of social existence by which, as I have already suggested, all churches set great store: sexuality, addressed through the legal regulation of marriage and procreation, and education, with special reference to the religious and moral content of the curricula and the status of educational institutions established by religious bodies. This last question shades into a broader one of great significance: whether, to what extent and in what ways the state may commit public funds to the financial support of such institutions and more generally of the churches sponsoring them. Should some form of fiscal exemption of church property suffice, or should priests and other religious personnel receive a public stipend or other subsidies? Should they be exempt from military service, or on what terms should they become a distinctive, well-regarded part of the military establishment? These are some of the problems at the hard end, so to speak, of the generic question of how, if at all, the state should extend its recognition and support to the churches. Time and again, over the last few centuries, in many countries, the settlement of those problems has become the object not only of hard bargaining between the church and the state but also of sometimes fierce contentions within each party.

What makes those and related questions so problematical is their complexity. In *Ulysses* James Joyce refers to Jesus's commandment, to give Caesar what is Caesar's, God what is God's, as 'a riddling sentence to be woven on the Church's looms'. In dealing with the state (as in dealing with other worldly powers) the churches are also trying to comply with another of Jesus's commandments, that his disciples should be *in* but not *of* the world. This is another riddle-ridden mandate; it could be argued that the great division of Christian religious institutions into churches and sects reflects the intrinsic difficulty of complying thoroughly with that mandate: roughly, the churches give priority to being *in* the world, the sects to *not* being *of* the world. But even in the framework of their own priority the churches perforce encounter persistent, serious difficulties – reminders, perhaps, of the half of Jesus's mandate they have implicitly downgraded. Even an apparently well-settled bargain may conceal problems which a change of circumstances reveals to be intractable.

Consider, for instance, a religious ceremony taking place on 4 May

1789, the eve of the opening of the Estates General of France, described by the historian Dansette.[8] He first shows us a procession of nobles and notables holding candles and chanting hymns, then points up among these people some individuals (for instance, Mirabeau and Robespierre) who were soon to lead a ferocious political battle against the very church to which they are apparently demonstrating their devotion. This anecdote indicates a critical *religious* danger of too close an accommodation between church and state; chiefly, that of inducing in statesmen (or aspiring statesmen, or for that matter people at large) only a shallow and precarious commitment to the church itself, likely to turn, under changed circumstances, to indifference or indeed to revulsion and hostility. But there are also *political* dangers; for instance, the supine, well-rewarded subservience of the Russian Orthodox Church to tsarist autocracy at length deprived it of most of its moral credit, and when the regime became embattled and tottered it found in *its* church only an unavailing, rickety source of support.

More generally, whatever advantages the state may draw from the legitimating services of the church may have to be paid for dearly. Those services transform political arrangements into central aspects of a broader, God-willed order of worldly affairs; they impart to those arrangements an aura of sanctity which protects them from the intellectual and practical challenges of critics and opponents of the political *status quo*. By the same token, however, religious legitimation tends to freeze that *status quo*, to restrain even the rulers from tinkering with it; in this way, it places a heavy mortgage on their freedom of action, their ability to improve or suspend arrangements, to confront new contingencies with new solutions.

Furthermore, religious legitimations of the political order tend to construct some kind of reciprocity between the rulers and the ruled. Often, they justify the privileges they vest in the former by making them responsible for rendering the latter some services (including the preservation of their customary entitlements). For instance, the late medieval Germanic literature of the *Fürstenspiegel* (literally 'mirror of princes') celebrates the powers rulers hold from God and asserts the related duty of obedience of the ruled; but it also admonishes rulers to look after the people's security and welfare. No matter how much practical leeway these injunctions leave the rulers, they expose them to the risk of delegitimization should their dereliction of their responsibilities become particularly flagrant and oppressive. Even in the great despotic empires, where religious legitimation seems to have been most powerful, such delegitimization can be disastrous, and leave the emperor distinctly naked; when, as repeatedly happened in classical China, the Mandate of Heaven which empowers the ruler appears to have been withdrawn, the imperial dynasty may be threatened.

Finally, religious legitimation, whatever its limitations, works best where one church holds an effective monopoly over, let us say, the production and management of 'meaning, norms, and aesthetic and ritual practices' for a whole society. But suppose this monopoly is broken, and a number of churches compete to supply those intellectual, normative and symbolic resources for the society, or each of them has (so to speak) cornered the demand for them each with respect to a different sector of society. Both these circumstances make it dangerous for the state to rely on religious legitimation; its effort to control politically all of society can be hindered if it associates itself too closely with one particular creed or church, for then what legitimizes it with respect to one sector of society may delegitimize it with respect to others.

In the course of Western modernization, the awareness of these several liabilities of religious legitimation contributed to pushing the state, to a different extent and according to different timetables in various parts of Europe (and then in North America) toward its progressive disentanglement from the church or the churches, or, more broadly, toward its own secularization. A secular state has been synthetically defined as one that 'guarantees individual and corporate freedom of religion, deals with the individual as a citizen irrespective of his religion, is not constitutionally connected to a particular religion nor does it seek to promote or interfere with religion'.[9] By the same token, a secular state is one that seeks to do without religious legitimation.

Interestingly, over the same stretch of Western history, similar considerations induced the Christian churches (in a manner and to an extent different from church to church, and from locale to locale) to accommodate themselves to the secularization of the state. The most important consideration was perhaps one foreshadowed by the episode from French history reported by Dansette: when the basic arrangements through which a given state conducts its business become contentious (for instance, when one contends over whether the state should be constituted as a monarchy or a republic), a church that legitimates religiously a given set of arrangements may unwittingly lose its moral credit with all those social forces committed to alternative arrangements, and jeopardize its own efficacy as an institution of salvation.

Basically, the demise of the European *anciens régimes* meant that the churches could no longer unproblematically identify themselves with all of a given national society by means of 'the alliance between the throne and the altar', or by other sweetheart deals with the society's traditional political elite. They could either take sides in the increasingly divisive and contentious political process and take the attendant risks, or they could try to distance themselves from the political process by (among other things) accepting more or less openly the secularization of the state. Often, they tried to combine both alternatives, for instance by allying themselves with whatever party showed the best promise of remaining safely in the majority for the longest time. But if, as one says, 'the Church of England is the Tory party at prayer', even this strategy is bound to impair its mission as far as the social groupings associated with the Liberal or the Labour parties are concerned. A variant of this strategy consists in the church sponsoring, more or less openly, parties of its own, intended to secure the best possible deals with it: optimally, by gaining power on a stable basis (as with the

Christian Democratic party of Italy between 1945 and 1993); alternatively, by opposing the damaging policies of other parties (as with the Catholic *Zentrum* in the German empire).

Further contingencies of the relationship

Let us return briefly to our argument concerning the disadvantages that the state may incur if it depends on the church for legitimation. A state unwilling to incur them does not have to *do without* legitimacy – that might also be disadvantageous. It may instead attempt to develop new, non-religious, specifically political forms of legitimacy. One of these consists in proclaiming that the state's power and its entitlement to dutiful obedience on the part of subjects or citizens are grounded in the validity of *law*, understood as a set of general, abstract, coercively sanctioned commands.

The appeal of this kind of legitimacy, which Max Weber called legal-rational and considered the most appropriate for the modern state, lies in the fact that the law as so understood is itself an aspect of the autonomous functioning of the state, which produces it according to its own internal rules, in the light of its own needs and preferences. Such legitimacy, not being imparted to the state from outside, has the advantage of not confronting it with potentially embarrassing requirements and criteria. Alas, for the same reason it is not morally very compelling. If the validity of whatever is a given state's law depends only on the observance of procedural rules, this observance guarantees at most the *legality* of its operations, and does not anchor it to any substantive principles that those subject to the state acknowledge as just and intrinsically valid.

There are ways of remedying this difficulty while continuing to rely on the law as a legitimating institution. The principal one consists in establishing a hierarchy among the law's contents, fixing the most significant rules in a special document (typically, a constitutional charter) which specifically grounds the legitimacy of the state. Such rules, protected from the vagaries of the state's day-to-day legislative choices, express the state's abiding commitment to certain principles (among these, perhaps, certain rights of citizenship) which have a particularly strong moral resonance.

Other responses take a different route. For instance, the state may be seen as legitimate because it gives political expression to the transcendent right to exist and to pursue its collective destiny vested in an emotionally potent supra-individual entity, the people or the nation. Or the state may be construed, in a more matter-of-fact manner, as a massive political instrument for the promotion of economic development and thus for increasing the material welfare of the population, seen as a mass of consumers of goods and services.

Finally, states may undertake to confer a kind of semi-religious legitimation upon themselves, without the mediation of the churches. Such an attempt goes against the secularization trend characteristic of modern culture, but if successful it may allow a state to benefit from the distinctive *consecrating* effect of religious legitimation without making itself beholden to an outside power centre. This strategy is embodied in various forms of symbolic politics, which occasionally confer a hieratic majesty upon particular political institutions and events. Often symbols drawn from religion proper are inserted within a political context – as when, for instance, the literary or visual imagery of 'sacrifice', whose religious components are suggested by the expression itself, is applied to the death of soldiers. Alternatively, political symbols are made to gain expressive potency from becoming associated with religious places and occasions.

American 'civil religion' is rich in these devices, and produces effects that outsiders find intriguing. I remember, for instance, how shocked I was at first by the obtrusive presence of 'Old Glory' immediately next to the altar of US Catholic churches. Later, I found amusingly instructive an anecdote related to me by a friend; she decided at one point to tell her father that as a result of her reflections on philosophical problems she no longer believed in God. Her father, a 'regular army' fellow, commented in dismay, 'But if you don't believe in God you no longer believe in America!'

These ways in which the political realm seeks to *colour itself sacred* generally observe two constraints. First, they concern almost exclusively those Walter Bagehot would have called the 'dignified', as against the 'efficient' part of the state's operation: in the latter part, political business is mostly transacted in a matter-of-fact, demystified fashion, coherent with the prevalent secular temper of modernity. Second, on the whole the rituals carried out in the 'dignified' part of the political realm do not antagonize the churches, because they are not focused on expressly non-Christian ideals and symbols.

Neither of these constraints applies to the brief period during which the French revolutionaries, as I have already mentioned, undertook to introduce the cult of the goddess Reason and other expressly political forms of creed and belief; or to the sustained employment by the National-Socialist Party of Old Norse and other pagan symbolism immediately previous to and during the Third Reich. (On the occasion of a visit by Hitler to Rome in 1938 the Vatican daily, *L'Osservatore Romano*, expressed dismay at the fact that within the Eternal City 'a cross other than that of Christ' – the swastika, of course – was being lavishly displayed.)

It should be noted that some of the interactions and interferences between religious and political power that we have been discussing concern not so much the state as a whole, but particular political factions. Nazi symbolism, for instance, patterned itself, to some extent, on that of the Italian Fascist party, and was in turn widely adopted by a number of European right-wing movements, some of which never managed to impose it on the state within which (or against which) they were operating. Even when movements of this kind conquer the state and widely display their symbols and enact their ceremonies, some symbols and some ceremonies remain reserved for an inner core of initiates – as with the SS Orders or the

Fascist Scuole di Mistica Fascista. (Incidentally, *chez eux* Italians used to refer to 'La mistica del mastica' – 'the mystique of mastication'.)

In these ways, then, states (or particular political movements) seek sometimes to *go into the religious business* on their own. Are there parallel examples of religious institutions *going into the political business* for themselves – that is, building up and deploying coercive resources of their own?

Of course, there are some phenomena relevant to this question that may be attributed to either side of the religious / political divide. Were the Knights Templar, for instance, primarily monks who liked to wear and use armour or primarily warriors with monks' habits? In general, however, Christian churches derive from their shared heritage, however differently interpreted from case to case, a serious constraint on the autonomous use of coercion for religious purposes. Even in its most terroristic phases, the Catholic Inquisition needed to hand over to the *secular arm* the wretches it persecuted and prosecuted in order to have them finally dispatched; and the shedding of any human blood in a Catholic church (including of course suicide or self-mutilation) desecrates it.

Two phenomena, however, reveal the recurrent hold upon Christian churches of an aspiration – or should we call it temptation? – to 'go political'. The first phenomenon, particularly prominent and persistent in the Catholic church, is the purposeful elaboration of a body of internal law (called canon law in that church), which imparts a strongly authoritarian cast to the relations between the various parts of the church – the papacy, the episcopate, the clergy, the religious orders, the laity. As canon law structures them, those relations come to resemble closely those between the rulers and the ruled in a non-democratically constituted, strongly hierarchical, bureaucratically organized polity. This of course raises the problem of how to reconcile these aspects of the church's identity with those that reflect a conception of it as a community, and those that have purely to do with grace and God's love. According to one view, voiced by the Protestant scholar Rudolf Sohm, no reconciliation is indeed possible: 'Everywhere church law has shown itself to be an attack on the church's spiritual essence. . . . The nature of church law stands in contrast with the nature of the church.'[10]

The second phenomenon is the tendency for churches to mobilize on behalf of their institutional goals the state's distinctive resource, organized violence. Time and again, churches have requested that the state engage that resource in order to repress forms of private conduct they deemed sinful, persecute and banish heretics, forbid other churches to broadcast their own creed and look after the spiritual welfare of their own faithful, lay siege to parts of a state's territory that had become the stronghold of alternative beliefs, curtail the rights of those suspected of holding such beliefs, suppress heterodox, atheistic or libertine publications, wage war on states that harbour and protect heretical faiths, collect ecclesiastical dues from unwilling taxpayers, foster and protect their own evangelizing efforts in non-Christian lands in the process of being colonized.

Note, however, that these operations, mostly very damaging to the development of civil society – and sometimes, in the medium to long term, to the moral standing of the churches themselves – have generally been the result of negotiations between them and the state, not initiatives taken autonomously by religious bodies, for to these, by their very nature, the medium of violence was not available.

This holds, of course, for the public sphere. In the private sphere – in families between spouses and between parents and children, in innumerable religious institutions between the clergy and the laypersons in their charge (from school pupils to young people elected by their parents to become monks or nuns) – all manner of moral and physical brutalities were routinely perpetrated in the name of religious principles, in order to enforce discipline and submission, perhaps in the expectation that these would dispose the victims to achieve salvation. But these forms of violence were expressly non-political, and represented, so to speak, the hard edge of that ability to sanction other people's conduct that constitutes the power phenomenon.

As I see the matter, however, in the case of religious power that ability rests mostly on constraints and sanctions mediated through understandings and convictions. The basic mission of Christian churches is an inherently complex, perhaps a contradictory one: they must both affirm the transcendence of the sacred *and* inspire in earthbound creatures a sense of reliance on it. They must both communicate to individuals a cosmic design of which they are a part and also make them apprehensive about that part; at the same time, they must assuage those apprehensions by inspiring the hope of redemption. However, they insist, redemption is contingent on the individual's conduct – Augustine said it all: 'He who created you without you will not save you without you.' Yet the church is there to guide that conduct, support it and remedy its failure through sacramental means, to help the individual to express a sense of hope, trust and atonement by means of prayer and other ritual practices.

Such a complex set of beliefs and precepts cannot in the end remain credible if a church, in its impatience with the error and the sin to which individuals are prone, too often and too crudely resorts to the state's violence in order to propagate true belief, direct and police right conduct. This, at any rate, is the message I would derive from the scene Dansette evokes – Mirabeau and Robespierre taking part in the procession while thinking, and perhaps muttering under their breath, murderous thoughts about the very church they pretend to honour.

The positive side of that message, conveyed by the experience of many disestablished, dissentient churches and sects, is that a religious body that expressly renounces and rejects the state's assistance, or is otherwise denied it, may root itself all the more deeply in the civil society, evoke a more thrusting loyalty from its followers, renew its sense of prophetic significance. However, some churches are more reluctant than others to seek this experience, and once more the Catholic church is a case in point. As late as the 1940s, a French cardinal referred to the arrangements prevailing between the church and the French state in the late nineteenth century as 'chères et bien-aimées habitudes'; even in Communist Poland, the church struggled stubbornly and successfully to obtain from the state concessions denied to any other corporate bodies.

One may remark that that cardinal was speaking ironically and self-critically; and that the Polish church managed, in spite of those concessions, to maintain a high nuisance value *vis-à-vis* the Communist regime as well as to convey to the population a strong sense of its own moral autonomy. *Yet*, as I write, at least some sectors of the French Catholic church are trying to secure for their educational establishments, from a government of the Right, financial advantages that the Left had long denied them; and, as I write, the Polish church is seeking to entrench in legislation invidious privileges for its own institutions and its own moral preferences.

One reason why the Roman church so insists on making deals with the state is that these deals serve two purposes: they assist the church not only in pursuing its 'external' task of evangelizing and saving souls, but also in securing resources for the 'internal' needs of a huge, expensively run institution, manned by extensively trained personnel who normally do not earn their keep through other services, and somewhat addicted to pomp and circumstance in its ritual practices, as is perhaps required to highlight its distinctively hierarchical structure.

A typology of accommodations

In this chapter, I have made much use of the metaphor of 'negotiation', in order to suggest both that church–state relations are two-way affairs, involving both parties in supply and demand, and that they are inherently open-ended and fluid. I have also emphasized that the historical context I have implicitly or explicitly referred to, that of Western Christianity, was marked by an inherent dualism. To close the chapter, I shall make use of a book by an Italian student of ecclesiastical law, Francesco Ruffini (1863–1934),[11] which corrects some of these emphases. Ruffini *de*-emphasizes the open-endedness of church–state relations by comprising their variety within a relatively small number of relatively stable patterns; and suggests that in early Christian times dualism was not much in evidence, except through the fact that *two* power centres were both seeking to unify the power field, each around itself. As Ruffini summarizes it, the whole story of 'relations between state and church' in the West falls into only two great phases: that of 'subordination and union', and that of 'separation and co-ordination'.

The first phase is still marked by the pre-Christian tendency to consider religious institutions as an integral part of the polity. In the Roman empire, in particular, all matters of cult and ritual constituted aspects of public administration, regulated by 'public law'; the emperor was also the 'supreme pontiff', and from a certain time on the addressee of a specific cult. As I have already mentioned, this last point led to difficulties as concerned Jews and Christians, and to their persecution as a politically rebellious element. The situation changed with the Edict of Milan (313), which allowed Christians to preserve their beliefs, to practise their own cults, and to constitute legally protected associations. About seventy years later, the Emperor Theodosius took a step further and proclaimed Christianity the official religion of the empire. This decision, however, confirmed the ancient view of religion as an 'affair of state' through and through: for some time, emperors exercised *vis-à-vis* the new official religion the same prerogatives they possessed previously in the context of pagan cults; they issued norms on matters of belief and ritual, supervised the administration of the possessions of the church and monitored the appointments to church offices.

The basic arrangement was, thus, the *union* between polity and church, and the prime beneficiary of it was the former. Ruffini, like other writers, employs the expression 'caesaropapism' (meaning that 'Caesar', the political ruler, is also 'pope') to characterize it. However, the church also benefited from the arrangement in its own terms. For instance, once validated by the emperor, the decisions of church authorities had the full force of law. Above all, political power could be brought to bear against heretics, and mobilized in the suppression of pagan cults and in the propagation of Christianity.

After the fifth century, this pattern (union or fusion between state and church, with the former dominant) continued chiefly in the Byzantine empire; and it is chiefly within the latter, until its end in 1453, that the pattern of 'caesaropapism' continued to hold. After the end of the Western Roman empire (476), political institutions became so weak and fragmented that they could no longer hold a dominant position with respect to religious institutions which, on the contrary, were waxing stronger and stronger. Over the next few centuries, only rulers who sought to rebuild something like an imperial framework (Charlemagne in particular) would, as part of that attempt, claim also some of the old prerogatives *vis-à-vis* the church. But the balance had swung the other way: while the key pattern in the relations between religious and political power remained their union, the former held the dominant position in the partnership, thanks to ascendancy of the bishop of Rome as the head of Western Christianity. It was often as if *he* claimed the mantle of the Roman emperors of old; but he did so in new, specifically Christian terms, emphasizing the spiritual nature, and thus the intrinsic superiority, of his power and his mission, and seeking to subordinate, not to suppress, political institutions.

This second, medieval version of the union of the two powers is labelled (by Ruffini and others) 'theocracy'. It was more than anything else a theological doctrine, a set of claims never seriously made good, except on two counts. It served as a justification for the particularly absolute nature of the power of the pope over the State of the Church (Rome, Latium and a historically variable collection of more or less adjacent Italian lands). And it served as an argument not so much for the actual conferment of large political prerogatives to popes and other religious leaders as for the lessening of the religious prerogatives of political rulers (particularly those concerning the appointments – the so-called 'investitures' – of bishops and abbots and the control over church properties).

In the later Middle Ages and the early modern era, the progressive consolidation of political powers in the hands of princes and other rulers led to a third variant of the union between state and church, which Ruffini labels 'jurisdictionalism' and considers a much attenuated version of caesaropapism. Rulers proclaim themselves Christian, commit themselves to the defence of the faith, and are religiously legitimated; but increasingly they intervene, through their own administrative apparatus, in various aspects of the existence of the church, in order to guard the interests of the state. For instance, they exclude foreign personnel from high church office; they monitor the administration of church property, they reserve the right to validate the decrees of ecclesiastical office-holders and even to verify their doctrinal correctness. After the Reformation, in Catholic lands monarchs negotiated with the pope over the extent of these prerogatives (which are very extensive, for example, in seventeenth-century France and in eighteenth-century Austria); in lands that had undergone the Reformation, rulers had much more leeway to build (and govern, to a varying extent) *national* churches.

But, as we have already seen, the break-up of the religious unity of the West by the Reformation presages a more momentous transition; in Ruffini's terms, the era of union between church and state is succeeded by the era of 'separation and co-ordination'. Implicitly or expressly, the state redefines its nature in such a way as to renounce any religious competences and relieve it of the attendant responsibilities; also, some Christian confessions denounce the state as intrinsically evil, or seek to distance themselves from it in order to reassert their nature as purely moral and spiritual communities.

As Ruffini defines the term, 'separation' means that the state seeks to relate to the church(es) as to any private association, commercial or cultural, in a spirit of indifference and perhaps of hostility to its (their) distinctive mission. In his view this is an inherently unstable pattern, which no state policy has ever embodied coherently and persistently, because the church holds in civil society a position that makes it quite unlike any private association. Since the 1920s, when Ruffini began to teach the course on ecclesiastical law on which his book is based, Communist regimes have in fact pursued at length, in the name of 'separation', a policy of sustained hostility toward the church(es). But this does not disprove his argument, since those regimes were marked also by their suppression of civil society.

In any case, according to Ruffini, 'co-ordination' between state and church represents a much more stable pattern. The term '*co*-ordination' itself, as applied to state–church relations, expresses conceptually an alternative to '*sub*ordination', and is meant to signal the abandonment of century-long attempts by each party to assert its dominance over the other or to absorb it within itself. The state, without renouncing its own secular identity, acknowledges the peculiar nature of the church by conferring on it a special status under public law; the church, in return, bestows its own recognition on the state, accepting certain limitations on what it can expect of it, and commits itself to certain services to the state (which, in our own vocabulary, have much to do with 'legitimation' and 'domestication').

As far as the Catholic church is concerned, co-ordination is generally achieved by means of concordats, that is, by covenanted agreements between the Holy See, as the supreme office of the universal church on the one hand, and a given state on the other. Concordats settle the status and prerogatives of the church in that state, in exchange for its recognition by the church, which explicitly or implicitly commits itself not to challenge the state's policies. Their contents vary considerably from situation to situation, and can be periodically revised. Though typically they need to be articulated through state legislation and to be implemented by state agencies, they have the status of internationally binding agreements *between* states, on account of the peculiar position of the Holy See as the ruling summit of a sovereign state.

As I see the matter, the notion itself of 'concordat' suggests the validity of the view here presented of church and state as the institutional embodiment each of a different form of social power. It suggests the naivety of Stalin's famous question at Yalta, 'The Pope! How many divisions has *he* got?' It confirms both the tendency of both forms to reach accommodations, *and* the inherent risks and limitations of these. States with religiously diverse populations sometimes find it difficult to reconcile their claims to represent the political interests of *the people at large* with the favours that concordats bestow on one part of it, that identified with its partner in the concordat itself. The church sometimes finds itself politically overcommitted not so much to the state with which it has reached a particularly favourable accommodation (on the face of it), as to the particular *regime* with which it has dealt; thus, it risks the displeasure of that regime's opponents, who may at some point supplant it with another one, less well disposed toward the church itself.

6

Creative Intellectuals
and the State

The desacralization of ideological / normative power

Over the last two chapters, our argument has followed a path toward greater and greater (relative) concreteness. Starting with a generic notion of ideological / normative power, we have first singled out religious power as its chief manifestation, then considered its institutional embodiment in churches, and Christian churches in particular.

Let us invert this itinerary for a moment, and consider once more Michael Mann's general argument about ideological / normative power (as we call it). This emerges in so far as, to quote him once more, in a given society a 'distinctive group' acquires a monopoly over 'meaning, norms, and aesthetic and ritual practices'. Originally, I have suggested, such monopoly tends to be associated with a focus on sacred realities and experiences, hence with what ordinarily goes under the name of 'religion'; the group that enjoys it and exploits it, however it may name itself, is or resembles a church.

But this situation may change. Starting from a shared religious matrix, where 'tout se tient', the three components – 'meaning, norms, and ritual and aesthetic practices' – may develop into relatively self-standing concerns, engaging (and empowering, as our argument goes) relatively differentiated groups; and some of these may cease to focus their activities on a separate, superior, sacred sphere of reality. Oversimplifying the matter somewhat, 'meaning' may become increasingly the province of philosophers and scientists; 'norms' the province of legislators and lawyers; and 'aesthetic practices' the province of artists.

This does not necessarily mean that those who live for (and off) religion find their living (and their power) threatened; it may remain understood that *ultimately* what counts as meaning, norms and aesthetic value continues to depend on prevailing perceptions of the sacred sphere, and that this sphere constitutes the exclusive concern – and the power basis! – of the 'charismatically qualified'. However, people not charismatically qualified may carry out more and more of the activities *proximately* concerned with cognitive problems, with the formulation and application of norms, with the symbolic expression of sentiment and vision. These people may in various ways seek to gain autonomy from, so to speak, 'the *ultimate* lot'.

Scientists, for instance, may state that they are not interested in the *what* and the *why* of reality, but only in the *how* of it; lawyers, inspired by 'legal positivism', may insist that their sole concern is with *jus conditum* – what norms are at a given moment, in a given place – not with *jus condendum* – what norms ought to be; and artists may content themselves with expressing and evoking intense and exalting but *earthly* experiences: adventure, glory or erotic passion, for instance.

A relatively stable understanding among all those involved in 'meaning, norms, and aesthetic and ritual practices', between those who are and those who are not charismatically qualified, can thus be achieved by layering, so to speak, the referents of the related activities. As long as the superiority of the upper, *sacred* layer, and the higher significance of the activities directly involved with it, is not directly challenged, those committed to the lower, *profane* layer can get on with it relatively undisturbed. But this relationship may not remain stable. One starts, say, with the notion of philosophy as the handmaiden of theology; but at some point one may argue that the former addresses and attains truth independently of the other, and that if the respective conclusions about something disagree, then there may be such a thing as a *double truth* about the matter; finally, one may end up inverting the original hierarchical relationship between the two lines of discourse, as when Kant writes about 'religion within the boundaries of mere reason'. At the beginning of a parallel story in the artistic realm, all music, in a given society, may be sung and played and danced to within the context of religious ritual; at the end, sacred music, reduced to a minor, specialized realm of musical experience, may have a hard time defending itself from the encroachment of techniques and understandings of music originating from the now dominant, profane realm.

This progressive suppression or inversion of the understanding between the two layers may be assisted by (but it may also cause) a shift in the priorities the environing culture and society assign to each layer. The standing of those activities originally conceived as less significant, because related to the profane layer, may be increased by their effectiveness, in so far as effectiveness itself has become a widely accepted standard of judgement, as against, say, 'symbolic appropriateness' or 'traditional value'. Consider the fictional dialogue between an Anglican bishop and a judge. Bishop: 'The most *you* Judge can do to a man is condemn his mortal body to death; but *I* have a say on the eternal fate of his soul.' Judge: 'Yes, Bishop – but when I say to a man, "you hang", *he hangs!*'

Note that here the judge does *not* challenge the higher significance of a soul's eternal fate. At length, however, the original understanding of the relationship between what we have called the two layers of reality may be attacked. Legal positivism, for instance, may move from encouraging the jurist to focus exclusively on *jus conditum* to a drastic devaluation and exclusion of any argument on *jus condendum* – say, any reference to 'justice' as a criterion for legal decision – as inescapably ideological.

As far as Western history is concerned, from the late Middle Ages, within the universe of activities dealing with 'meaning, norms, and aesthetic and ritual practices', one may detect a broad trend toward the progressive autonomization of what we have called the profane realm and the relative marginalization of the sacred realm.

What accounts for such a development? To begin with, we have argued all along, a group securing something of a monopoly on the activities in question gains a quantum of social power; thus groups on either side of the sacred / profane divide have an interest in asserting the higher significance of their distinctive concerns and in downgrading alternative concerns and the related practices and understandings. But if any group can play this game, what systematically favours one group as against its opponent (say, positivist lawyers as against moral theologians) may be the correlation between the former group's interest and some broad tendencies of the environing society. In the case of the post-medieval West, the broadest tendencies were those towards social change and towards structural differentiation, and they definitely *dis*favoured what we are calling the sacred layer. Why?

Sacredness, as we have seen, stereotypes, holds constant; those attending to it are not prone to experimentation and tinkering, and discourage such activities in others; in other terms, sacredness tends to keep change from occurring. But if change occurs *anyway*, possibly driven by processes that have little to do with 'meaning, norms, and aesthetic and ritual practices', such change may in turn marginalize the sacred, reduce its relevance to a context in the grip of a self-sustaining dynamic.

Also, the sacred sphere is one characterized by unity; at any rate in the Judaeo-Christian tradition, it emphasizes the oneness of the Deity, the dominance of the Deity's will over all of reality, the universality of sin and of the promise of redemption. Such a conception has difficulty comprehending and appreciating the increasing differentiation of society and culture characteristic of modernity, the emergence of a plurality of distinct, self-referring spheres of experience. That development inspires in most representatives of the tradition an acute sense of loss. The factors driving modern differentiation, whatever they were, favoured instead groups that single-mindedly attended to their diverse concerns, emphasizing their autonomy and their grounding in different, self-standing principles and values.

The formation of distinctive groups that share the cognitive, normative, expressive concerns originally exclusive to the 'charismatically qualified', but which unlike those do not systematically refer (and *de*fer) to a unifying, sacred, stable and stabilizing centre of reality, can be interpreted in other terms. One may suggest, for instance, that Christianity, or at any rate certain Christian denominations, positively enjoin individuals to identify and to pursue values and principles intrinsic to each sphere in which they operate, and expressly prevent religious authorities from restraining the resulting dynamic engagement of individuals with the world. Whatever interpretation one adopts, it should recognize one remarkable fact. On the one hand, the groups operating in the profane layer emphasize their own distinctiveness with respect to those operating in the sacred layer; on the other, paradoxically, they often project a quasi-sacred conception of their core concerns, and adopt a semi-sacerdotal image. Lawyers and judges liken themselves to 'priests of Themis' and sometimes wear hieratic garb; many learned professions describe the places in which they operate as 'temples' of this or that god whom they represent and cherish; some modern intellectuals like to project themselves as the re-embodiments of sacred prophecy, artists as the virtuosi of a semi-religious way of life, earthly and indeed redoubtable as it may seem from a conventionally religious point of view. (See the closing sentences of James Joyce's *Portrait of the Artist as a Young Man.*) In sum, there are reminders, in the activities of profane suppliers of meaning, norms and aesthetic experience, of the original religious matrix and context of those activities.

Who are 'creative intellectuals'?

This chapter singles out for consideration one particular category of individuals, which I label 'creative intellectuals'. It considers to what extent such a category can be said to hold a specific form of ideological / normative power, and the relationship between that form and political power as institutionally embodied, once more, in the state. The conceptual bound-aries of the category, alas, are very hard to determine; in particular, the definition of 'intellectuals' has been the object of lengthy and heated sociological controversies in which I have no intention of engaging. I shall try, however, to give some idea of the empirical content of the category *as I use it* in what follows.

For a long time there has existed in all Western societies (and in others too, of course) a relatively large set of people whose main occupational commitment (carried out outside the churches) has been to cultivate, transmit and generate intellectual and artistic values, to guard, increment, refine, criticize the cultural patrimony of society, and in particular the assumptions 'ordinary' people are expected to make about the nature of reality, the broad course of history and the grounds on which individuals and groups can claim moral worth.

The expression 'creative intellectuals' refers to a *subset* of such people, those who in a given context are engaged in setting standards, in innovating the content and form of artistic pursuits, in criticizing the conventional assumptions about intellectual validity and moral worth, in extending the boundaries of publicly validated modes of understanding, vision, aesthetic appreciation and feeling. Who does this cannot be determined by defini-tional fiat, partly because intellectuals disagree among themselves about who, among them, is in fact 'creative' in that sense. Given the nature of the modern division of labour, however, the likelihood is that certain niches within it will offer their occupants a better opportunity to play the role of 'creative intellectual'. Editors of 'quality' national literary and political periodicals, say, are better placed to play it than crime reporters in local dailies; professors of humanities, law, or the social sciences in important universities are better placed than researchers in chemical laboratories.

On that count (among others), intellectuals compete for positions in those niches. In order to make a difference to how the environing society defines and rewards intellectual, artistic and moral worth, perceives and evaluates the course of its own collective development and prospects for its collective destiny, intellectuals feel they need and deserve to become part of established institutions, and to thus to have access to and possibly to control effective channels of communication with the general public and of influence on public agencies.[1]

To this extent, to narrow down further the meaning of 'creative intellectuals', one may emphasize that the referent group is chiefly composed of people who operate in a realm Germans call *die Öffentlichkeit*: the public sphere. In this realm the differences created among participants by their respective disciplinary affiliations (if they are, for instance, scientists or scholars), by their commitment to distinctive artistic media or by ideological loyalties, are to some extent transcended by their intent to shape the generality's opinion, moral sensitivity and taste, to orient the collectivity, to make sense of individuals' circumstances; *and* that intent is pursued, in principle, through discourse, through the mutual confrontation of the participants' competing views and preferences.

In the public sphere, intellectuals generally expend resources of credibility, reputation and standing that they have acquired elsewhere. They can successfully enter it only if they have proved their productivity and creativity in the respective fields of enquiry and of artistic endeavour, and deserved in the first place the recognition and the admiration of other practitioners in those fields. Once in the public sphere, intellectuals compete with one another to assert the superiority of their viewpoints, to make *their* difference as it were.

However, intellectuals share an interest in enlarging the scope and deepening the influence of the public sphere. Thus, within the European *anciens régimes*, in particular, intellectuals sought to free the formation and circulation of ideas (including new conceptions of the possible form and content of artistic products) from restrictions imposed by traditional political and ecclesiastical institutions. Subsequently, they generally supported the enlargement of access to the public sphere via the promotion of literacy, the establishment of new places and occasions where the broad public could be brought into contact with objects of intellectual and artistic interest. Furthermore, confronted with the emergence of organized party politics, intellectuals sought to establish within each major political alignment a kind of *micro* public sphere, where they would elaborate the ideology and the platforms of the alignment, and develop appropriate forms of artistic expression.

There is another interest creative intellectuals share, and it concerns specifically the *power* dimension of their position and their identity. So far as they are concerned, both the broader public sphere, and the narrower ones, ought to be shaped hierarchically, in the sense of maintaining a fairly sharp distinction between the protagonists – the intellectuals themselves – and everybody else, that is, the more or less broad public: the book or periodical readers, theatregoers, listeners, viewers. Admission to the first lot, as I indicated, ought to be competitive, and those admitted to it should be willing to slog it out among themselves for further recognition; but the point of gaining recognition is to make it easier for intellectuals to get a hearing from an audience conceived as largely passive, as needing to have its opinion formed, its views formulated, its options laid out for it.

Two phenomena complicate this hierarchical relationship, in the public sphere, between the protagonists and the audience. First, the notion of initially earning a reputation and then wielding it as a means of guiding a passive audience is often simplistic: the audience's response does not simply reflect and amplify a pre-constituted reputation, but to some extent itself makes and unmakes reputations, on the basis of processes of preference formation and expression which the protagonists themselves often find disturbingly unpredictable. Second, that hierarchical relationship is itself mediated through various arrangements, which involve people who are themselves neither intellectuals nor audience members. Writers need publishers and journal editors, composers need orchestras and theatre managers, architects need builders, artists need patrons. This interposes an organizational and a financial aspect in the relationship between the intellectuals and what they think of as *their* publics, and those aspects unavoidably impose requirements of their own, which intellectuals may see as interfering with their personal understanding of their activity and distorting their access to the public.

A current complication in this regard is that the contemporary public sphere is largely constituted by industrialized, highly capitalized media, which function chiefly according to business criteria, and are run by individuals who, intellectuals suspect, would not know *true* intellectual or artistic worth if it hit them in the face, and who furthermore tend to hog all public attention themselves. As a result, those interferences and distortions are immeasurably increased. Paradoxically, at the very time when the public sphere has attained its maximum size, and is in a position to exercise the greatest influence on the cultural preferences and the perceptions of the people at large, intellectuals often feel unable to play their favourite, protagonist role within it.

Let us assume that, for the reason just given or for others, the public sphere does not unproblematically offer creative intellectuals a site within which to play a power game entirely of their own; that they are frustrated in their attempt directly to shape the perceptions, the standards, the visions prevalent within the public. This may be one reason why intellectuals often concentrate their attention on another potential target of their creative efforts, another medium of the influence they seek to exercise – the state.

Giving splendour to the realm

There are of course other reasons, some of which I shall mention while considering what creative intellectuals typically expect from the state. But, as in the case of the church, I shall instead discuss first what they *offer* the state. In other words, we envisage once more the relationship between two forms of social power as the varying result of a process of negotiation in which each party both lays claims on the other and also offers it inducements to meet those claims.

What, then, can creative intellectuals offer the state? They can in the first place, to use a somewhat archaic expression, 'give splendour to the realm'. The intellectuals' services (as embodied in poems, anthems, histories, buildings, pictures, monumental statues, operas) can assist the political centre in justifying its powers and in making their exercise more effective. They do so both by surrounding the core aspect of rule – organized violence – with a halo of righteousness, and by emphasizing its invincibility. Those artefacts recount a ruler's exalting lineage, and evoke his or her dynasty's heritage of glory; they depict the many manifestations of benevolence shown to him or her by God, by fate, by fortune, and they emphasize a given ruler's personal qualities of bravery, cunning, wisdom, piety, virility, justice, fortitude, magnanimity, mercifulness, generosity. Enemies are shown plotting against a ruler and then cowering in defeat; new lands are shown asking for rule to be extended to them.

Sometimes, however, the focus is not just on the ruler and on that ruler's strictly political achievements, but on broader aspects – the broadest being nothing less than initiating a *novus ordo*, restoring peace to the world at large, guiding a whole society into a new era of material and moral well-being and of surpassing cultural attainment. An early instance where intellectuals lent themselves to attributing such scope to rule is as discussed by Paul Zanker in his work on 'the power of images' in the era of Augustus:

> Together with the 'restoration of the *res publica*' and the development of his new political style, Augustus stood for a comprehensive program of societal 'healing'. The leitmotifs were the renewal of religion and the mores, of *virtus* and worth of the Romans. Never before or since has the establishment of rule been accompanied by such a comprehensive program of cultural policy and by such a suggestive visualisation of the values which inspired it.[2]

Intellectuals are particularly interested in making claims for the renewal of cultural values associated with a ruler, since they are both protagonists and beneficiaries of the advancement of the arts, the refinement of literary taste, the uplifting of the spirits. This broad emphasis allows them to place their powers of artistic representation and embodiment at the service of less personalized systems of rule, focusing them on particular moments of their history – Magna Carta, the Glorious Revolution, the Declaration of the Rights of Man, the US Constitution – around which a rich imagery can be built, capable of evoking in subjects and citizens sentiments of pride, allegiance and trust, directly addressed to the system and purportedly recognized and rewarded by it. Works of art of various nature, from bas-reliefs on the friezes of public buildings to ballets and films, can represent anonymous individuals as protagonists of significant political events, and especially of military ventures: the Burghers of Calais, the *Poilus*, the British Tommies, the GIs, the martyrs of the Fascist, Nazist and Communist revolutions, the Unknown Soldier, the *Voortrekkers*, the rebellious sailors on the *Potemkin* battleship.

If they are to produce the effects expected of them, the artefacts in question must bear witness to the wealth and generosity of their sponsors; sometimes they consist in one-off productions (theatrical representations, fireworks, grand entrances in cities) which suggest how recklessly rulers are willing and able to waste resources. However, in each case the artefacts must also bear the marks of 'true art', as these are understood when and where they are produced. In the Western tradition, this has long meant that in order effectively to 'give splendour to the realm' the works of creative intellectuals must to some extent innovate on current artistic and literary practices. Typically, a ruler – take Louis XIV, or Peter the Great – will expect the construction of his palace or capital city to draw from all of Europe the best it can currently offer in architecture and the visual arts; but he will also insist that the final product must convey a novel conception, a design of unique beauty and potency. The novelty and the uniqueness may in some cases be purely a matter of scale, in others rest on authentic stylistic innovation or the boldness of the techniques employed; in any case, the whole undertaking can only work if it evokes a particular feeling of wonder, whether through its gracefulness, its monumentality, or the cleverness of the conceit it embodies. Besides increasing the intrinsic significance of the products in question, its aesthetic achievement has a further import: it becomes more likely to be noted, envied and imitated abroad.

This does not mean, of course, that the artists can *simply* do their best, allow themselves to be as creative as they can. The nature of the task they are lending themselves to places constraints on them. The chief constraint is the commitment to producing *effect*, to induce promptly and reliably a feeling of wonder, awe and possibly submission. A frequent result is a tendency to monumentality and grandiosity in architecture and the visual arts, to the epic style in literature. More muted and perhaps intrinsically more rewarding registers of artistic expression, which could evoke and induce other ranges of feeling, are not at a premium when legitimation is being sought. There are two further constraints: those who are to benefit from that effect often seek to have it produced as cheaply as possible; and they sometimes think *they* know best how to produce that effect. On both counts, the artists are likely to experience a lot of meddling and interference with their practices.

Constructing political communities

The services from creative intellectuals to the state that I have just discussed are very close in kind to the legitimating and 'domesticating' political services of the churches; the former can either complement the latter or, in a secularized environment, replace them. In both cases what is on offer to the state is the possibility of evoking some amount of morally motivated compliance and commitment, relieving it to some extent from the burden of continually exhibiting and exercising its capacity to repress and punish oppositional or deviant conduct on the part of subjects and citizens.

Notice, however, some differences. Churches are largely tradition-bound in what they can say and how they can say it; Christian liturgy, in particular, re-enacts the same cycle of sacred events year in year out, and arranges the same ways of (among other things) teaching the faithful to obey their leaders; furthermore, as I have already suggested, religious legitimating practices often refer to ancient reciprocities between rulers and subjects, which the former might prefer to be forgotten. The works of creative intellectuals are not similarly constrained by the past; stylistically, if anything, they tend towards innovation; and the fact that each new creative generation tends to produce its own works allows also their legitimating activities to be, to an extent, 'reprogrammed' with close reference to the recent past and the current difficulties and opportunities on the political scene.

Hence a closely related difference arises: religious legitimations are perforce focused on the abiding qualities of the political system, which they supply with a kind of permanent, background justification; those provided by creative intellectuals, even when they recognize and celebrate continuities in the political system they seek to legitimate, can take on board changes of regime, of policy, of circumstances. For instance, from time to time they can place a kind of negative emphasis on a different foreign power, accusing *it* of being (typically, of having *always* been!) the chief obstacle to the realization of the objectives of the political system. Finally, artistic and intellectual legitimations can bypass some constraints that the Christian tradition places on church legitimations: the celebration of war, the incitement to hatred of the enemy and the exultation in their extermination, the emphasis on victory, conquest and glory as self-validating political goals, can be much more explicit in the former.

As concerns a second major service they offer the state, creative intellectuals are, so to speak, on their own; for this service becomes particularly relevant in the course of modernization, which to some extent marginalizes the churches and makes *their* service to the state of less moment. What is involved here is the creation of new political communities, particularly those on a national basis.

In western Europe, centuries of policies of conquest, annexation and acquisition, chiefly guided by dynastic interest, simplified at length the political map, and left in place a relatively small number of centres of rule; but on the territories of some of these were settled ethnically, religiously, linguistically and culturally diverse populations. The imposition of territory-wide frameworks of rule, and the development of markets of similar scope – two overlapping tasks of the greatest significance for the political authorities – could only be assisted by the formation of new understandings of the shared identity of such populations, which would make of them not only the object of externally imposed rule, but also the *unitary constituency* of a valued system of political arrangements. This would allow the state to rely upon, to mobilize for its own purposes, significant sentiments of mutual belonging, of solidarity, generated within and sustained by the civil society. On this and on other counts, the state seeks to project itself as the political expression and the political guarantor of a pre-existent political community. Ideally it seeks to project itself as the state *of* the nation, rather than claim that the nation belongs to and is a product of the state.

This is historically untenable; 'in the European context, state building historically preceded nation building'[3] – and in any case the notion itself of nation-*building* belies the conception that the nation is an original, self-activating entity which seeks to manifest and to assert itself politically through the state. However, making a historically untenable case appear plausible is a task for imagination and persuasion; and this is where creative intellectuals come in. They imaginatively reconstruct the historical itinerary that has led (or indeed, in many cases, *should lead*) to the formation of the new, larger political entities, and persuasively interpret it as the slow, laborious fulfilment of a destiny. They unearth (sometimes, they forge) ancient literary documents in which a people has allegedly expressed its sense of identity, its awareness of shared interests, its noble virtues, its vocation for war. They derive from such documents the lineaments of a literary language fit to take its place among the better-established European languages, and which, they advocate, should replace the current vernaculars as the means of literary expression and civil intercourse. (Incidentally, the explicit or implicit claim that this language's intrinsic superiority over 'mere dialects' justifies its elevation to national status again demonstrates the intellectuals' ability to argue persuasively objectively untenable cases. After all, as somebody has remarked, 'a language is a dialect which has an army and a navy'.) They write in this language epic poems, ballads, children's stories, operatic librettos, novels and histories which extol long-forgotten heroes and execrate long-forgotten villains, celebrate victories and deprecate defeats. They depict the beauties of the people's country, chronicle the advance across it of a new, proud 'consciousness of kind', articulate claims to *irredenta* (unredeemed) territories. They fashion symbols of unity, pointers to destiny, by drawing on the country's past, its geographical features, its legends. They vaunt the moral and cultural superiority of the people, its scientific achievements, its inventors, explorers and missionaries. They embody the same messages in frescos, portraits of past (real or imaginary) characters, sculptures, operas, choral music, in the design of monuments and buildings, in the contents of academic works about law, history, politics, literature. Sometimes their products have no explicit political content or intent; but they may be internationally acclaimed as outstanding works of scholarship or scientific discoveries or artistic masterpieces, and as such make a powerful indirect contribution to the task more expressly pursued by other creative intellectuals.

One may connect the conceptual distinction between the first offer of creative intellectuals to the state (legitimation services) and the second (the construction of a collective identity, the fostering of collective morale) with a historical transition – that between the dynastic, absolutist state and the incipient national and then democratic state. Or one might think of this as a transition between two modes of legitimation, the first of which still mobilizes a number of sacred symbols (not just from the Christian tradition: the Este, the ruling dynasty of Ferrara, were supposed to descend from Hercules, the Habsburgs from Aeneas and thus from Venus),[4] and confers on rulers a kind of transcendent significance; the second is more explicitly secular, and is focused on immanent political values (especially unity and military might).

In any case, there is a further difference between the two intellectual and artistic enterprises. In the first case, a relatively small number of creative intellectuals, the most eminent representatives of a still narrow literate stratum, suffices for the task of recounting, celebrating, framing within a suitably exalted environment the activities of a small ruling elite. The efficacy of the second enterprise depends on the co-operation of much larger numbers of intellectuals; most of these, however, play no creative role, but connect those who do with an increasingly large literate audience, to whom the creative message must be delivered. Here, then, relatively few creative intellectuals generate potent symbols, and a relatively large number of intellectual hacks amplify and broadcast those symbols to the larger audience. Mostly they find their niche in a country's growing educational system, which provides them with a living and with a captive audience, cohort after cohort of pupils and students; others act and sing in provincial theatres and opera houses, edit and write local gazettes and newspapers. But similar low-grade intellectual functions are exercised also by those working as lawyers, doctors, pharmacists, notaries, judges, public officials, or even by members of traditional groups of notables. The mechanism of amplification is sometimes very direct: thanks to the press and to the educational system, it may take only days for, say, the last patriotic poem by Lamartine or Kipling or Prati to be recited first to and then by hundreds of thousands of elementary-school pupils. More complex ideological messages, such as those encoded in the histories by Michelet or by Treitschke, may require a more protracted process of diffusion and assimilation, culminating perhaps in the ways questions are phrased in the examination papers of *lycées* and grammar schools, or in the phrasing of newspaper editorials in Chambéry or in Leeds.

Diverting the citizenry

In the last chapter I suggested that churches perform some of their legitimation functions by providing those afflicted by burdensome political duties (paying taxes, seeing one's children off to the wars, bearing the ravages of foreign armies invading or of domestic armies billeting themselves) with some compensation or consolation in the form of an assurance of virtue or a promise of reward in the hereafter. A third service intellectuals offer to perform for the state has a roughly similar content, representing the second half of the Roman formula for keeping the *plebs* reasonably content – 'panem et circenses', bread and circuses. (The Bourbons of Naples had a more complete, obscene formula for holding the populace at bay, the three 'f's': 'farina, forche, fiche' – 'flour, gallows, sex'.)

Rather than focus the minds of readers and spectators on the sometimes doubtful advantages of their subaltern participation in the political life of the country, intellectuals sometimes promise to keep those minds off political affairs, fastening them instead on private cares and pleasures. Their works seek to assuage the former and to enhance the latter, to console and to divert; in both ways, they distract the attention of their target audiences from the political scene, relieving the authorities from the burden of meeting inconvenient expectations.

They can do so in more or less dignified ways, possibly according to the specific segment of the public they address. Members of the more educated and economically more secure classes may be addressed by works that emphasize private, pre-political values, foster an existence self-consciously centred on the moral and intellectual cultivation of the personality, and discourage too much attention to the sound and fury of the political arena. At the other extreme, the supposed taste of the broadest masses for raw gratification and cheap sentimentality may be pandered to by salacious entertainment or by overly dramatic, trashy literature and theatre assiduously provided by specialized literary hacks.

In our century, of course, the mass circulation periodicals, the cinema, radio and television constitute the chief instruments of a similar 'distracting' function, performed by an increasingly large and specialized body of intellectuals, within which the hierarchical distinction between the few creative ones and the many broadcasters is reproduced and emphasized. While the modern media assist in positively legitimating the systems of rule within which they function, it can be plausibly claimed that their chief political effect is that of offering their audiences such an overwhelming fullness of apolitical stimuli that their attention is perforce diverted from the public scene; as a result, the populace becomes to an extent depoliticized. A peculiar twist on this effect is represented by the media's tendency to turn political affairs themselves into spectacles and into spectator sports, to over-personalize the content of political conflicts instead of supplying audiences with relevant information about issues and alternative policies.

This last point is reminiscent of an essential aspect of modern politics in constitutional systems – its adversarial nature, the fact that typically they involve a confrontation between a governing and one or more opposition parties. The emergence of modern party systems adds a new dimension to the relationship between creative intellectuals and the state; the intellectuals tend to align themselves with one of the contending parties, and to direct to these, to a greater or lesser extent, the services we have discussed so far. Their chance of having those services made use of (and rewarded) by the state may come to depend largely on the contingent results of party politics; at any given time creative intellectuals with political interests and aspirations are divided, roughly, into those associated with the party in power and those associated with the opposition(s).

This phenomenon raises a range of significant problems which we cannot consider at length. For instance, under what conditions intellectuals openly and exclusively commit themselves to a given party and depend entirely on its fortunes for a chance at political effectiveness; alternatively, they can seek to become apolitical or establishment figures, whose chance of, say, being asked to design a public building or to become poet laureate is as great whichever party is in power. Intellectuals must ask themselves how much distinction they can acquire in a given line of creative work if they associate themselves too closely with a party. Yet, under certain conditions their party commitment may be rewarded so handsomely by like-minded intellectuals in control of career contingencies that it can offset a relatively poor professional standing. (The contemporary Italian academic system, for instance, is full of intellectual nonentities who have attained positions within it purely on the basis of their party affiliations. Interestingly, this is at least as likely to have been the case for left-wing intellectuals, particularly in the humanities, as for those associated with the parties of the centre.)

What creative intellectuals expect of the state

In any case, in the context of party politics it becomes possible for intellectuals to offer political power a further service: not just legitimating rulers, or assisting in shaping collective identities, or diverting the public's attention from political matters, but, in their capacity as party ideologists, *inspiring and framing policy*. Of course certain categories of intellectuals are more likely than others to step forward with this kind of offering – first to party leaders as such, then possibly to the same in their capacity as the country's governing elite. Jurists, economists, historians and social scientists are more likely than musicians or painters or archaeologists to see themselves (and to be seen by others) as possessing the combination of vision and expertise, of moral commitment and realism, required for playing the role.

It is difficult not to see this particular *offer* of intellectuals to the state (via parties or otherwise) as expressing at the same time a thrusting ambition: to make the state serve their ends, by defining the state's own.

On this account, our mention of this last service that creative intellectuals declare themselves ready to perform may as well serve as a transition to our next topic – what claims, in their express or implicit negotiations with the state (or with political parties), do intellectuals lay on their counterpart?

To introduce a first answer to this question we may make explicit one point left implicit in the earlier account of the relationship between (as I have put it at one point) sacred and profane intellectuals. The point, to put it briefly, is that historically the former fought hard against each successive encroachment on and denial of their monopoly over 'meaning, norms, and aesthetic and ritual practices', against every step in the progressive differentiation and autonomization of an intellectual personnel specialized in profane 'meaning, norms, and aesthetic and ritual practices'. Church intellectuals mostly did not take kindly to the view that within such matters one could distinguish, to use my own phrasing, a sacred and a profane layer; or to the later claim that the profane layer was entitled to equal standing with the sacred; or to the further argument that the knowledge they held had been thoroughly compromised by the invidious advantages it had long enjoyed, rested in fact on obscurantism and superstition, was being overtaken by the advance of secular science, and might as well be done away with.

As this sequence indicates, church intellectuals were fighting, in the long run, a losing battle. But fight it they did; and since the field of battle was often institutional rather than strictly intellectual, they fought it to some extent by mobilizing the power of the state (the supreme mundane institution) on their own behalf. They had uppity laymen declared heretical, and prosecuted as such (Dante was at one point sentenced *in absentia* to 'be burned by fire to such extent that he die' probably because he, a layman, dabbled in theology); they caused the state to censor and license publishing; they visited the terrifying curiosity of the Holy Inquisition on scientists and academics; and so forth.

The state was often all too obliging in its response to the promptings of the church on these matters. Yet, in some cases it acceded to some of them reluctantly or not at all. One reason for this was that rulers were seeking to become less dependent on the clergy for manning their own offices, but could do so only to the extent that they established, or allowed to flourish, institutions where laymen could be trained and prove their intellectual mettle (schools, universities and, later, academies). The enterprise of rule was being redefined as needing large inputs of sophisticated knowledge at all levels from immediately below the top. Law was considered for centuries *the* relevant form of sophisticated knowledge; and although for a long time many lawyers graduated *in utroque jure*, that is, both in Roman and civil law and in canon law, the first component was increasingly recognized as more relevant to the political, diplomatic and administrative aspects of rule. Also, religious legitimations and justifications of political rule were considered less and less viable as the state took to defining its own mission in more and more secular terms; after the Reformation, they became more and more burdensome and divisive. They might still be made use of, but a heavy price could be paid for that – consider for example the huge intellectual and economic losses suffered by the kingdom of France for its persecution and expulsion of the Huguenots.

Secular intellectuals, I have argued, were able and willing to provide new forms of legitimation; and here the price to be paid by the rulers was affording some protection, however qualified, to their institutional bases – again, universities, academies, the press. Increasingly, states found *this* price worth paying. Indeed, some of them competed to offer charters and arrangements that would prove more attractive to a transnational elite of artists, scholars and scientists; and, explicitly or implicitly, the first condition they emphasized was the degree of liberty of the institutions in question from the intrusive and intolerant guardianship of the church. (This was probably the operative meaning, for instance, of the motto of my own Alma Mater, the University of Padua, 'Universa universis patavina libertas'. It is often suggested that Galileo would have spared himself much grief if he had not left the Venetian Republic.) Related measures ranged from the suppression of the local Inquisition, to the express regulation of censorship, to the general assertion of a right to the free formation and expression of opinion.

None of these concessions was totally unproblematical for the state. For instance, it could be awkward for a state to stop censoring publications for blasphemy and at the same time reserve the right to prosecute writers for *crimen laesae* (the crime of *lèse-majesté*). Besides, state and church mostly shared an interest in the suppression of libertine and / or obscene literature. In spite of this, most states followed a more or less halting progression toward conditions that increased the autonomy of intellectuals because they perceived a connection between, say, freedom of the press, growing literacy and public enlightenment on the one hand, and economic advance on the other. In other words, at some point many rulers saw it as a significant part of a political 'modernization package' to relieve creative intellectuals from the sense of jeopardy they inherited from centuries of uneasy relationship with the church(es).

More recently, creative intellectuals have often asked the state to relieve them from a very different set of pressures, those originating from the market. Mass literacy, the expansion of the educational system, the slow increase in the average disposable income of the population, the rise in the portion of that income (and of the leisure time) that could be spent on cultural consumption, the development of the modern media – all these closely associated phenomena, which have created a market for the products of creative intellectuals, have had an ambiguous impact on them.

On the one hand, those phenomena have freed intellectuals from the necessity of seeking the patronage either of the churches or of the traditional upper strata, since their activities can now find some resonance in broader and broader swathes of the population. On the other hand, the mechanisms for creating that resonance obey rules, and adopt selective criteria, that according to some creative intellectuals hinder what they consider their mission – the pursuit of expressive innovation, the increasing sophistication of knowledge, the critique of existent modes of feeling and imagination. As far as many of them are concerned, those mechanisms reward the wrong forms of intellectual and artistic activities, for they consider their results as 'commodities', and reward their producers accordingly. On this account, markets for cultural products tend to stereotype genres and expressive modes of proven success, or alternatively they encourage a frantic search for superficial innovation. They aim to shock existent sensitivity, or to pander to it, instead of refining it and extending it. They over-reward scientific undertakings of which they expect a commercial fallout and under-reward more 'basic' ones.

Also, the organizational forms that address the market for cultural products – the film studio, the broadcasting network, the publishing empire – have acquired autonomous significance due to the cost of building and operating them, the enormous economic rewards they compete for, and the complexity and sophistication of the technology they mobilize. As a result, creative intellectuals can less and less treat the media as media, as neutral channels for giving resonance to what they have to say. It seems to them as if, on the contrary, either the public themselves (through such instruments as ratings) or the media technicians are increasingly dictating the content and form of the intellectuals' efforts.

This new dependency on the market is not, creative intellectuals complain, what they had sought to achieve in the past, as they fought censorship, rejected the philistine criteria of narrowly educated upper-class sponsors, and reached out to broader publics, all the while holding forth the ideal of art for art's sake, of science for the sake of science. They would prefer to abandon the market to the hacks and the media technicians; but they can only do so without jeopardizing both the values they stand for *and* their own personal interests if their efforts are supported outside the market. As far as they are concerned, specially designed institutions should take responsibility for safeguarding and increasing the cultural heritage of society by assisting the creative intellectuals' continuing experimentation with new ways of conceiving and expressing emotion and experience. In an affluent business society this task should be shared between 'soulful corporations' and private foundations on the one hand, and specially chartered state agencies on the other.

These agencies should be independent of other parts of the state's administrative system, in order to protect their policies from the vagaries and irrelevancies of day-to-day political business. Their operations should reflect the values of the appropriate sections of the intellectual community, which only distinguished members of it can authoritatively articulate; however, they should support also less distinguished members who pursue new ways of expressing those values. They should seek to give wide public resonance to the relevant creative activities, if only to justify the funds committed to them, but not allow current public preferences to frame rigidly the form and content of those activities. At the same time, they should not allow their policies to be captured by small, self-promoting coteries, whose claim for attention and support rests only on their willingness to shock and outrage, rather than to educate and cultivate, current public sensitivities.

Needless to say, these multiple criteria are hard to satisfy, for basically they reflect two contrasting demands addressed to the state by intellectuals: they want both to be independent, and to be supported; they want the state to be generous towards them, but not to follow a narrowly political approach in deciding how to do so. The difficulty is made more acute by two facts: first, the prospect itself of support, however meagre, generates a competitive search for it among increasing numbers of claimants; second, contemporary intellectual and artistic communities are notorious for generating an unending succession of incompatible understandings of accomplishment and worth between which it is difficult to arbitrate. One answer to this last difficulty consists in making different forms of support available to different sets of claimants, possibly through different programmes or different agencies, some of them state-funded, others established by corporations or foundations.

This indicates that a considerable range of requests is associated with the primary claim to protection advanced by creative intellectuals towards the state. 'Protection' suggests that the claim has primarily a negative content: the state should simply ensure that the church, lordly patrons, the market, should withdraw, leaving intellectuals to pursue their own commitments according to their own lights. Yet, as the last paragraphs suggest, this claim shades easily into a more positive one for support, charging the state with ensuring that intellectuals enjoy the appropriate conditions for their pursuits. Similar positive implications can be attributed to what I have formulated earlier as the creative intellectuals' *services* to the state; normally, they do not volunteer, for example, to 'give splendour to the realm' for free, much less at their own expense, but expect to be employed to do so or to be otherwise supported while doing so, and indeed compete with one another to that effect.

This form of support can be variously combined with what intellectuals can derive from other sources, such as private patronage or indeed the market; often it does not take the form of direct state employment, but is mediated through various arrangements. Musical directors of symphony orchestras, for instance, are generally employed not by the state or the local government, but by the orchestra itself as a corporate entity, and it is this that the state or the city directly subsidizes. Furthermore, particularly renowned conductors reserve the right to *play the market*: they charge fees for performances (sometimes, I hear, extra fees for encores!) even when conducting the publicly funded orchestra they direct; they frequently hire themselves out to other orchestras; they collect royalties on recordings of their performances. Or painters may benefit from public support simply because they practise their art in studios maintained in public buildings and are charged below-market rents for them; this, however, leaves them free, if their paintings find a purchaser, to charge for them what the market will bear.

When they have little or no access to a market, and have to depend on more or less direct support from the state or other public authorities, the preference of intellectuals is pretty much for *prebendary* employment. In this case the remuneration bears a rather loose relationship to the work actually performed, and is supposed to be commensurate instead to the cultural significance of the activity performed, to the cost of *keeping* the intellectual in a style appropriate to the intrinsic dignity of his or her pursuits, to the loss the society would presumably suffer if a given kind of activity ceased to be practised at all; and so on.

One jaundiced way of summarizing these and other preferences of intellectuals is by saying that they will do anything to avoid being paid for what they produce that people *actually want*, and at the *price* people are willing to pay for it. In this sense, what intellectuals want is to be 'kept'. An even more jaundiced coda to that summary judgement is that the above are the preferences that modern intellectuals mostly develop (and elaborately justify) to the extent that they have tried *and failed* to 'make it' in the market. And it is a fact that many great creative intellectuals, from Dickens to Charlie Chaplin to Matisse, have indeed withstood the test of the market and come out unscathed from their confrontation with its supposedly corrupting standards. They have not so much given their publics what they were willing to pay for, as defined for them what they could expect of artistic experience.

Those made uneasy by such criticisms of the pretensions of intellectuals (as I am myself, for they may well be directed also at many academics) may reflect, however, that the business of intellectuals (beginning with priests) has ever been to provide goods and services that are intrinsically superfluous, and that only such superfluities mark a society as human, and within the course of historical experience differentiate one society from another.

A less generic justification for placing the support of creative intellectual activities on a non-market basis and directing to it a flow of resources extracted (when all is said and done) through coercion is by thinking of their existence as a 'public good' – not different in this from defence, or justice, or a healthy environment. In my view, what television does to the moral and intellectual temper of contemporary societies when it operates exclusively according to market criteria is a sufficient example of the damage one can expect from *not* treating the pursuit of cultural values, at least to some extent, as a public good, and providing for it accordingly – whether or not this creates a 'prebendary mentality' in some categories of intellectuals.

Intellectuals as awkward customers

In the remainder of this chapter I shall consider some reasons why the relations between creative intellectuals and the state are subject to recurrent strains, which is one reason why those relations vary fairly widely from one situation to another. I shall conduct this argument from the standpoint of the state, starting from the hypothesis that from time to time the political elites ask themselves (to use our own vocabulary), 'What are we to do about those creative intellectuals?' (Generally they are likely to use less respectful names – the Italian post-World War II politician Mario Scelba, for instance, would speak of *il culturame*. More colourfully, Spiro Agnew, Richard Nixon's first Vice-president, liked to speak of intellectuals as 'nattering nabobs of negativism'.)

If there is an undertone of anxiety and / or irritation in that question, very likely it refers to a small minority within what could be called the intellectual constituency at large. The bulk of these either make no valid claim to creativity or, when they do make such a claim, have somehow found an accommodation to (and possibly within) the state; they are content at best to act as its more or less generously rewarded communication agents or at worst to leave it alone. Thus that question typically selects for attention, within that broad constituency, a small cluster of individuals who hold on to a particularly exacting, and perhaps exalting, conception of their vocation as creative intellectuals.

A number of aspects of this conception make their relations to the state troublesome. If we stick to the metaphor according to which intellectuals negotiate their relationship to the state, offering it a quid pro quo, we might say that some of them at least turn out to be awkward customers. Why is this so? In the first place, the historical itinerary in the course of which creative intellectuals have gained their primary freedom, the freedom from church sponsorship and control, and more generally from a religious institutional framework, has left its mark on their collective memory. Although, I have suggested, intellectuals were significantly assisted by the state in that itinerary, from time to time they had to take the risk of challenging religious authority, questioning conceptions of creative work too closely tied to ritual contexts, loosening the hold of tradition on the content and form of their activities, crossing established boundaries between types of artistic and intellectual production, violating conceptions of themselves that reduced them to the status of skilled subordinates. They have from time to time talked back, played the fool, circumvented or bypassed authoritative expectations, insisted on previously unprecedented extents of freedom, made fun of their sponsors and censors, derided their ignorance, incompetence and ill will.

To a greater or lesser extent, the relations of creative intellectuals to secular patrons and sponsors, including political authorities of various kinds, have followed the same pattern, and yielded the same result (though there have also been disastrous setbacks). By and large, thanks *among other things* to their willingness to take risks, challenge, criticize, even to make themselves obnoxious, intellectuals have been able to extend the reach and depth of the prevailing modes of imagination and perception, to formulate and symbolize ever new understandings of the nature of things and of the fate and significance of human beings.

Very often the direct targets of these criticisms have been *other* creative intellectuals; but these were made into targets largely by their having become establishment figures, who represented canonized, authoritatively sponsored and endorsed forms of creative work. Thus even the recurrent, bitter internecine struggles among artists and thinkers sometimes have had a more or less expressly oppositional content, directed instead to the powers that be. As a result, creative intellectuals have come to associate with their own self-respect a measure (sometimes a large measure) of disrespect for those representing alternative positions, and a willingness to express that disrespect in a more or less provocative, corrosive and outspoken manner. At the very least, they have learned to keep a kind of inner distance, a degree of mental reservation, *vis-à-vis* the established powers – the church, the uneducated masses flooding the market for cultural goods, the state itself.

As far as the latter is concerned, creative intellectuals tend to associate themselves politically (if with anybody) with opposition parties, protest movements, dissentient currents of opinion and often, within these, with the more extreme factions and views. For instance, they seem to be forever subscribing to declarations denouncing this or that official government position, harassing the current authorities, expressing solidarity with persecuted minorities. The targets of these attacks sometimes observe with bewilderment, or with bitterness, that among the attackers are the holders of prestigious university chairs, the beneficiaries of sizeable grants or of expensive public investments in the arts or in scientific research. In other words, they observe in creative intellectuals a redoubtable, unendearing tendency to bite the hand that feeds them. This is, I suggest, just an expression of a more deep-seated and significant tendency of creative intellectuals to take an oppositional posture – a tendency that contributes to making them, as I said, into awkward customers.

Closely associated with that tendency, and working to the same effect, is the creative intellectuals' further tendency to take themselves awfully seriously. A neat indication of this comes in a passage from Jean-Paul Sartre's account of his childhood in *Les Mots*: 'I was told the story about Charles the Fifth, stooping to pick up Titian's painting brush. It did not astonish me. Big deal! That's what princes are for.' Creative intellectuals sometimes seem to presume that their vocation confers on them a privileged relationship to a set of higher values of universal significance – truth, justice, morality, beauty – and vests them with a special responsibility to assess mundane matters (including political ones), and to instruct and judge those who handle them, in the name of such values. Very often they make use of the authority that they claim to derive from that relationship in order to endorse and validate the ways such matters are handled by those in charge of them; but sometimes they find such people wanting, and fulminate against them, or express bitter disappointment in their neglect of those values.

What is significant here is not so much the further manifestation of the oppositional posture I have already discussed, as the particular tone it takes of self-satisfied moral assurance, sometimes its intolerant and fanatical character. It is as if, reviving consciously or unconsciously one aspect of their distant heritage as 'charismatically qualified' people, creative intellectuals were taking up the role of the biblical prophet, bitterly attacking the powers that be for betraying the covenant between the Lord and the Children of Israel. In more modern terms, the leadership of a sitting administration often finds what it considers an outspokenly partisan position being voiced against itself as if it consisted, instead, of a set of undeniable, intrinsically valid values and truths, straightforwardly expressed by their (self-)appointed intellectual guardians. These seem to be forever grandstanding to a higher audience, which practically-minded politicians may find it hard to perceive, but to which, they are told in hectoring tones, it is their duty to defer. Shelley wrote somewhere that poets are 'the unacknowledged legislators of the world'. Perhaps: but some of them at any rate, and some of their associates in the practice of other arts and intellectual pursuits, seem keen to become *acknowledged* as such unacknowledged legislators.

The same phenomenon takes place, once more, on another level of political life, that of the party struggle. Intellectuals often consider themselves the keepers of a party's conscience, among other reasons because they are the only members truly conversant with its ideological heritage; they use that heritage as a platform from which to attack the party leadership for political initiatives which in their view betray that heritage, necessary as they may be as tactical moves for forming alliances, gaining power and remaining in power. They can make themselves difficult to the extent that, by virtue of their professional qualifications as communicators and 'men of ideas', they control the party press and/or command a respectful audience among the rank and file. This may make their righteous finger-wagging a serious embarrassment for wayward leaders, who are sometimes unable to challenge intellectuals on their favourite terrain of sustained, quotation-studded ideological debate. Furthermore, particularly within Marxist parties that they see as slipping toward 'minimalist' perceptions of their mission, intellectuals sometimes organize 'maximalist' factions, or even lead in the formation of splinter parties, always in the name of higher values and holier truths. One may sometimes wonder whether these claims to ideological purity are justified, and to what extent they are (also) instrumental to the pursuit of undeclared interests; but even when taken at face value they can do great damage to civility in political life (within and between parties), and in any case they contribute to making creative intellectuals a potentially troublesome presence on the public scene.

There is a further implication of the intellectuals' declared commitment to higher values, but sometimes also of some institutional aspects of their vocational practice. Sometimes they have a frame of reference, a network of associates, which transcends the boundaries of the polity in which they operate and in which they aspire to some kind of political efficacy. Many of them travel and cultivate relations abroad, speak and read foreign languages, belong to international associations, sometimes pursue careers in foreign universities or in an international system of research institutions, like to think of themselves as citizens of a world-wide community of scholars or artists. If the expression 'rootless cosmopolitanism' had not been turned into an anti-Semitic euphemism by its use in the Soviet Union, one might well use it to characterize a tendency of many intellectuals, both Jewish and non-Jewish, to maintain a relatively loose relationship to their own political base, a tendency that may well inspire a certain diffidence towards them on the part of the political guardians of that base. This is all the more likely in so far as the values and principles – even political ones! – to which intellectuals so emphatically refer are universal, or at least European or Western or Christian or socialist, instead of national (*echt deutsch* or whatever); for this may make them reluctant to say 'right or wrong, my country', or to commit themselves to 'fight for king and country'. Or they may consider their country itself as valuable only to the extent that it serves as the political and military instrument of interests higher than those of its own survival and its pursuit of power – interests that the intellectuals themselves seek to define and to hold forth as a standard by which to judge political life. Thus, sometimes their sense of political realism and / or their political loyalty seem in doubt; on both counts, they appear somewhat unreliable or indeed potentially troublesome as participants in *real-life* politics.

The same conclusion can be drawn from a further set of considerations. The state, as the chief institutional embodiment of political power, generally seeks to maintain good relations with other centres of social power – for instance, as we have seen, the church; or, as we shall see, the economic elite. Often, it also has a broad interest in not disrupting certain understandings between social groups, not challenging certain cultural and moral preferences diffuse within its own population. But the vocational practices of creative intellectuals, and the demands they place on the state, can disturb those arrangements between the state and the rest of society. Their insistence on the freedom of the press, for instance, may constitute a dire threat for churches struggling to preserve the beliefs and morals of their faithful from free-thinking and immoral books and periodicals. The virulent attacks of non-established artists and writers on canonized, academic art and literature in the name of aesthetic experimentation frequently offend a country's solid, middle- and upper-class element, for it impugns their taste, their sense of what is aesthetically noble and worthy, as 'philistine', 'conventional', or 'bourgeois'. The military elite may be repelled by the intellectuals' repudiation of traditional understandings of artistic and literary accomplishment, by their undermining of patriotism and of the values of the warrior's ethic, and frequently by their adoption of an 'unmanly', disorderly, Bohemian lifestyle. Their disparagement of the commercial and industrial mentality, their distaste for market processes, irritates the business classes although often it seduces their scions. In all these ways creative intellectuals make a nuisance of themselves from the standpoint of rulers seeking to maintain reasonable arrangements with important social groups; for, if the state seems to indulge the intellectuals' propensities, those groups may feel perturbed if not threatened by what they consider the state's irresponsible complicity with moral, aesthetic and intellectual subversion.

Thus, even when the rulers may have no objections of their own to new modes of feeling and perception proposed by intellectuals, they may find themselves compelled to disassociate themselves from them in order to protect their flank, so to speak, by remaining on good terms with other social forces. Sometimes, however, intellectuals represent a more direct inconvenience or threat to the state. For instance, in the framework of the programme of moral regeneration undertaken by Augustus, and to which according to Zanker the majority of intellectuals committed themselves, Ovidius Naso's self-consciously licentious poetry stood out as an express challenge to the ruler's purposes; and this may help account for the fact that the poet had to spend several wretched years in exile in a remote, dreary outpost of the empire on the Black Sea. In modern times, the term 'libertinism' had at least two meanings – not just the one associated with salacious books and pictures and with a sexually liberated lifestyle, as one might say today; but also a broader one referring to an irreverent and sometimes bitterly critical attitude toward established religious beliefs and institutions. From the standpoint of most rulers, 'libertine' intellectuals particularly committed to this second meaning were bound to constitute a considerable potential nuisance for they threatened their cosy relations to *their* established church.

Intellectuals as an 'easy mark'

These considerations suggest, then, that at least some categories of creative intellectuals confront the state as a particularly problematical counterpart – excessively self-important, potentially disloyal, and so forth. However, other considerations suggest that, to phrase the point colloquially, intellectuals tend to be something of an 'easy mark' for the state; that their political challenge is generally not that difficult to suppress, to contain, or indeed to ignore.

Two lines of reasoning suggest this. In the first place, the terms of the bargain between the state and creative intellectuals have been shifting to the disadvantage of the latter. Historically, they had been obtaining the state's institutional support of their activities in exchange for the legitimacy-conferring power of the images they produced, of the myths they invented and propagated. However, at any rate in the second half of the twentieth century, the Western state sought to legitimate itself chiefly as the political instrument of industrial development and of increasing economic welfare. In this capacity, it has made considerable use of intellectuals, but these have been of a different nature from those I have labelled 'creative': they have been economists, planners, managers, policy scientists, technocrats of various kinds. Furthermore, the production itself of images and myths (including those put to political uses) has been industrialized by a more and more significant branch of the capitalist economy, the media; and the latter has generated and made use of vast new categories of intellectual workers, again with little in common with 'creative' intellectuals in the meaning I have adopted here.

Accordingly, these have seen their distinctive capacities become less and less relevant from the state's standpoint; at the same time, they continue to depend on arrangements largely established and underwritten by the state: in particular, institutions of higher education that provide credentials and employment and bodies that provide subsidies. (Even private bodies are mostly financed by the state through fiscal concessions.) Needless to say, in these circumstances it is difficult for creative intellectuals effectively to *negotiate* their relation to the state: their hand is simply too weak.

A second line of reasoning (which, as we shall see, overlaps with the former) leaves aside the state and considers some developments internal to the mental and institutional sphere constituted by creative intellectuals, the upshot of which is, again, their political weakness. Earlier in this chapter I have suggested that secular intellectuals have gained significance in the modern world, as against ecclesiastical ones, because they have ridden (so to speak) a distinctive modern trend towards differentiation. Being less committed to the view that the cosmos is one, and a single process of creation and redemption imparts a unitary meaning to it, they have emphasized instead the severalness of its aspects and explored the logic inherent in each; they have variously partitioned, for instance, the universe of artistic experience and asserted the autonomy of the media of artistic expression. As artists relentlessly 'pushed the inside of the envelope' of each medium, an explosion of creativity resulted; but a double political price has been paid for this. First, with regard to the differentiation between clerical and secular creative intellectuals, an increasing differentiation among the latter was added, until it became impossible for them to function – and to represent themselves to the state – as a unitary body (as churches continued to do). Second, it became impossible for anything resembling a stable hierarchy to establish itself among intellectuals; those working, say, with the same artistic medium might at any given time acknowledge the leadership exercised by someone among them, but such leadership always could be challenged – indeed, it was bound to be. There is a tendency for one 'artistic or intellectual pope' to emerge from time to time in a given country and field of intellectual or artistic endeavour – Toscanini was 'Mr Music' in the America of the 1940s and 1950s, Sartre was a towering intellectual figure in France over the first couple of decades after World

War II – but even such figures do not strongly control the internal reward system. As a result, from the standpoint of the state creative intellectuals generally appear, at any given time, as a loose cluster of small tribes which barely communicate with one another, and even internally are poorly structured, so that none can represent itself authoritatively to the political elite. Furthermore, the relations of these tribes to the state mostly consist in appeals for support, and tend to place them in competition with one another. This is particularly so at a time when, as I indicated, intellectual and artistic production can be industrialized, and the tribes that continue to engage in it on a handicraft basis risk being run out of the market.

These political weaknesses of creative intellectuals are to a large extent due to an aspect of their activities that has become more and more conspicuous over the last century. Many years ago Hannah Arendt noted that the public significance of the sciences as a form of collective knowledge had been undercut by the fact that scientists, for intrinsic reasons, no longer could express themselves in a public language; in fact, they were increasingly unable to communicate even with one another across the boundaries of narrower and narrower specialities, let alone enter the public sphere and argue comprehensibly the relevance of their pursuits to problems of general significance. Something very similar has happened to the arts and to broader intellectual pursuits; they have become increasingly self-referential, preoccupied with problems significant only to their practitioners, unable or unwilling to address collective concerns in a manner accessible and relevant to wide publics. Over the long run they have undoubtedly continued to widen and deepen the modes of understanding and perception available in the culture at large; but in the short run the modern commitment to artistic experimentalism, in particular, tends to widen the distance between the driving edge of discovery in a given art and what its potential audience defines as aesthetically worthy and inspiring. That commitment entails what one may call the contemporary artist's adversary relationship to tradition – and tradition is exactly what that potential audience relies upon for that definition. As a result, contemporary artists, so to speak, abandon most of that audience to various forms of mass cultural consumption, from the endless revisitation of 'the classics' (say, via posters and compact discs) to the frenetic worship of the latest media-packaged video star. An associated result of the distinctive experimentalism of contemporary 'high art' is to deprive it, so to speak, of bargaining counters in its negotiations with the state; the emotional resonance that, say, Verdi's music could find in the masses in the nineteenth century, and which made it among other things a potent vehicle for patriotic emotion, was denied in the following century to that of Dallapiccola, Stockhausen or Boulez. Crudely put, 'their stuff don't sound good'. You can't credit it as a medium for expressing and evoking universally recognizable emotions. The average film soundtrack is much better at it; and *that* you can now produce by computer, given sophisticated software and a reasonably gifted tune-maker.

We have considered some aspects of the situation of creative intellectuals that, as I put it, make them into awkward customers and those that make them into easy marks for the state. What is the balance between those contrasting aspects? On the whole, I suspect the latter ones are more significant, chiefly on account of a fact I have mentioned a few times, the last just a few lines ago. It can be argued that all over the world, but especially in the more advanced parts of it, contemporary social and cultural developments have been increasing the significance of what the French call *l'imaginaire*, the realm of symbols, of perceptions of self and reality, of modes of feeling and vision. This is the stuff that creative intellectuals deal in, and to that extent such a development should increase their social significance, and thus perhaps their autonomy and, in our vocabulary, their disposition and ability to act as 'awkward customers' *vis-à-vis* the state and other power centres. However, *l'imaginaire* is also a realm where colossal businesses at the driving edge of technological and industrial advance – those dealing with information and communications, and particularly the electronic media – have imperiously installed them-selves, and lead the dance, employing in the process the new specialists in the creation and manipulation of *l'imaginaire* itself. The best among these are brilliantly talented men and women, comparable in sheer brainpower and artistic originality to any of the 'creative intellectuals' we have been talking about. But they are selected, trained, rewarded and managed chiefly in the light of criteria of technical prowess and productivity, and they operate in units totally committed to the making of profits and / or the shaping of public opinion for commercial and political purposes. This new body of intellectual personnel no longer shares with the ecclesiastical clerisy and their secular counterparts, the creative intellectuals, a commitment, however vestigial, to universalistic values, a sense, however attenuated, of critical detachment from purely mundane involvements. It is in the process of displacing both clerical and secular intellectuals from the centre of the cultural process, making them dispensable, or at any rate further diminish-ing their sense of autonomy *vis-à-vis* worldly powers, beginning with the state itself.

7

Economic Power

Two power situations

Erving Goffman, a master of the art of revealing that things aren't quite what they look like, once drew an intriguing example from a lion-tamer act in a circus. If the act is successful, the spectator may assume that the tamer has trained the lion to recognize the commands he shouts at the animal – for instance, 'Jump on the red stool!' – and dutifully to act upon them. In fact, as Goffman would have it, something rather different is going on: by positioning himself in the cage, the tamer simply compels the lion to move, and makes sure that there is only one way he can do it – to jump to the red stool. The lion-tamer apparently gets the lion to do something he wants (which the lion, left to himself, would not want to do), and in that sense he exercises power over the lion; but in the process no proper commands are being listened to, recognized or obeyed by the lion. He, in fact, does not know or care what the tamer wants of him; he remains in charge of his own movements, but performs them in circumstances that the tamer controls, and to that extent and on that account complies with the tamer's wishes.

This example, in Goffman's rendering of it, suggests that there are two rather different kinds of power relations. One kind is most clearly represented by political power: here one party to the relationship can activate another by issuing commands, which displace in the other's mind its own programmes and preferences, and can thus commit the other's activities to the implementation of its designs (or prevent them from interfering with those designs). In the second kind, the party subject to power may go on pursuing its own interests, acting upon its own designs; but does so within constraints that automatically advance and foster the power holder's interests. In a company town, for instance, would-be employees normally have no choice but to seek employment with *that* company; in an isolated town with only one store, most consumers have no choice but to pay *its* prices; in an area where only one bank operates, its terms of credit will have to be accepted by all those seeking credit. This last example is that given by Weber in a text, from the early drafts of *Wirtschaft und Gesellschaft*,[1] which emphasizes the difference between these two kinds of power situation, and considers economic power as the most significant embodiment of the second, which he labels 'domination by virtue of a constellation of interests' (as against 'domination by virtue of authority').

A closer examination of this phenomenon requires that we distinguish two questions. First, under what circumstances, within the economic sphere, can it be said that some unit possesses power over other units? Second, to what extent does such (economic) power represent a form of *social* power, that impinges upon the broader structures and processes of society? We shall consider both questions in this chapter before turning in the next to our main theme – the relations between economic and political power.

Our first concern, then, is to determine whether and to what extent the functioning of the economic system allows or indeed compels the formation of power differentials between the system's units. Our referent here is an *economic* system proper, which to begin with we may characterize rather formally, coming up with an image of it that corresponds closely with that of a *capitalist* economy. An economic system, that is, consists in a large set of independent though interdependent units (firms, households, single producers or consumers) which 'traffic' with one another in a formally peaceable manner on the market; that is, they exchange their respective outputs for money, at mutually agreed prices; they also compete with one another, each seeking to make its output more valuable to prospective exchange partners than those of other units.

By so acting the units spontaneously generate vast, open-ended networks of ever changing transactions, whose terms, in principle, depend purely on what each unit has to contribute to the overall process of production and distribution. The system as a whole has no general designer, overseer or controller; its varying states derive solely from whatever action each unit performs on the market, in the pursuit of its own interests and in the light of the resources available and the opportunities open to it.

Since both the exchanges taking place between units, and the processes internal to productive units, can only be conducted rationally in so far as they are expressed in money, the system's proper functioning requires that an outside agency, endowed with coercive power, guarantees the universal acceptability and the (relative) stability of the value of money. The same agency must also stand ready to enforce, whenever necessary, duly agreed contracts by means of which the units dispose of their own outputs and acquire those of others; finally, it must secure, if necessary by applying force, the units' ability to accumulate resources and to dispose of them according to its own preferences. In other words, the state, as a set of institutions managing political power, has a place *next to* the system thus construed. However, in principle this is a state with minimal tasks, none of which is of direct economic significance, in the sense of involving it immediately in the production and distribution of goods.

The question is, is there a place for power *within* the economic system so construed? That is, is it possible for any unit to secure its own economic advantage other than by obtaining from other units, on the market, the going rate for the contribution its output can make to their functioning and ultimately to the attainment of the consumers' satisfaction? Can any unit, in the system as described, compel others to make available to it resources which it does not *compete* for on the basis of its ability to pay for them, or compel them to acquire its own output at prices higher than those of its actual or potential competitors?

The standard answer in economics is 'no', and it is probably correct as far as it goes. Entrepreneurs, by stealing a march over their competitors with technological or organizational innovations, may over the short term enjoy a 'rent position'; but in a regime of open competition they will soon find their innovations imitated, and / or find themselves overtaken by other innovators. Employers who take excessive advantage of their employees will find themselves deserted by them, and merchants who sell substandard wares at non-competitive prices will be deserted by their customers. Skilled workers who charge high rates for their services will unwittingly entice other workers to learn or improve upon their skills, and this competitive supply of the same services will lower their prices.

All this of course applies, according to the standard argument, *unless* political arrangements, such as the granting of monopolies and patents by authorities, or the erection of legal barriers against the entry of workers into privileged professions, distort and thwart the competitive process. In other terms, there can be no such thing as *economic* power proper; unearned economic advantages can only be secured if *political* power is brought to bear on the economic process, on the initiative of either mischievous and ignorant political authorities or of businessmen bent on conspiring against the public.

Correct as it seems on the face of it, this response lends itself to two objections. First, however valid it may be for *the economic system* abstractly described above, the thesis that 'there is no such thing as *economic power*' is (prima facie) not valid for real-life economic systems as we know and love them. For these systems differ hugely from the above description; and a critical difference lies precisely in their engendering and harbouring systematic inequalities of economic power among units. It is impossible to get an elementary grasp on the nature and dynamic of real-life economic systems without recognizing that certain individual entrepreneurs, groups of firms, branches of industry and occupations are systematically and persistently at an advantage over others in securing capital, designing products, promoting innovation, undertaking research and development, obtaining returns on investments, entering arrangements with other units, finding export outlets, gaining market shares, hiring and retaining high-grade personnel, restraining and controlling labour activity.

They are not simply better at it; they determine what *it* is going to be, and in doing so they lay tight boundaries around the actions of other units, confining them to the status of peripheral or marginal suppliers. They are, as the expression goes, *price makers* rather than *price takers*. To some extent, in obtaining such advantages, they avail themselves of privileged relationships to government (as we shall see). But frequently the relationship works the other way round; that is, economic units may acquire political clout by virtue of the success of their specifically economic policies, especially those that allow them to grow in size without (immediately!) falling prey to bureaucratic inertia, to maintain an aggressive strategy of industrial innovation and market expansion while securing economies of scale, to become self-financing and thus escape the sanction of capital markets.

Economic power

In his essay on 'The domination effect and modern economic theory' (1950), the French economist Perroux draws from a number of considerations concerning such phenomena a number of conclusions that are worth quoting at some length:

> Economic life is something different from a network of exchange. It is, rather, a network of forces. The economy is guided not only by the search for gain, but also by that for power. . . . In order to express [this] I have constructed a tool of analysis . . . which I call . . . for lack of a better name, the *domination effect*. Between two economic units, A and B, the domination effect is present when, in a definite field, unit A exercises on unit B an irreversible or partially irreversible influence. . . . For example, a business firm in many cases influences decisions concerning price and quantity made by another firm, client or competitor, the inverse not being true or not to the same degree. Or an economic sector engenders a lowering or raising of costs and prices from which it does not receive influences comparable in breadth and intensity. Or one nation imposes on another goods or services or a general pattern of institutions of production and exchange.[2]

If these clearly recognizable facts of economic life contrast with the standard conception of the economic system, which excludes the possibility itself of economic power, this is largely due to a lack of attention to the conditions required for the tenability of that conception. For instance, the theoretical argument for the inexistence of economic power is based (among other things) on the assumption that the number of productive units interacting on the market is large, and can continually increase; yet the fact is that units seeking to enter real markets in contemporary economic systems generally face massive and ever increasing costs of entry.

Many important developments in twentieth-century economics, and particularly various theories of imperfect competition, have acknowledged these realities, and thus the existence of such a thing as 'market power'. However, more archaic forms of economic thinking, instead of taking on board such a phenomenon, prefer to ignore those same realities or to reinterpret in such a way as to reaffirm that 'there is no such thing as *economic* power'.[3] Unfortunately, highly refined formulations of such thinking are currently at an advantage in economics because they can theorize in rigorous and elegant fashion the functioning of the economic system, while remaining inapplicable to real-life economic processes. As a result, much main-line economic thinking insists on discounting theoretically the phenomenon of economic power. Such thinking, furthermore, both informs and is informed by the hegemony of conservative social and political thinking characteristic of the last quarter of the twentieth century, and this adds ideological usefulness to their intellectual prestige.

There is a second reason for recognizing the existence of power relations within the economic system, and this obtains even if the standard construction of it is accepted. It consists in acknowledging some significant differences among system units, and in particular the difference between units constituted around lumps of capital, and units whose market activities, instead, consist exclusively in the sale of labour power. Even if these two types of resources are brought together on the market through contractual arrangements, those arrangements necessarily reflect a significant, unavoidable *power differential* between the two basic types of unit. This differential, however, obtains at the collective level, rather than at the individual one; it is *vis-à-vis* employers as a class that employees as a class are at a systematic disadvantage. For this reason, that differential is liable to be ignored by an 'atomistic' approach, which focuses exclusively on individual actors and fails to recognize to what extent their conduct is assisted or constrained respectively by their access to or exclusion from certain resources.

To the extent that the economic system is internally differentiated in those terms, a number of other differences follow. For instance, it is commonly said that the system as a whole is characterized by a distinctive logic, the pursuit of profit. This is true; but that logic directly drives the conduct of only a minority of units, normally referred to as firms or enterprises; only these can meaningfully seek profitability in their market operations. Units of the *other* kind, and in particular the majority of households, are present in the market only as sellers of labour power to enterprises and as purchasers and consumers of the products of enterprises. They may operate rationally in this capacity, for instance budget their expenditures in such a way as to maximize their marginal utilities; but it makes no sense for them to engage in capital accounting and in other practices required for the pursuit of profit, which remains the privilege of enterprises. Enterprises are normally constituted around privately appropriated means of production, but these can actually serve the pursuit of profit only if the hired labour power of units of the *other* kind is expended upon them.

Thus, in a sense the two types of units *need each other*; but the resulting relationship, even if it is brought about through an employment contract, rather than through coercive means (as in slavery or serfdom), is an asymmetrical one. It is capital that hires labour, not vice versa. The intensity and the urgency of the need to enter the employment contract is normally much greater for employees than for employers. Adam Smith makes this point as follows: 'Many workmen could not subsist a week, few could subsist a month, and scarce any a year without employment. . . . In the long-run the workman may be as necessary to his master as his master is to him, but the necessity is not so immediate.'[4] Various institutions (from collective bargaining arrangements to unemployment benefits to minimum wage legislation) may reduce the asymmetry and allow employees to bargain for better terms; but while this means that even employees are expected to seek their own interest, they continue to do so within a context controlled by the employers. They are thus necessarily subject to the kind of power Goffman's tamer exercises upon the lion, the relationship of domination which may arise, according to Weber, from 'a constellation of interests'.

In his critique of Böhm-Bawerk's attempt to expel the concept of power from economics, the German economist Preiser evokes Weber's definition of power, which he quotes as 'the possibility of enforcing our own will *even against resistance*', and argues as follows:

> From this point of view power presupposes that the economic agent has the possibility of stipulating conditions, that he may accept or refuse offers, that he can evade pressure; such a possibility presupposes in its turn either qualifications higher than average, i.e. some specifically rare skill, or a material basis such as ownership of material goods or certain rights. In this sense there can obviously only be one group *without* power, namely the propertyless wage earner. In relation to him all other economic agents have power. This manifests itself in . . . the different position [of the propertyless wage earner] on the labour market: an essentially rigid supply faces an essentially elastic demand. . . . Elasticity of demand does not mean that the employer always has the upper hand; his demand may, momentarily, be very rigid. But eventually he can react by changing his methods of production, or in other ways. That is why we say that demand is 'essentially' elastic; we could also have said 'in the long run'.[5]

A further aspect of the inherent asymmetry of the employment relationship is pointed out by Heibroner:

> Under a wage labor system workers are entirely free to enter or leave the work relationship as they wish. They cannot be forced or dragooned into work or compelled to stay at work if they wish to quit. . . . However, the freedom from impressment equally enjoyed by labor and capital does not betoken an equality of their respective entitlements. The wage labor relationship includes a legal provision that is wholly at odds with the equal footing on which the owners of labor power and capital apparently confront one another in the market place. The understanding is that the product . . . belongs to the owner of the capital resources that are used in production, not to the owners of the labor resources who receive a payment – their wage – and who have no legal claim to their product.[6]

Finally, the structure of the employment relationship, once established on terms that more or less directly express the market inferiority of the employee, makes the asymmetry even clearer by subjecting the employee to managerial authority and discipline. In Italian law, the technical term for that relationship is 'contract of *subordinate* labour'. This points up that the expenditure of the employee's labour power, since it normally takes place within an organized complex of capital goods and other resources that belong to the employer, is carried out under the control of the same employer and/or the employer's agents. This is of course required for the enterprise's rational functioning, which is in turn a necessary (not a sufficient) condition of its attaining a profit. In Weberian terms, this adds to the employer's 'domination by virtue of a constellation of interests', grounded on his or her ownership of means of production and on the employees' exclusion from them, an equally grounded but more explicit and visible 'domination by virtue of authority'. That is, the employer normally operates by issuing commands to subordinates, and the conduct of the matter 'to a socially relevant degree occurs as if the [subordinates] had made the content of the command the maxim of their own conduct for its very own sake'.[7]

This line of thinking, at variance with conventional views of the economic system and of the nature of the social relations characteristic of it, is generally associated with the thinking of Marx. In fact many elements of it predated Marx, and all of them are shared by post-Marxian thinkers such as Max Weber.[8] Marx construed the economic system in a distinctive manner, seeking to establish not only the inherent inequality of the employment relationship, but also its subtly and yet relentlessly exploitative nature. Furthermore, he argued that the system harboured internal contradictions that made its breakdown and its revolutionary supersession by socialism inevitable. These distinctive components of Marx's thinking have turned out to be largely untenable; yet he remains a valuable source of insights into the realities of economic power. As Frank Parkin suggests, in a statement applying both to capitalist and to socialist societies: 'The relevant question is not whether surplus extraction occurs, but whether the state confers rights upon a limited circle of eligibles to deny access to "means of life and labor" to the rest of the community'.[9] The key Marxian insight, one again that Weber shares, is the emphasis on the significance of *property* – or, in Weber's terminology, of 'appropriation'. It may be worthwhile to elaborate further the bearing of this phenomenon on the question of power.

Powerful property

The essence of property is that it divides society into haves and have-nots, for it confers on the former the faculty of excluding the latter from access to objects (including non-material objects, such as skills, rights and other forms of secured expectations) which are part of the public world both haves and have-nots inhabit.[10] We can think of this exclusion, in the first instance, as a purely negative faculty, which simply keeps apart individuals who continue to exist, so to speak, on the same plane.

In a book intended chiefly to criticize the social theories of Talcott Parsons, Alvin Gouldner construes the social advantage accruing to property owners in an original manner. Parsons had constructed a sophisticated imagery of society at large, but of modern society in particular, as a complex plurality of overlapping 'social systems' which tie together actors into relations of mutual obligation, the prototype of which is constituted by role relations. However, Gouldner remarks, this view neglects the significance of property, and particularly of large property holdings. These allow their owners to stand back from other actors and, by resting on their resources, to enter relations that do not commit them to reciprocity.

> 'Social space', then, may be conceived of as divided into two types: one type consists of parcels or areas preempted by 'ownership', the other of the 'free space' that has not been thus enclosed. It is in the free social space that 'social systems', as they are conceived by Parsons, are established. A 'social system' is therefore a *residual* organisation of social relationships, in that it may deal only with those things that are 'left over' after property rights have been established. . . . Property is an encumbrance on social relations. It is . . . a claim treated as prior to those involved in the role relations that constitute 'social systems'. Property constitutes the 'givens' or the limiting conditions for the construction and development of social systems. . . . Property is thus the infrastructure of social systems.[11]

However, property of a certain kind and size does not only confer on the owner what one may consider the negative advantage of standing aside from normal social commerce. It confers a positive advantage, becomes the pivot of an asymmetric relationship whose components lie instead on top of one another, when the objects owned have two characteristics. First, they represent the product of the shared efforts of a plurality of individuals; second, they are indispensable as a support and instrument of further such efforts. People who own such objects, which lie as it were at the intersection of the past and the future, can control the existence (and direct the activity) of people excluded from them, by dictating the terms under which they can gain *some* access to those objects. It is in this sense, and to this extent, that the former acquire power over the latter. Marx phrased this point particularly sharply in his so-called *Critique of the Gotha Program*:

> The fact that labor is conditioned by nature entails that a man who possesses no other property than his own labor power, under all conditions of society and culture, must be the slave of those other men, who have become the owners of the objective conditions of labor. He can only work with their permission, hence live only with their permission.[12]

The notion that social power grounded on property is a development of a broader, conceptually prior phenomenon, has been argued otherwise. Franz Neumann, for instance, writes:

The legal meaning of private property comprises two radically different conceptions: power over an external piece of nature . . . and power over other men derived from power over nature. It is only the second meaning of private property with which the political scientist is concerned: with proprietorship in the means of production. This type of property gives power.[13]

Neumann's statement projects a classically Marxist image of the power-conferring objects: 'pieces of nature', which happen to be indispensable, in a given society, to the task of producing and reproducing the material conditions of human existence. In one of his later works, expressly intended to criticize and modify the conceptual armour of Marxism, Alvin Gouldner on the one hand focused more specifically on capital as the distinctive modern type of privately owned means of production, on the other hand defined capital so broadly that Neumann's 'pieces of nature' become only a particular, and somewhat archaic, form of it; in particular, 'education is as much capital as are a factory's buildings or machines'.[14] At the same time, in Gouldner's definition of 'capital', what one may call the negative, exclusionary significance of property reasserts itself as the proprietor's right to *withhold* the object that he or she owns:

Capital . . . is: any produced object used to make saleable utilities, thus providing its possessor with *incomes*, or claims to incomes defined as legit-imate because of their imputed contribution to economic productivity; these claims to income are enforced normally by withholding, or threatening to withhold, the capital-object. . . . [Typically] capital enforces its claims to income . . . by modifying others' access to the capital-object, or threatening to do so.[15]

But reasoning about property does not constitute the only avenue to a recognition of the existence of economic power. Robert Blau's *Exchange and Power in Social Life* holds property in the background while, as the title indicates, it foregrounds another critical institution of the economic sphere – exchange.[16] Blau considers to begin with a plurality of autono-mous units (individual or collective) entertaining primarily relations of exchange with one another. That is, each unit has (or can produce) a different set of resources, some of which are surplus to its own require-ments; it can thus make over these resources, in a given quantity, to other units which lack them, and thus induce those units to make over to itself resources of other kinds of which *it* has a deficit and those units have a surplus. In principle this situation generates among the units a 'horizontal' network of flows of differentiated resources, exchanged on terms ultimately reflecting the significance of the contribution that each unit can make to the welfare of all others.

But consider two particular units, A and B. A has a resource set ($a1$, $a2$, $a3$, $a4$, . . . an), and B a resource set ($b1$, $b2$, $b3$, $b4$, . . . bn). On this condition, it may be the case that only exchange relations obtain between

A and B, each making over to the other some of its surplus resources. However, it may also be the case that:

- B cannot do without some of the resources in A's set; on the other hand
- A *can* do without any of the resources in B's set. Furthermore
- there are no other suppliers than A of whatever resources in A's set B needs; and, finally
- B is not in a position to *coerce* A to make over to itself the resources it needs from A's set.

Given these circumstances, one can easily see, B is in a bad fix. It may experiment with ways to preserve its autonomy and its presumptive equality with A as a component of the exchange network. For instance, B may seek to produce autarkically those of A's resources it needs. It can seek to *do without* them (as Blau remarks, some forms of ideology may serve this end, by characterizing those resources as not worth having, damaging to B's identity or in contrast with its *real* interests). Or it can try to make the resources it can supply to A indispensable to it, for instance by organizing a cartel of suppliers. But if each of these strategies fails (and the conditions stipulated above assume that they have failed, or will fail), B has – Blau argues – only one way out of its fix. It must accept a diminution of its own autonomy and of its sense of equal standing with A. It may do so by becoming particularly deferential and obsequious towards A, or by declaring itself a grateful and dutiful member of A's retinue of clients and supporters, or by committing itself to do A's bidding in its own relations to C, D and E.

To a different extent, all these constrained responses by B to what I have called its fix distort its relationship to A, rendering it asymmetrical, and (in the end) subjecting B to A's power. The power in question may take political form, but whether it does or not, its roots lie in B's condition of economic inferiority. And although the analytical route we have followed to it has started from the phenomenon of exchange, one can see how it converges with a line of reasoning emphasizing instead property and employment, by thinking of A as a group in sole possession of capital goods, and of B as a group formed by those who possess solely their labour power.

Social consequences of economic power

In this way, we have answered positively the first question posed at the beginning of the chapter – whether there be such a thing as economic power. The second, it may be remembered, concerns the extent to which such power, so to speak, spills over the boundaries of the economic system and affects broader social structures and processes.

In principle, the answer to this question must be that *it depends*. One can think of a society where the economic system (as characterized above) is not the sole or even the primary site of the processes of production or reproduction of material life; where most such processes, instead, are embedded within the institutional frameworks, say, of religion or of kinship, rather than carried out by means of networks of exchange among independent market units. Also, there have been and there are societies where some, or many, people are made to work for others not by means of employment contracts, but through some form of total dependency, as in slavery. If such a society has a place at all for something resembling the economic system, the effect on its total existence of specifically economically grounded power phenomena may be very limited.

It is not difficult, in fact, to think of and to discourse reasonably about societies of this nature, different as they may be from our own, for arrangements of the kind I have just indicated have probably been prevalent the world over until at most a couple of centuries ago. It is more difficult to think realistically about another kind of society, differing from both the former, and from societies similar to ours. In societies of this kind, the general impact of specifically economic power is small because the material processes entrusted to the economic system in our own society are not so much carried out otherwise, but rather are insignificant, marginal to social existence at large, for most of the people's physical and moral energies are invested in other kinds of activities – say, worship, warfare, play or sex.

However, according to Marx's mordant criticism of Bastiat, only a superficial appraisal of certain historical circumstances may suggest that in them non-economic activities were institutionally central and economic ones insignificant:

> Truly comic is Mr Bastiat, who imagines that the Greeks and Romans had lived purely off plunder. Yet, if someone is to subsist on plunder over centuries, there must always exist something to be plunder or the object of the plunder must continually reproduce itself. It thus appears that also Greeks and Romans had a production process, that is an economy, which was the material basis of their world just as much as the bourgeois economy is the material basis of the contemporary world.

In the same text – a footnote to the first volume of *Das Kapital* – Marx extends this criticism to a reviewer who had recognized the validity of Marx's views on the relations between the economic basis of society and the ideological superstructure, but only as concerns modern society,

> not however for either the Middle Ages, where catholicism dominated, or for Athens and Rome, where politics dominated. . . . Yet it is clear that the Middle Ages could not live off catholicism nor the ancient world off politics. On the contrary, the ways in which they made a living explains why in one case politics, in the other catholicism played the central role.[17]

Whether there is one or there are two kinds of society where the general social import of properly economic power is minimized – by entrusting material concerns to frameworks that do not closely resemble the economic system, and / or by minimizing the social and cultural significance of economic concerns as such – there is little doubt that that import is huge in the societies with which we are more familiar. For here economic concerns are dealt with by means of a complex set of distinctive, elaborate, sophisticated institutions (property, contract, money, markets, the corporation, collective bargaining, banking, insurance, hire-purchase, the professions, company law, and so on). These institutions can be considered the 'software' of an economic system; in the early 1990s, when an undertaking was made to reconstitute on the capitalist pattern the economies of the east European countries and of the former Soviet Union, where such institutions had no close equivalents, their critical significance soon became apparent. Furthermore, economic concerns have become utterly central to the social process at large in the societies with which we are more familiar. We can easily see this if we consider the role that money – the essential economic medium – plays in aspects of everybody's everyday existence apparently remote from the economic realm.

Households, police stations, charity organizations, political parties, couples on dates, schools, prisons – all these units we do not think of primarily as performing economic activities are tied into the economic system, if by nothing else, by the necessity of budgeting their activities in money terms. There may not be a 'cash nexus' between, say, a national health service and an individual making use of it; but the service itself is a complex of establishments which acquire the services of nurses and doctors and the products of pharmaceutical companies at the going price, and have to balance those outlays against a flow of resources which comes to them in money form.

Furthermore, purposefully designed economic units supply goods and services on which directly depends the satisfaction of the most diverse needs of individuals, from personal security to transport, entertainment or education. To the same extent, most individuals secure the satisfaction of those needs only to the extent that they command a flow of income, which in most cases comes from their being employees, former employees, or the dependants of employees. In sum, in societies like ours, it is not only the case that *money talks*; rather, it talks a uniquely persuasive and authoritative language, with which everybody is expected to become at least acquainted just to survive.

Some accounts of the significance of economic power

One may ask oneself why this should be so, what causes the processes and structures of the economic sphere to assert themselves so imperiously within social existence as a whole. Let us briefly consider three main answers to this question from 'classical' social theory.

Tocqueville's answer would probably impute this development to a profound mutation in the moral and intellectual temper of Western

countries. Over the last century or two of the *anciens régimes* the populations of those countries became steadily more secular-minded, more indi-
vidualistic, less attached to tradition, more resentful of previous social
hierarchies, more egalitarian, more interested in material well-being. All
these changes made Western populations receptive to the appeals and
challenges of new ways of producing and distributing wealth; these, as a
consequence, established themselves imperiously at the centre of society's
institutional landscape.[18]

Marx's answer would point to the inherently dynamic character of the
so-called Money–Commodity–Money cycle, the molecular component of
the capitalist system. It only makes sense to go from Money to Money via
Commodity if the cycle eventuates in *more* money than it started with; by
the same token, however, that cycle tends to become self-sustaining, more
money breeding ever more money; it is through the endless, restless
reiteration of the cycle that capitalism undergoes its expansion – until,
Marx thought, its own contradictions explode and cause its supersession
by socialism. Although *one* critical commodity – 'abstract labour power'
Marx calls it – intervenes in the cycle and makes possible its endless
repetition, it plays that role by embodying itself in other commodities, that
is, objects produced with an eye not to their inherent 'use value' but to
their 'exchange value', what they can fetch on the market. On this account,
a central aspect of the process is constituted by 'commodification'; that is,
more and more goods and services must be produced and supplied with a
view to selling them. As more and more 'use values' are expelled from the
social process and replaced by 'exchange values', the hold of the capitalist
mode of production on society at large expands and deepens.

Weber once called modern capitalism 'the most fateful force in the
modern world' because it embodied a distinctively dynamic form of rationality. Its development, however, was part of a broader process of rationalization, which had other significant expressions – in particular, the
development of the modern state, and within the latter the expansion and
the increasing sophistication of the bureaucratic form of administration.
There were deep affinities between capitalism and bureaucratization, and
the modern transformation of the social world at large was largely due to
the rationalizing impetus they shared. Of the two, in Weber's view,
capitalism was intrinsically the more dynamic phenomenon: mechanisms
similar to those analysed by Marx were continually forcing firms to
innovate their production processes, to develop new markets, to address
(and to generate) new social needs.

However, bureaucratization, increasingly dominant both in the political
realm (where it was supported by another transforming process, democratization) and in other social realms, had an intrinsic tendency to standardize
action, to reduce the autonomy of actors, to constrain innovation. This
tendency was resisted within the economic system in so far as it functioned
on the basis of competition, and thus compelled entrepreneurs relentlessly
to seek innovation in the search for profit. For Weber, the key question of

the future was how long such entrepreneurial resistance to bureaucratic levelling and co-ordination would last. As far as the past and the present were concerned, however, he had little doubt of capitalism's tendency to expand its reach over society at large.

These, then, are our givens. The economic system has an intrinsic tendency (ignored by main-line economic theory) to generate a power structure within itself. It has also an intrinsic tendency to extend its reach more and more widely over society at large. A corollary of these two propositions seems to be that economic power has, so to speak, an extra-economic edge; that it necessarily constitutes a distinctive and important form of *social power*.

Michael Mann phrases this point as follows in the conceptual introduction to his book on forms of social power: '*Economic power* derives from the satisfaction of subsistence needs through the social organisation of the extraction, transformation, distribution and consumption of objects of nature. . . . Those able to monopolise control over production, distribution, exchange, and consumption . . . can obtain general . . . power in societies.'[19] However, from such a generic position it is possible to develop different arguments concerning the general social significance of economic power and in particular its relation to political power, which is of course *our* concern in this book. If we consider again the three 'classical' authors mentioned above, we see Marx resolutely claiming that the group – the class, in his own vocabulary – in possession of economic power is also, by the same token, the 'ruling class'. The other two authors, however, beg to differ.

Consider Tocqueville's view of the matter, which turns out to be a rather complex one. In volume 2 of *De la démocratie en Amérique*, where he considers the general tendencies of Western society in his own time, Tocqueville argues, in the first instance, that the universal passion for well-being makes 'industry' the key form of economic activity, and on that account industrialists tend to represent a new form of aristocracy. 'The particular class which occupies itself with industry',[20] which had once been 'an exceptional class', threatens to become 'the principal class, and, so to speak, the sole class'.[21] In a later chapter, however, Tocqueville suggests that, for industry to expand, governments must undertake ever new tasks in order to provide it with the required 'infrastructures' (as we would phrase the point today) and with various other services. This allows government to gain a degree of control over the social process which rivals that of industrialists. As Tocqueville puts it: 'Rulers increasingly possess themselves of, and put to their own service, the greatest portion of the novel force which industry constitutes in our own times. *L'industrie nous mène, et ils la mènent.*'[22] Taken by itself, however, this formulation is perhaps too trenchant – it reveals Tocqueville's notorious taste for aphoristic phrasing – and might best be considered in conjunction with the previous quote. Together, these statements express a dynamic tension inherent in societies characterized both by an economic system of the kind described above and by liberal-democratic political structures. Economic power is indeed a form of social power of such significance as to embody a more or less open claim to general social superiority; but normally political power resists this claim, opposing its own to it. The contrast between those claims, never completely resolved by the wholesale realization of either, allows a range of possible solutions and accommodations.

This situation is reflected in Max Weber's thinking about our theme. As an interpreter and critic of his own society, Weber was acutely aware that the relationship between economic and political power is inherently contingent; according to him, who liked to declare himself 'a class-conscious bourgeois', his own class, the German bourgeoisie, had signally failed to claim, *vis-à-vis* the groups entrenched in the political power structures of the post-Bismarck Reich – the Kaiser and his entourage, the *Junker* element which controlled the army and the higher reaches of the bureaucracy – the amount of political initiative and responsibility to which its own economic (and cultural) achievements entitled it.

More generally, as we have seen above, Weber saw at the heart of modernity two related but distinct and partly contrasting rationalization projects: respectively, the bureaucratization of authority (evidenced chiefly though by no means exclusively in the political sphere), and the advance of modern capitalism (and especially industrial capitalism). His own worst fear, once more, was that in the future the first trend would overwhelm the second, depriving the economic sphere of the autonomy it needed in order to select and reward an entrepreneurial class effectively committed to risk and innovation.

These 'classical' arguments to the effect that (as I read them) Marx had an oversimple view of the relationship between economic and political power find a more recent echo in an essay by Franz Neumann (written in 1950) which I have already cited. The essay provides a very summary account of the main historical conceptions of that relationship, and suggests that within Western history the close institutional co-ordination of the two power forms has been the rule; in fact, economic superiority and political superiority have been barely distinguishable aspects of the overall position of social advantage of privileged strata. Schematically, in 'the ancient conception', 'although the source of political power is economic power [and particularly the control of land], political power permeates all social activities and all spheres of life. The economic power position merely provides the motor of political power which includes all power relationships.' As against this, in 'the feudal conception', '[i]n the ideal-typical form, political power does not exist. It is merely a function of an economic power position: the ownership of land. From it flow judicial, military, religious, legislative and administrative powers.'

It is only in 'the capitalist conception' that political and economic power become institutionally separate from one another; only the differentiation of the respective spheres allows the economic system to achieve the physiognomy sketched above, and to uncover and cultivate its distinctively dynamic form of rationality. What I have characterized, above, as 'the economic system' is in fact the historical product of such a differentiation process, whereby economic power emerges as a distinct form of social power, relatively self-standing with respect to political power, and typically constituted, in Weberian language, by 'a constellation of interests', rather than through visible hierarchies of command and obedience.

Two contrasting 'moral syndromes'

Paradoxically, however, the same differentiation process raises the problem of how the two spheres, and the respective power forms (or, more concretely, the political and the economic elites), are going to relate to one another.[23] On a number of counts, each power form seeks sometimes to subordinate the other to itself, asserting the superiority of its own distinctive potentialities and the priority of its own requirements. Jane Jacobs has recently restated a number of reasons for this tendency by means of a new construct, that of the 'moral syndrome'.[24] A moral syndrome is a distinctive set of approved character traits, of valued dispositions to act and think, which the practitioners of a given kind of social activity think ideally suited for it and against which they claim to measure their own moral stature. Jacobs works out two syndromes, the 'commercial' one and the 'guardian', and formulates them as two contrasting sets of moral injunctions:

THE COMMERCIAL MORAL SYNDROME
Shun force
Come to voluntary agreements
Be honest
Collaborate easily with strangers and aliens
Compete
Respect contrasts
Use initiative and enterprise
Be open to inventiveness and novelty
Be efficient
Promote comfort and convenience
Dissent for the sake of the task
Invest for productive purposes
Be industrious
Be thrifty
Be optimistic

THE GUARDIAN MORAL SYNDROME
Shun trading
Exert prowess
Be obedient and disciplined
Adhere to tradition
Respect hierarchy
Be loyal
Take vengeance

Deceive for the sake of the task
Make rich use of leisure
Be ostentatious
Dispense largesse
Be exclusive
Show fortitude
Be fatalistic
Treasure honor

Jacobs imparts a self-consciously archaic flavour to her argument; she gives it the literary form of a Platonic dialogue, and sets it up as a contrast between models of virtue chiefly applicable for individual members of elite groups – essentially, traders and dynastic rulers, that is, the holders of traditional forms of, respectively, economic and political power – and on these counts her argument is not straightforwardly applicable to our concerns. But she analyses also some of the social practices and institutional arrangements associated with each syndrome, and in doing so mobilizes a number of modern and contemporary examples. Besides, the title itself of her book, *Systems of Survival*, suggests that its concerns go beyond the ways in which each elite group has traditionally argued the moral superiority of its own design for living and devalued the other's.

In any case, by emphasizing the incompatibility between the 'moral syndromes' of the respective elites, Jacobs chiefly makes a case for the tendency of the two forms of social power to oppose one another, each seeking to suppress the other's autonomy or to subordinate its workings to its own designs. Such a case can be made also in other terms: for instance, by emphasizing the objective contrasts between the interests typically pursued by the two forms, or the configuration each power form tends to impart to the larger society (including the circumstances of non-elite groups). But one should also consider the two power forms' tendency to accommodate one another, to enter relatively stable co-operative arrangements. One can variously account for this tendency, imputing it for instance to the interest all elites share in securing their privileges and advantages from the possible onslaught of the masses, or to the functional interdependence of the differentiated spheres, neither of which can profit, in the end, from suppressing entirely the other's autonomy and thus damaging its distinctive form of rationality. From the vantage point of the turn of the twentieth century, one can see this second consideration validated by the (on the whole) poor results socialist countries obtained from their 'command economies'. In 1950 Neumann could write quite neutrally that '[t]he Soviet Union presents a clear-cut marginal case where political power not only has made itself supreme but has become the fount of whatever economic power positions exist'. Forty years later, it was apparent that such an arrangement had irremediably damaged the vitality of the economic sphere.

To conclude, I would reassert that there are contrasting tendencies in the relationship between political and economic power; and one might say that over the last two centuries the vicissitudes of that relationship have constituted the main stuff of politics, both domestic and (to a lesser extent) international, and have embodied themselves in very different constitutional designs and institutional arrangements. Neumann's article attempts a very schematic account of those vicissitudes; the next two chapters will, in nearly as schematically a fashion, give a conceptual treatment of the main issues in the relationship, by asking again what the two powers typically demand of one another. Since within the horizon of our treatment political power is mainly institutionalized in the state, it is the relationship to the latter of economic power that we shall primarily consider.

8

Business and Politics

Political requirements of the economic system

Above, we have construed the economic system as a plurality of economic actors 'trafficking' with one another on the market, each on its own behalf. The existence itself of such a system rests on institutional foundations which only the state can secure, through the ultimate sanction of organized, legitimate coercion. The prime foundation is private property, for only this can ground the severalness of economic actors, their standing aside from one another as independent units that deal with one another through mutual, negotiated adjustments, rather than by complying jointly with some overriding scheme of production and distribution.

Economic actors define themselves as each the exclusive guardian and beneficiary of a discrete parcel of appropriated resources, each relating to others through valid acts of disposition concerning such resources; and again the validity of such acts needs to be coercively sanctioned. In other words, contract – the institution by means of which the system's components construct the changing networks that structure it – also requires a political sanction.

We have noted, however, that the appropriated resources vary in their nature, the most significant difference being that between means of production on the one hand and labour power on the other. Such a difference, we have argued, establishes a most significant power differential between economic actors, and that differential in turn determines to what extent various contractual partners are actually free when they dispose of their resources in their mutual traffics. If those resources consist exclusively in their labour power, then their freedom is substantially limited, and the leverage upon the condition of the possessors of means of production is correspondingly increased. If this is so, then political power, to the extent that it guarantees the existence itself of the economic system (as we have construed it), also guarantees the existence of economic power. It does so by allocating differentially the factual advantages economic actors derive from the state's distinctive capacity for organized, legitimate coercion. Built into the nature of property is a privileged claim upon that coercion. Thus the cash value, so to speak, of the economic actors' expectation that the appropriate political agencies (the police, the judiciary, the executioner, the prison system) will deploy coercion – in its ultimate domestic manifestation as the exercise of penal jurisdiction – in order to uphold and defend their possessions varies necessarily with the amount and nature of those possessions.

In his polemic against Talcott Parsons's overuse of the concept of 'social role' as a tool for sociological analysis, Gouldner remarks:

> Ownership . . . seems to have some very remarkable attributes, which are not at all common to other social roles. In particular, it has an ease of access to social enforceability. The inviolability of property rights is more closely monitored and protected by the legal and state apparatus, in the normal course of events, than any other 'right' except that of protection from bodily harm. The use of the state's force to protect property is not at all an instrument of 'last resort,' but a *routine* method of enforcement. Normally, one does not bargain, negotiate, remonstrate, or appeal to a thief; one calls the police. This implies something about the priorities that the state assigns to the protection of property rights.[1]

The significance of this point is wide, particularly when the property in question consists in industrial assets – the economically and socially most significant form of property in our type of society. For such property allows the owner to extend employment to the propertyless on terms which, I have argued, are in principle systematically favourable to the owner, and comprise the explicit subjection of employees to the managerial powers vested in the owner or the owner's agents. Thus the legal protection of property comes to guarantee a considerable modification in the presumptive equality of contractual partners, the fact that the employee, to use again an expression from the Italian Civil Code, commits him- or herself to perform '*subordinate* labour'. As Parkin argues:

> the industrial firm . . . is the locus above all others where authority relations are inseparable from property rights. When workers occupy their factory and lock out management, the offence for which they are liable to be arraigned is not disobedience, which is a mere offence against authority, but unlawful trespass, which is an offence against property. . . . Managerial command over labor . . . takes place within a legal framework in which the inviolability of property is already guaranteed. . . . Clearly no-one would imagine otherwise than that the state would be the principal guardian of property. . . . The images of the policeman, the courthouse, and the prison cell are almost inseparable from the idea of property.[2]

To sum up, the holders of economic power expect the state to ground in its law their very identity as property owners, and to sanction their contractual claims towards one another and towards economically powerless individuals. As I have stressed, these expectations are chiefly addressed to the state understood as an apparatus for coercion, and concern various critical components of its structure: not just 'the policeman, the courthouse, and the prison' listed by Parkin, but the legislature itself. In a more elaborate version, this argument could be extended to other, more or less significant institutions of the economic sphere – from money, the market and the firm at one end to bankruptcy and inheritance at the other – and could consider the part played by the state, in its various aspects, in establishing them and monitoring their effects.

I will give one example of where such an elaboration might lead. In contemporary economies the most significant productive assets are vested not in physical individuals or families but in corporations; these are generally the most significant actors in the economic process.[3] There is a great deal of controversy over the part played respectively by proprietary and by managerial interests in orienting the typical corporation's strategies. But there can be no controversy about the fact that corporations are of necessity, directly or indirectly, the products of public policy. Only a complex set of sophisticated legal arrangements can create such artificial individuals, allow the natural individuals who originally conferred resources upon the corporation not to respond with their whole patrimony for its activities, empower the corporation to accumulate and manage further assets, and so forth.

Of course those arrangements, the making of which is necessarily a state activity, constitute no more than frameworks within which the concrete activity of organizing, financing, managing the corporation takes place; and of course that activity has many significant determinants of a non-legal nature and obeys in the first place an economic logic: so far as I know, the creators of Standard Oil, or of the Dupont Corporation, or of General Motors were not lawyers. Yet the specific content of those frameworks does make a difference: the contemporary discussion about 'models of capitalism'[4] traces at least some of the persistent, significant differences between the so-called Rhenan and the so-called Anglo-Saxon model to public policy choices embodied respectively in, say, German commercial law and American company law.

Constraints on public policy

I have argued so far that economic power depends on, and claims, the state's support of the institutional conditions of its existence and its func-tioning – beginning, as we saw, with property and contract. One may wonder whether its *dependence on* that support weakens its *claim to* it. It does, both conceptually and in specific concrete circumstances, in the sense that at some point a given state may appear rather unwilling to comply with that claim. It can for instance, through a policy of agrarian reform, expressly withdraw its legal endorsement from certain kinds of assets and explicitly undertake to distribute them to previous non-owners. Or it can weaken the contractual superiority of employers by allowing or encour-aging employees to join unions, by institutionalizing collective bargaining, by widening and strengthening the 'safety net' constituted by its own welfare activities, or by empowering a public agency to monitor industrial work conditions and safeguard employees from particularly damaging consequences of their contractual inferiority. Above all, it can, through its taxation policies or its strategies of industrial development, lay constraints upon the productive initiatives of the owners of industrial and other assets, inducing them to vary in some measure from those they might undertake if they sought purely to increase those assets or to maximize their yield.

In these and other ways, states often incur the accusation of being bent upon 'socialistic', 'demagogic' or 'confiscatory' policies, hostile to business and deaf to their sacred duty to protect property. But mostly the policies in question reflect the contrasts of interests between various economically powerful groups, which compel public policy to favour some groups and disfavour others. In any case, only within fairly narrow limits can the state actually turn its back on the claims of property for legal and political protection or seriously abridge the freedom of operation of the economically powerful. A case in point may be contemporary Sweden, the country in Europe committed to the most thrusting and self-conscious social-democratic project (high taxation levels, generous welfare provisions, Keynesian economic policies and so forth), and yet a country whose industrial system has not ceased to be dominated by a small oligarchy of powerful corporations.

One might ask what reasons there are for thinking that the state *cannot* seriously turn its back on the economically powerful, totally refuse to acknowledge their claim for a political endorsement of their power through the establishment of appropriate institutions. I shall offer three different (though overlapping) answers to this question. First, a broad historical answer, based on an argument (not an uncontroversial one) by North and Thomas.[5]

Most European national states existing today – the argument goes – are the products of a prolonged military struggle taking place in the first two centuries of the modern era, between political units formed in the Middle Ages, whose governments competed to increase the territorial scope of their rule at each other's expense. To sustain the struggle, those governments had to command increasing revenues, and their ability to do so depended among other things upon how they dealt with an essential task of governments at large, to establish and enforce property rights.

According to North and Thomas, such rights can to a different extent satisfy a criterion of 'efficiency' which they articulate as follows: 'each individual desires to maximize his wealth and . . . has the exclusive right to use as he sees fit his land, labor, capital and other possessions; . . . he alone has the right to transfer his resources to another; and . . . property rights are so defined that no one else is either benefited or harmed by his use of his property'.[6] As can be seen, property rights established and enforced by governments in keeping with this criterion are also an appropriate institutional component of the economic system as we have construed it. Furthermore, such rights have two additional features: first, they are necessary if a national economy is to experience sustained economic growth; second, they lend themselves to supplying governments, through taxation, with the regular and relatively high volume of resources governments need to finance military expenditure and support other administrative activities.

According to the argument in question, in the sixteenth and seventeenth centuries two major European governments, those of England and of the Netherlands, institutionalized property rights more in accordance with the 'efficiency' criterion. As a consequence, on the one hand growth got going in the respective economies, on the other those governments assured themselves of a reliable and high flow of resources for public expenditure. Basically, they made a deal with the economic powers that be, granting to them appropriately designed property rights in return for revenue. By contrast, two other governments, those of France and Spain, maintained 'inefficient' property rights and fiscal arrangements, and these on the one hand impeded or retarded economic growth, and on the other exposed those governments to repeated, paralysing financial crises.

Here I will go beyond North and Thomas's argument – and perhaps against the grain of it, for it seems inspired by what I consider rather implausible fears of a state wholly deaf to the appeals of economic reason and totally unconcerned about the 'efficiency', or lack of it, of the property rights it establishes and protects. Spain and France have survived as political units but, to a different extent and at different points in their history, they have had to learn from England and the Netherlands how to institutionalize 'efficient' property rights; and so have, in various fashions, many other states. In so far as this is the case, one might indeed say that the 'lesson of history' North and Thomas expound has been taken on board by Western states at large, and lays persistent, significant constraints on their conduct *vis-à-vis* economic power.

At this point, my first answer, which appeals to a view, however simplified (and, as I warned the reader, controversial), of historical facts, merges with a second one, more directly concerned with the nature itself of the Western state. The very design of its structure, it seems to me, binds the state to observe a line of demarcation, which may well lack stability, between itself and the civil society; and the latter simply cannot subsist without a set of distinctive institutions, among which those of the economic sphere (private property, contract, the market and so on) play a vital role. Such institutions may need the state as ultimate guarantor, but their subsistence in a realm separate from that where the state predominantly operates is intrinsic to the very nature of the state, as a set of differentiated, specifically political institutions complementary to that realm. The classical formulation of this principle is the early modern distinction between *imperium*, political authority, and *dominium*, the right of property. These two institutions had in common the absolute character of the respective claims: but they differed in that the former was to be vested exclusively in the sovereign, as the public subject *par excellence*, while the second was, so to speak, dispersed and decentralized among a plurality of private subjects, each of whom enjoyed a *dominium* protected even *vis-à-vis* the sovereign himself.

Subsequently, the same principle was to be articulated, in various manners, in the constitutions of most Western states. These documents differ considerably from one another, sometimes they change, and of course they do not provide too reliable a guide to political practice; but it cannot be insignificant that most of them acknowledge, more or less explicitly, the institutions of the economic sphere as a valued feature of the societies that the state ordains and protects.

A third answer to the question why the state *cannot* seriously, and for long, turn a deaf ear to the claim of the economically powerful for a suitable institutional environment is pragmatic in nature, and can be given in two complementary versions. In the first, *negative*, version, it behoves the state to establish and enforce the economic system's essential institutions because otherwise it risks having some critical economic resources desert the country and seek a more hospitable political abode beyond the state's boundaries.

According to Albert O. Hirschman's *The Passions and the Interests*,[7] arguments to this effect were already made, more or less expressly, in the early stages of the Western commercialization process: the new forms of wealth, based on money, restrained the notorious rapacity of rulers, because unlike landed possessions these forms of wealth were intrinsically mobile and thus less liable to seizure and to other forms of arbitrary dispossession. Rulers threatening to usurp such wealth would thus be punished by having it flee from their jurisdiction. In our own time, the same argument is routinely phrased with reference to, say, the international (or, in current terminology, 'global') nature of financial capital or to the necessity that a given state maintain its creditworthiness by complying with the policy dictates of the International Monetary Fund.

The *positive* version of this third answer is complementary to the negative version, and overlaps with an aspect of North and Thomas's argument. Basically, *it pays* for a state to create and maintain a suitable set of institutions for the economic system, for the latter is (potentially, at any rate) the goose that lays the golden egg of economic development and by so doing underwrites a state's own financial needs. The satisfaction of these, in turn, allows the state to play an independent role in international affairs by building up its industrial base, strengthening its military potential, and so on.

What *is* a set of institutions suitable for economic growth, of course, will largely depend on its changing requirements. Thus, the conferral of corporate legal identity upon commercial ventures used to be an exceptional step, which the state would take only in very special circumstances, such as the opportunity to colonize at arm's length vast and rich overseas territories (as in the case of the East and the West India Companies). It turned into a much more routine affair when corporations became the instrument of choice for gathering savings from a large number of potential investors and committing them to normal commercial and industrial undertakings requiring larger amounts of capital than individuals and families or more conventional forms of partnership could muster. (In the United States, the state of Delaware, in particular, became famous for the ease with which it conceded the advantages of incorporation.)

To give another example, the peculiarly close relationship between banks and industrial firms in modern Germany is the result, among other things, of public policy choices intended to make the country take the lead in the second historical wave of industrialization, centred on chemical and heavy industry and requiring large amounts of capital. (One can interpret in the same manner Bismarck's policies concerning 'the social question', which comprised both repressive measures toward independent labour organizations and some social insurance provisions. In the latter, many students see the first major initiative in the direction of the modern welfare state.)

I have sought to address the question of what induces states to meet the demands laid upon it as concerns the key institutional requirements of the economic system. Essentially, I have answered that it is both in its nature and in its interest to do so. This answer should not be given too self-confidently and too rigidly, for there have been circumstances in which states have responded in a niggardly or inconsistent fashion to those demands, choosing to accommodate instead those of economically weak but politically mobilized strata, or to pursue goals – especially foreign policy goals – that made little economic sense.

Even in dealing with such cases, however, the above answer may preserve some validity, in the light of two considerations. First, in situations where, on the face of it, a state *seems* to downplay the institutional requirements of the economic system, it may in fact (I have already suggested) be favouring in its policies one set of economically powerful forces over others. Just consider the systematic differences in interests between, say, landed and industrial or commercial wealth; or between sectors of a national economy needing customs protection from international competition and other sectors that stand to benefit from free trade; or between sectors that stand to gain from inflation and those hurt by it. In Marxist language, one might say that by making itself useful to one particular 'capital fraction' the state necessarily short-changes others. Second, in those cases where a state has actually turned its back on the demands of the business class at large, it is important to determine how the rest of the story went. Very likely it will turn out that it was subsequently confronted with an 'investment strike' (possibly assisted by the policies of its own central bank), the flight of domestic capital overseas,[8] a devaluation of its currency, a subversive attack on its institutions and its leadership and / or the arrival of the United States Marines.

Further claims of the economically powerful

With these reservations and qualifications, the statement that it is both in the nature and in the interest of the state to provide the economic system with suitable institutional arrangements may be complemented by considering two further sets of claims typically raised towards the state by the economically powerful.

The institutional arrangements considered so far consist largely in a promise by the state to use its coercive powers, whenever necessary, in defence of certain fundamental interests of economic actors, such as the exclusive control over their possessions, the freedom to dispose of their own resources according to their own judgement, the certainty that their contractual partners will perform their obligations, and so forth. Often, the institutions of the economic sphere do not expressly envisage the economic capacities of the individuals they concern (their being investors, entrepreneurs, wage labourers) but simply their quality as subjects of rights, which they share with citizens in general. (Characteristically, in some countries the Civil Law Code comprises also the legislation concerning commercial and industrial affairs, instead of assigning this to a separate Commercial Law Code.) In any case, typically those institutions do not commit the state to any positive intervention in economic affairs, but limit themselves to establishing a framework for the conduct of private economic activities.

This state activity, however, has always been complemented by others intended to assist more positively in the formation of the economic system and to favour the holders of economic power; and the second major claim of economic power on the state concerns activities of this kind. Any serious reconsideration of the *true story* of Western economic development, in particular, leads to the abandonment of, as Neumann puts it, 'the mythological conception of the laissez-faire state'[9] – or of the 'night-watchman state', to use another common metaphor – and thus shows the limits of North and Thomas's exclusive concern with the institutional design of property rights.

Time and again, far from simply laying down and policing legal frameworks for the conduct of private economic activity, the state has deployed in the interest of the domestic economic system all its unique resources – not just the provisions of its legislation and their enforcement by the judiciary, but also the facilities of its executive branch. The state has engaged in that interest its power to tax (and thus to influence the spending patterns of the public) and that of levying tariffs on imports, the monetary policy of its central bank, the surveillance capacity and the order-keeping powers of the police, the bottom-line intervention of the army in industrial disputes, the decisions of planning authorities. It has committed huge flows of public resources – commandeered through taxes, imposts, customs, the public debt, tributes from abroad – to the construction of infrastructures chiefly useful to producers, and acquired colonial possessions intended to lower their production costs or to provide them with captive markets. It has secured for firms credits at lower than market-rates of interest, paid for their products at higher than market-prices, entered contracts with them on sweetheart terms, financed their export drives, underwritten their research and development costs, exempted them from fiscal and other public obligations, established special agencies to deal with their requirements and given them privileged access to public information and to administrative decision processes. It has allowed firms to form cartels and to agree the prices of their products instead of competing over them, policed those agreements, made life difficult for firms not party to them. It has stood surety for firms in the face of threatening creditors, 'socialized' their losses, rescued them from failure. In the interest of the business class, the state has forbidden or hampered the formation of unions, has defamed, persecuted, prosecuted, bribed labour leaders and organizers, repressed workers' protest, forbidden and disbanded demonstrations, allowed the rapid immigration of blackleg workers, broken strikes *manu militari*, borne the costs of shifting manpower from rural to industrial employment. Finally, through their budgets and their fiscal and monetary policies, states have sought to control the aggregate level of demand of domestic economies, to contain inflation, to achieve a positive balance of trade, to maintain a certain relationship between the value of its own currency and that of the currencies dominant in the international market.

These forms of positive state intervention in the economy – others could be added to the list – have increased in number over time, in a progression that can be schematically explained as follows. While some forms have from the beginning accompanied the establishment and functioning of the economic system, others became necessary as various national economies successively undertook to industrialize. New industrialization ventures often required the state to assist them through its customs policy and by expending public funds to build infrastructures or to jump-start critical branches of industry with its contracts. Sometimes the political elites were indeed responsible not just for servicing, but for initiating capitalist development. For instance, reviewing the history of the Italian economic system in the modern era, De Cecco writes:

A modern economy, with a large industrial sector, was considered by almost all parts of the Italian ruling elite as a necessary feature of an important modern nation. . . . All powerful European nations had an industry, an army and a navy, a road network and a railway network, banks and post offices. Italy, if it wanted to achieve a status comparable to that of other large European countries, had to have all these things. The Italian ruling elite thus set about to acquire them and by 1922 they had succeeded. . . . Capitalism was introduced into Italy by politicians, bureaucrats, generals, and admirals, who needed to furnish the new Italy with the requisites of the modern state.[10]

Furthermore, within more mature national economic systems, approximately from the second half of the nineteenth century, a process of capital concentration began to interfere with the automatic workings of the market, which became less capable of striking an equilibrium in the economic process. New state policies had to be developed to counteract the new tendencies and to meet the system's persistent need for regulation.

In the twentieth century, further forms of state intervention were adopted to a number of ends: to put domestic economies on a war footing; to counteract their tendency to undergo periodic crises, some of which threatened to put them into a tailspin; finally, to target them positively towards a set of new objectives to which, in the wake of World War II, Western nations widely subscribed. These objectives were variously characterized as sustained and balanced economic growth, 'guided' technological change, the transition to a post-industrial economy, the demonstration of the superiority of capitalism over collectivism, the further internationalization of the economic system.

Some of the forms of state intervention adopted in this context would have been unthinkable before the mid-twentieth century, since previously most states lacked the resources, the know-how, the constitutional machinery, the administrative capacity, or the political will, necessary to undertake them. Many new forms were experimented with during World War II, and subsequently, together with yet newer forms, became part of a complex set of political measures and arrangements concerned with what came to be called the 'management of the economy'. The fact that the set had largely originated in the context of war left two legacies: the policies in question continued to pay close attention (particularly close in some cases, such as the United States, Britain and France) to industries more or less directly connected with the business of war; and, although those policies were focused on the domestic economy, they treated the openness of the national economies to each other both as a significant parameter and as a development to be fostered.

During the so-called 'long boom' following World War II, the new shape of the relationship between the state and the economy was viewed by power holders on both sides of the relationship as a historical breakthrough, and generally applauded by the broader public.[11] Even such phenomena as state ownership of industrial assets, and some forms of 'planning' for development and of express 'concertation' of incomes policy by officially empowered bodies seemed to be widely accepted by public opinion. At the height of the boom, towards the end of the 1960s, a German economist, Knut Borchardt, phrased as follows the developments that such consensus acknowledged and applauded:

> It is clear that also in Western countries the decisions of state officials have gained much greater significance, and will certainly preserve it in the future, for the share of the state in the social product has grown and its competence to guide production and consumption has increased. We have a growing sector of non-private production, concerning not just intermediate but also end-products. We have a growing sector of collective, unpaid consumption. Although presently in most Western countries the push toward public owner-

ship is less visible, there remains a tendency to make available more and more products and services at prices lower than market prices. . . .

[This] state activity is in no way bound to contradict the principles of a profit oriented economy; rather, state interventions accord with the regularities which characterize the decisions made in the private realm, and often have the task of securing the material conditions for the operation of that realm and, more concretely, for the realization of the profit expectations of firms.[12]

In the last two decades of the century, however, the workability of the new relationship between the state and the economy, its costs, its side-effects, have become widely controversial. What is at stake is the part to be played respectively by the state and the market in the management of national economies, as well as (increasingly) in the participation of those in the global economy. The controversy is all the more serious because it bears also on a third set of claims economic power lays upon the state, which needs to be briefly examined.

The claims in question concern the general social environment in which the economic system is to function; in the rhetoric of the claims and complaints that business elites address to governments, they are expressed by such recurrent terms as 'atmosphere', 'climate', 'ambiance'. The state, besides assisting the system more or less directly in the ways we have just reviewed, should give high priority to its requirements also in managing its political environment. The first requirement is a negative one: the management of the society should only to a limited extent be expressly political, and remain entrusted to a large extent to what are perceived as the spontaneous workings of the market. The economic system can prosper only if its distinctive mode of operation – the self-seeking transactions of discrete, mutually independent though interdependent units – is allowed to extend its reach to a large and possibly growing number of aspects of the social process; by the same token, the state should not conduct itself as the total manager of that process.

This means, among other things, that the state should not be possessed of a total design of the society, should not orient its activities to a general, paramount goal – unless that goal consists exactly in maximizing the autonomy of the economic system and the moral priority of economic concerns. It also means that the state's interventions in the distribution of the social product should respect the significance of the market as the key mechanism of that distribution, modifying it at most marginally. (This means of course that the power relations that exist in the market, despite the conventional understanding of its workings, are to be left alone.)

Even as a partial manager of the social process, furthermore, the state should observe various further requirements of the economic system. The autonomy and welfare of the system can be threatened not only by an excessively intrusive state, but also by the uncontrolled explosion of the social conflicts engendered by its own workings. The key conflict still results from the power asymmetry between the capitalist class and the employee class and revolves both around the allocation of the product of their interaction and around the authority relations structuring that interaction. But other conflicts juxtapose themselves to that – for instance, the challenge of women to their persistent disadvantage as concerns the more rewarding forms of employment; the anomic behaviour of marginal, disaffected groups (youth, the unemployed, ethnic minorities); the resistance of traditional and / or unconventional forms of life and work to their displacement by the market and by technological advance; intergenerational and cultural tensions.

Economically powerful groups expect the state to control all these conflicts, if necessary by repressing them, otherwise partly by institutionalizing them, partly by ameliorating the conditions that tend to accentuate them. In its capacity as an agency operating on behalf of the public interest, the state should attract from the social body at large some loyalty, impart to it a sense of collective identity that can in turn dampen the contrasts that characterize that body when considered purely as an assemblage of individual and collective components oriented chiefly to antagonistic interests. To evoke that loyalty and inspire that sense of identity, political elites normally thematize certain issues rather than others, emphasize interests pertaining to the social body as a whole, mobilize symbols and ideas focused on the nation, understood as a collectivity sharing one history and one destiny.

They may also commit public resources in order to give material expression to solidarities binding the nation across differences of class, regional location and generation. In doing so, they may alleviate in economically weak groups conditions inducing them to despair, resentment, disaffection and hostility, which if allowed to fester might otherwise eventuate in open social conflict. The economy works best when its arrangements for allocating and managing resources and for producing and distributing wealth are not the object exclusively of a strained and reluctant compliance nor are openly challenged and contested. To this extent, the holders of economic power may consider it a positive duty of the state to put in place and finance arrangements that correct the distributive outcomes of the market in the name of equity or on behalf of the principle of citizenship.

Broadly for the same reason, they may also consider well spent the resources that go into maintaining a public educational system, for this may produce a series of effects directly or indirectly favouring the economic system. Such a system offers families an opportunity to secure or improve the position of their children in the stratification system by allowing them to acquire the appropriate qualifications and credentials. It inculcates in pupils and students habits of self-discipline and obedience and a disposition to engage with one another in a competition process, and to consider legitimate its results even when unfavourable to themselves.[13] Because, under modern conditions, it is increasingly involved in the socialization of the new generations, the educational system suggests itself as a suitable device for creating in the population a sense of collective identity. Furthermore, it imparts to pupils and students bodies of skill and of knowledge on which, to a greater or lesser extent, their future occupational life will depend, and which by the same token the economic system finds, so to speak, prepackaged in the individuals entering the labour market. Finally, the higher reaches of the educational system are geared to the production of new knowledge, some of which can be critical for maintaining the economic system's capacity for innovation and thus its international competitiveness.

To what extent these various expectations laid upon the educational system are actually met is of course an open question, and possibly a distinctly problematical one, among other reasons because there may be some conflict between specific expectations, and some trade-offs may be necessary. Furthermore, expectations other than those I have attributed to the economic system often converge upon a country's educational institutions, seeking to determine the division of labour among them, their curricula, the ways in which they are to be financed and managed, and so forth. For this very reason, however, it is likely that the economic elites will take a keen interest in those and other educational matters. These, by their very nature, are particularly relevant to the shaping of future social conditions; and these in turn are of special relevance to contemporary economic elites, involved in undertakings that typically take many years in coming to realization, and thus particularly require a predictable social environment.

Some contemporary tendencies

This preoccupation with continuity and stability, encoded in two themes emphasized above (the moderation of social conflict, the provisions for the education and training of the future generations), sometimes acquires a harder edge. Business elites begin to question the compatibility of a liberal-democratic constitution and of the resultant policy trends with the indispensable conditions for the functioning of the economic system. They complain, for instance, that the polity's commitment to full employment, coupled with the institutionalization of collective bargaining, necessarily leads to excessive inflation rates; that welfare expenditures are getting out of control, imposing excessive fiscal burdens on the public, engendering irresponsibility and greed among their beneficiaries, placing an ever increasing amount of resources beyond the reach of the market mechanism; that the competition among the parties for electoral success and among the media for larger and larger audiences is rendering the public sphere too turbulent, heightening the expectations of the populace, making it quarrelsome, impatient and unruly, inciting envy and demagoguery.

From diagnoses of this nature recurrently flow some predictable policy proposals, all intended (in a typical phrasing) to 'restore business confidence': rolling back (or slowing down / stopping the advance of) the welfare state; curbing the excessive power of unions; re-educating the public in the virtues of self-restraint, compliance with rules, respect for authority; reasserting the superiority of national as against sectional interests, the moral legitimacy of earned advantages; awakening the public to the damages of excessive political intrusion in economic affairs; allowing managers to manage, consumers to choose and savers to invest, all according to their own lights; protecting duly empowered political elites from too close a scrutiny on the part of public opinion, thus allowing them to devise and enforce long-term policies. Proposals of this nature may be advanced in a more or less aggressive and intolerant manner; they tend to become particularly bloody-minded when (in the judgement of those making them) conditions adverse to business confidence last a long time, and not only threaten (however defined) 'normal' levels of profit but jeopardize the very possibility of doing business. Faced with runaway inflation rates, a high incidence of public disorder, sustained 'de-subordination' of the lower orders and frequent and lasting disruptions of the production process, business circles may begin to clamour for more decisive forms of remedial and repressive action on the part of the state. If these are not forthcoming, they may intimate, more or less openly, that all bets are off, that their own patience with a constitutional polity apparently incapable of maintaining minimal levels of order, or indeed harbouring subversive designs, has reached its limits, and they have no choice but to look for relief to a 'strong man' and his faction, to the army, or to foreign intervention.

Under less extreme conditions, threats of this kind are formulated only by minority groups within the business community. In most Western countries, through most of the second half of the twentieth century, the rest of that community has remained committed to a more moderate line. It has admitted the necessity of state policies that give some expression to social solidarity in order to maintain consensus around the *status quo*, and involve the state in the management of the economy; however, as I have already suggested, it has also insisted that such policies should preserve the central role of the market in accumulating and allocating resources. The mix between these components of the line has of course varied considerably from time to time and from place to place; but towards the end of the twentieth century it increasingly emphasized the reservations and objections of the business community *vis-à-vis* many kinds of state intervention and its preference for 'letting the market rip'.

Even ignoring this shift, the very variety of the claims reviewed in this chapter entails that the relationship between economic power and the state has been open to a range of diverse adjustments. Consider once more, in particular, the numerous forms of state intervention in the economy which I have listed above as objects of the second kind of claims. Historically, as the list grew longer and more diverse, the compound effect of its components upon the economic system as a whole became more complex and sometimes contradictory, and it became increasingly a matter of choice (and occasionally perhaps of chance) *which* components would be comprised among the economic and social policies of a given state. As I have already suggested, often such policies sacrifice the interests of some economic forces to those of others, and sometimes what appears as a given government's 'anti-business bias' expresses in fact its favour for one over other sections of the business class.

Economic power – both that of the business class as a whole (and to a lesser extent of organized labour) and that of single sections of it – intervenes to affect the choice among alternative state policies. It is often brought to bear on governments by associations specifically organized to lobby political decision-makers on behalf of numerous economic units, but sometimes by single firms. Occasionally, these may affect the political and administrative decision processes simply because they are particularly skilful and aggressive in accessing, cajoling, blackmailing and bribing the decision-makers. But normally economic units, singly or in association with one another, affect those processes to the extent that they possess economic power: that is, to the extent that they can seriously perturb the country's economy if they suspend their investment plans or shift them abroad, revise their pricing policies or their product mix, reduce the size of their workforce, declare an operating loss and suspend the payment of dividends, default on their obligations, become vulnerable to hostile takeovers, or threaten to go bankrupt. Of course the business class as a whole possesses this kind of power in abundance, as Charles Lindblom has argued most persuasively.[14]

This does not mean that the state is purely the passive, servile recipient of pressures from the holders of economic power. As I indicated, it must choose from a wide repertory of policies of intervention, and normally the various components of the business class advance diverse and often contrasting requests for state action. On both counts the political elite has a certain ambit of choice, and can orient its policy also to properly political considerations, which may benefit also groups relatively deprived of economic power, or give priority to concerns of a non-economic nature. Furthermore, preferences for particular kinds of interventions become associated with various parts of the state's institutional machinery, which compete to shape the state's policy in line with those preferences.

In liberal-democratic systems, the state's ambit of choice is structured by the competition between parties over the composition of government and over its agenda – especially, of course, its economic policy. In principle, this means that the economically powerful can influence that agenda by assisting a given party's drive for electoral success and by opposing the other parties, by establishing particularly close relationships with this as against that body of actual or potential government leaders. But this kind of politicking must be used cautiously; when it is too overt and unsubtle, it can backfire, exposing its beneficiaries, in the eyes of the public, to the charge of being in the pockets of the bosses, and bestowing on its victims the advantage of appearing to be on the side of the angels.

Also, modern forms of business have such complex significant and pressing political requirements that it is not wise to entrust their satisfaction entirely to such chancy matters as electoral outcomes, the bargaining between coalition partners, or the question of which politician holds which post at a given time. On this account, business forces (major ones in particular) like to keep lines of communication open to both political majorities and minorities, both government and opposition; they maintain, so to speak, a diversified political portfolio. Also, many of their political efforts are directed not so much at politicians as such, but at the top officials of various administrative bodies – from ministries to special agencies and various kinds of public or semi-public bodies – who generally operate outside the glare of the public domain, tend to outlast their 'political masters', and to prepare and inform the decisions the latter apparently make. On this account, the economically powerful seek to establish privileged relationships to those bodies, to supply them with information, to affect the career of their personnel; in this way, they attempt, as it were, to pre-select the policies they will advise politicians to adopt. However, as I have already indicated, those bodies may have preferences of their own, and the policies they favour in their contacts with politicians are the joint product on the one hand of such preferences, on the other of the claims and demands of the business sector the bodies are expected to police and support.

Typical attitudes of the business elites towards their political counterparts

In spite of this, the interactions between the economic elite (operating either directly or through lobbyists or the appointed officials of producers' organizations) and the political elite inevitably play a significant role in the formation and implementation of public policies relevant to business interests. In planning and executing those interactions, the political elite acts upon certain typical dispositions and attitudes that it entertains toward the economic elite, and which reflect more or less directly the contrast between the 'commercial' and the 'guardian' moral syndromes depicted by Jacobs. But the contrast is here biased by the conviction that only the former is a properly *moral* syndrome, while politicians are moved by a set of considerations deserving no respect.

Thus, the holders of economic power like to think of themselves as representing the 'healthy part' of the nation, whose capacities and qualifications are continually tested in competition for (ultimately) the consumer's dollar. They may recognize that in liberal democracies politicians, too, have to compete, but their target (the voter's ballot) can too often be attained by uttering lies and false promises, inciting the populace's prejudice and envy, appealing to sectional interests, threatening to make partisan use of the state's powers. They, and the bureaucratic officials who assist them, are mostly illiterate in economic affairs, never having had to meet a payroll, or known the hard discipline of the bottom line in a balance sheet. As a consequence, politicians recurrently succumb to the temptation to print money or to squeeze the taxpayer in order to meet the state's financial commitments, never mind what damage inflation and high rates of tax do to the business climate; alternatively, politicians and bureaucrats mindlessly allow the public deficit to accumulate. Typically, politicians cannot see any further than the next election date, if that far; their awareness of business conditions is limited to their local constituency; often, they pander to the broadest, least enlightened, least morally responsible and least economically self-sufficient strata within the electorate.

Furthermore, politicians are said to have a predilection for wasteful, irrational uses of economic resources. They do not understand, for instance, that by regulating the market for house rentals in such a way as to overprotect tenants, they may make it unprofitable for landlords to enter that market, and thus destroy the latter. Senior politicians and statesmen have a knack for expensive, ostentatious *prestige* projects meant to stand as a future testimony to their passage on the political scene, and lavishly commit public funds to these projects. As to bureaucrats, their training, their social extraction, the culture and structure of the administrative environment in which they are making their careers, keep them mostly unaware of the necessities of the business world, unresponsive to its stresses and challenges.

In the minds of the economically powerful, such standardized images of politicians (and of most bureaucrats) are systematically counterposed to their own self-images, which needless to say are largely admiring. All the same, you cannot do business, nowadays, without coming to terms with multiple, complex, ever changing public regulations, without gaining access to information and to financial resources in the hands of public agencies, without influencing somehow the choices of government members. On this account, economic power must be brought to bear on the operation of the state through networks of contacts, by means of unceasing negotiations; in this process business elites bracket to some extent their own self-righteous view of their political and administrative counterparts for the sake of making deals, establishing and maintaining privileged arrangements, even generating a certain amount of mutual acceptance, liking, implicit under-standing, trust between themselves and the other protagonists of the negotiations. When the distance between the two parties is too great to be bridged by their direct acquaintance, social and cultural affinity and ongoing conversation, go-between figures, who share some of the charac-teristics of, and understand how to communicate with, each party, may turn into most valuable links.

It is unfortunate from the standpoint of legality and of other official values that in this process politicians and bureaucrats on the one hand and the economically powerful public on the other often exchange resources (information, exemptions from regulation, funds) for private advantages (kickbacks, bribes, campaign support), for typically such exchanges make both parties vulnerable to one another, and to that extent are an effective way of establishing between them a degree of reciprocal commitment and trust. Things do not always work this way, for many business people deeply despise corruptible politicians and bureaucrats; but they also hate incorruptible ones.

Whatever the manner of the interaction between its protagonists, the relationship between political and economic power has a dynamic, open-ended aspect, especially under contemporary conditions in advanced industrial countries. For here, as I have stressed, the economic system relies to a particularly large extent on political regulation, guidance, assistance and sanction, and each of these political activities can take a number of forms. The business of policy is to choose among these, and the policy of business is to influence, and as far as possible to determine, that choice. But the chance to do so is itself the product of a relatively open-ended process, given the variety of economic interests that compete in order so to influence or even determine policy. As I have already suggested, the process may allow both politicians, and the public bodies nominally under the politicians' control, to develop and pursue their own understanding of the correct and useful way to deal with specific economic problems, rather than simply to act upon the policy inputs originating from established economic forces.

A further dynamic aspect of the relationship between economic power and the state is, of course, that it works both ways. The time has come to consider the claims the state typically imposes upon economic power.

9

The Economic Costs of the State

A Weberian typology

In the chapter on basic sociological categories of economic activity in *Wirtschaft und Gesellschaft*, Max Weber devotes a lengthy paragraph to the 'financing of political organizations'.[1] Here he reviews systematically the many, diverse solutions given throughout history to the following major problem: through what arrangements do institutions primarily involved in political activities provide themselves with economic resources? He conceptualizes those arrangements (which I shall mostly refer to as 'extractive' ones) in such a way as to emphasize both their diversity from one another and the tendency of each to recur through history, since frequently arrangements apparently very different from one another combine features of two or more of the 'ideal-typical' solutions that Weber outlines and classifies. The result – a systematic typology of the 'financing of political organizations' – is such an impressive conceptual exercise that I cannot do better than try to convey to the reader its main contents.

First, Weber distinguishes between solutions which are *unstet*, that is, they operate occasionally rather than on a continuous or periodic basis, and those which are *stetig*, that is, they are stable, recurrent. Within the former category, those that are most significant for *political* organizations (as against, say, religious ones) fall in turn into two main types.

On the one hand, a political organization may avail itself of the contributions that its components willingly make towards the costs of its operations: for instance, the gifts that individuals make to their betters, when these are engaged also in political activities – chieftains, princes, feudal lords. The intended uses of such contributions may themselves be expressly political – for example, to finance the chief's participation in a crusade, or his ransom after a failed military venture – or they may arise from other contingencies – for example, to provide the lord's daughter with a marriage dowry.

On the other hand, a political body may finance itself by means of extorted tribute, the booty secured from piracy and so on. Such arrangements fall within the category of *unstet* provisions because they depend on the fortunes of raiding expeditions or other risky undertakings, although some polities (Weber gives as an example 'the Ligurian pirate state') managed to survive on them for lengthy periods.

Much more significant are, of course, arrangements that regularly connect a political organization with a reliable source of economic 'utilities' (*Nutzleistungen*). Such arrangements fall under three main headings.

First, the organization may seek routinely to provide for its needs by means of economic activities conducted not by itself, but by others. It can oblige these to perform work of political significance, for instance as soldiers, or jury members, or induct them into *corvée* labour on public works (canals, bridges, roads) or in mines. Or it can commandeer part of the yield of activities others engage in on their own behalf, whether this yield takes the form of natural goods or that of money. Peasants, for instance, may be required to make over part of their crops to officials who directly support themselves from them, or sell them.

The most significant way of assigning part of the financial returns of economic activities to the support of a political organization consists of course in taxation – a phenomenon of such complexity that even Weber, in this text, does little more than designate its main varieties: taxes proper (on property or income); fees exacted from those making use of specific services provided (generally on a monopolistic basis) by the political organization; imposts levied on certain kinds of transactions (e.g., custom duties, excises or turnover taxes). The political organization can collect these moneys directly through its own offices and channel them to its centre, allow them to be collected by office-holders who retain them for their own use (perhaps after buying the office in question from the organization), or farm out their collection to independent individuals who advance part of the expected yield to the organization itself and keep that yield for themselves.

Second, the political organization may seek to produce itself the resources it needs. A ruler, for instance, may finance its army, or hire a mercenary one, from the proceeds of his or her dynastic domains; or a state may establish a monopoly of certain lucrative economic activities, say the production and / or sale of tobacco, salt or matches.

There is a third alternative: the political organization can single out for special treatment some of the larger social groups (characterized, for instance, by the size of the members' patrimonies), and impose on them particular economic burdens. These, however, are likely to be associated with some economic privileges, for instance the exclusive practice of some trade or craft, or the permission to operate cartels or monopolies, or the exclusive access to certain honours.

Why states must 'extract' resources

In the framework of this book, Weber's typological treatment, sketchily summarized above, concerns one very important aspect of the relationship between political and economic power: *how* does the former extract resources typically controlled by the latter, or at any rate guarded and generated within the economic system? Much of this chapter, however, addresses a related but different question: *why* does such an extraction process take place, what political interests does it generally serve?

I would answer, in the first instance, by placing the whole relationship of political to economic power, in all its historical variations, against the background of a basic contradiction, which can be phrased as follows: politics has economic costs (just think of the dictum 'c'est l'argent qui fait la guerre'), but it is essentially unproductive. I have already quoted Marx's ironic formulation of this insight:

> Truly comic is Mr Bastiat, who imagines that the Greeks and Romans had lived purely off plunder. Yet, if someone is to subsist on plunder for centuries, there must always exist something to be plundered, or the object of the plunder must continually reproduce itself. It thus appears that also Greeks and Romans had a production process, that is an economy.

Behind this insight lies an even more basic one, which can be articulated as follows. First (at any rate in Marx's view), the fundamental economic activity is production; second, production always involves, at bottom, an interaction between human beings and natural forces and entities; third, this interaction, although it can be metaphorically represented as a matter of humans giving commands to, or beseeching, nature, or making deals with it, always involves humans physically grappling with nature, getting their hands dirty in order to become part of, and to benefit from, its workings. (See Marx's own image of labour as the 'metabolism' between man and nature.) Schiller's drama *Death of Wallenstein* phrases poetically this aspect of the condition of the human species:

> It falls into the strong arms of nature,
> this gigantic spirit, which obeys only itself,
> knows nothing of contracts, and deals with it
> not on its terms, but solely on its own.

The necessity for humans to get their hands dirty if they are to survive has several implications. One is the significance of two questions: *whose* hands get dirty? to *whose* benefit? The private appropriation of parts of nature allows the answers to refer to two different subjects, or classes of subjects. In other terms, property in the means of production allows *some* to benefit from the fact that *others* get their hands dirty.

Another implication is that, if taken literally, the expression 'command economy' – often used to refer to collectivist, centrally planned industrial economies – does not make much sense. If nature obeys no commands, but must be dealt with on its own terms, that expression cannot meaningfully address the ultimate economic process, but refers instead to (some of) the arrangements under which individuals engage in that process. A further implication is the contradiction I have already pointed out: political activity, being essentially intersubjective, cannot itself produce the resources it consumes. It is perforce parasitical upon another realm of activity, this one expressly centred on the production of resources.

An even stronger expression than 'parasitical', 'predatory', has been used recently by political scientists to characterize metaphorically this aspect of the relationship between politics and economics.[2] Rulers of all kinds, from tribal chieftains to the top politicians in liberal democracies,[3] have been characterized as intent on preying upon the labour, the savings, the enterprise of the members of the civil society; these in turn are characterized as engaged in generating resources, as responsible (directly or indirectly) for that interaction with nature on which the economic process ultimately rests.

This construction of the prototypical relationship between rulers and producers (and traders), still to be found in as sophisticated a thinker as Claude-Henri de Rouvroy, comte de Saint-Simon, reflects of course a value judgement, rating the *doux commerce* as morally superior to the armed violence in which the practitioners of politics are liable to indulge. Carl Schmitt has criticized the ideological bias of this value preference. Jane Jacobs's book, to which I have already repeatedly referred, shows that, in spite of their contrasts, both positions embody a 'moral syndrome' – respectively, it will be recalled, the 'commercial' and the 'guardian' syndrome. Long ago, the French historian Guizot argued that they have even more in common, that is, they *both* amount to ways of pursuing wealth. However, in one case the pursuers seek a short cut to wealth in threatening or exercising violence on others, with all the risks that this involves both for its perpetrator and for its victims; in the other case the pursuers take the slow road to wealth: they identify other people's wants, sharpen their own skills and mobilize their own resources in order to supply those wants on terms favourable to themselves. According to this argument, modern times are characterized by the emphasis laid upon this second approach, which promises to make the first one a matter of the past.

The predatory tendency of rulers can express itself through a wide range of relationships. Nomadic populations with a military bent may periodically overrun the lands on which are settled more peaceable, agricultural populations, and withdraw to their own heartland laden with booty, leaving those populations burdened not only by the disruption their production activities have undergone but also by the obligation to pay tribute in nature or specie. Small groups of warriors may establish a racketeering relation to the majority of the population of the territory on which they themselves remain settled, creaming off by means of feudal dues or other exactions whatever surplus the population manages to produce. Established territorial rulers may exact heavy tolls from traders crossing their territory, sometimes going as far as seizing the goods they carry in their entirety, other times making sure the difference between what those goods will fetch, once carried to their destination, and their own extortions is just sufficient to induce the traders to keep up their traffic. Rulers may borrow money from local or foreign lenders and then partly or wholly default on their debts, and thus sometimes ruin their creditors. If a system for collecting and administering public resources exists, they may draw freely on those resources in order to finance their private expenditures.

Constraints on extraction

These and similar depredations cannot be indulged in indefinitely, however. If they are overdone, peasants will abandon their holdings, refuse to cultivate them, or die of starvation; the landlords who can no longer themselves exploit their own rural dependants, already wrung dry by a predatory ruler, will become restive and gang up against him, or declare allegiance to a usurper; traders will develop new routes or secure their goods by means of defended convoys; lenders will refuse to make further loans, or demand exorbitant guarantees; and so forth.

Confronted with these possibilities, rulers generally seek to reduce the part that sheer, violent depredation plays in their rule, in order to stabilize it and transmit it to their successors. They seek to restrain those of their associates who hold on to a purely military, bloody-minded conception of their own role, and impose on those associates and on themselves certain limitations upon the extent and manner of the respective depredations. For instance, they differentiate sharply between the exactions practised, in gathering resources within the territory they normally rule, *and* those that they practise or authorize in outlying areas, which remain subject to raids, conquest and colonization. (Some of the more savage depredations recorded by Roman history, for example, were carried out by Roman officials on populations not as yet romanized.)

Rulers, furthermore, may normally acknowledge certain customary or expressly agreed upon limitations upon their exactions, while claiming the right to exceed those limitations under particularly pressing circumstances. They may deflect from themselves some of the odium their financial demands arouse by entrusting the collection of tribute to particular elements within the population whom they affect to despise. (The episode of the 'publican' in the New Testament indicates what degree of moral jeopardy and social exclusion such elements may incur.) They may lay the blame for the damage their own exactions inflict on the economy – for instance, for the recurrent famines and the attendant epidemics – on specific groups (hoarders, profiteers, Jewish financiers) or on the conspiracies of their foes.

Occasionally or systematically, rulers may bestow on particularly vulnerable and potentially threatening sections of the populace some compensatory benefits – bread, circuses, or a petty (material or symbolic) share in the booty from conquest. A more complex version of this arrangement – exemplified by some African kingdoms – consists in the laying of an effective claim by rulers (through their own staff) to most of the surplus produced within the society; it is then conveyed towards the centre of the political system, and *then* redistributed throughout the population as an expression of the rulers' bounty.

Such policies modify to a greater or lesser extent a purely predatory relationship between the politically powerful and the economy of the societies over which they rule. Somewhat cynically, they can all be seen to respect a single, elementary principle – don't kill the goose that lays the golden eggs. Elementary as the principle may be, many rulers have failed to observe it. According to Eisenstadt, the 'political systems of empires', in particular, *have* repeatedly killed the goose that lays the golden eggs. In such systems:

> the ruling elites endeavored to control all the potential centers of investment (especially in trade and industry) and taxed them heavily. In this way, the rulers usually undermined the economic value of investment activities, depleted their strength, reduced the economic importance of centers of investment, and diverted a good portion of investment to land. Moreover, through excessive taxation and excessive expenditure of administration, court, and wars, the rulers often undermined the purchasing power of the masses, shrank their existing local markets, stimulated inflation, and directed the flow of capital away from the country.[4]

Often, in order to secure their immediate access to critical resources (manpower, staples, species), the bureaucracy controlling an imperial system sought to run its economy as a single unit, to extract as many resources as possible and to commit them to the empire's increase or defence. To this end, the bureaucracy hindered the formation of markets, where the resources might have fallen under the direct control of a body of entrepreneurs which mobilized and recombined them. Thus, in the medium or long term, it made it impossible for the economy to generate enough new resources both to maintain its political structures and to provide for the society's reproduction.

But even such a situation should not be seen too straightforwardly as one where political elites irresponsibly preyed upon, and irreparably damaged, the economy's intrinsic disposition to generate and regenerate wealth. Generally, the economically powerful element within empires – the magnates, let us call them – were themselves little disposed to risk and enterprise, or oriented to markets. They, too, preferred to immobilize the resources under their control by constructing self-sufficient estate economies, engrossing rural manpower, placing it outside the reach of the imperial tax collector and army recruiter, and preventing it from developing a system of autonomous peasant units.[5]

Thus, in imperial systems, the political elite and the magnates were often on a collision course. Neither wanted a market economy. But the former wanted to run the whole economy as a single *oikos*, a gigantic unit working for the benefit of the ruler and of his direct associates; to this end, for instance, prices were decreed authoritatively by the emperor and individuals were assigned compulsorily to this or that occupation. The magnates preferred an economy constituted by a number of large and, as far as possible, self-sufficient *oikoi*, each under the exclusive control of a member of their class. These contrasting options were of course matched by the two parties' preferences concerning the location of decision-making powers and of the capacity for organized coercion: the ruler sought to concentrate both towards himself and his court or his *curia*; the magnates sought to appropriate political and military resources and to keep them decentralized.

In any case, one need not accept the view of predation as *the* relationship between rulers and economic agents; one may think of it instead as *one* such relationship, with several significant variants (some of which I mentioned above). Even if, as I suggested, political activity typically requires the expenditure of resources that it cannot itself produce, so that it must draw upon the results of a different, specifically productive, activity, this does not mean that the relationship between the two realms of activity necessarily goes only one way, the former exclusively exploiting and encroaching upon the latter, which gets nothing in return.

Nor is it appropriate to think of the injunction 'don't kill the goose ...' as the only constraint upon the process whereby economic resources are drawn upon by political power. This, on the contrary, whenever it is strongly institutionalized, tends to develop a positive concern with the health of the economy, although this concern may express itself in ways that do not always accord with the requirements of an autonomous, efficient economic system. There are a number of reasons for such concern, but the most significant are probably one reason pertaining to a given political system's external relations, and one regarding instead its domestic affairs.

I have already cited a memorable dictum that formulates sharply the first reason: 'c'est l'argent qui fait la guerre'. The organization and management of armed might is the key political concern *and* it requires the expenditure of economic resources. Furthermore, the expenditure required tends to be large and wasteful, on a number of counts. Some amount of military might *always* has to be held in readiness, no matter how infrequently (if ever) it is to be made use of. At any rate under modern conditions, this is not a matter just of maintaining indefinitely the armed forces as they are at a given time, but of *continually* upgrading them, re-equipping them, retraining them; this entails, alas, throwing on the scrap heap a great deal of yet unused material, in and of itself perfectly sound, and the related skills, simply because they no longer embody advanced military technology.

If war is actually waged, furthermore, the goal of prevailing over the enemy takes absolute priority over all other considerations, including economic ones. In other words, when a clash of arms is going on and new military resources need to be produced, the criterion of *effectiveness*, the attainment of a given purpose at whatever cost, trumps the economic criterion of *efficiency*, which enjoins an optimum ratio between inputs and ouputs; or, as Weber puts it, 'a war economy tends to be a go-for-broke economy'.[6] Even in peacetime, and more so in wartime, the attitude of military personnel towards the resources they employ, at any rate when they are not immediately connected with the tasks of defence and offence, tends to be a careless or even wanton, 'devil take the hindmost' one, and leads to a great deal of waste. (It is generally ruinous for a community or a household to be used as billets for soldiery, even when a country's own troops are concerned. Only an officered, barracked, disciplined garrison may have some positive effects on the local economy.)

Finally, the economic demands of wartime tend to have a disruptive effect on the economy at large, for war may necessitate the call to arms of a great number of able-bodied workers, the mobilization and training of a raw workforce, a particularly heavy-handed interference of political authorities with the workings of the market, the disruption of trade relations with other countries, and the priority of military commitments in the gathering and investment of public and private resources.

For all this, again since 'c'est l'argent qui fait la guerre', it behoves political authorities to restrain their predatory instincts vis-à-vis the economy and to lend considerable attention to its requirements. This is all the more so under modern conditions. Previously, rulers might field an army (perhaps a mercenary one) or equip a fleet by dipping into their own treasure, pawning one of the dynasty's territories, levying extraordinary taxes, or borrowing from foreign lenders; they might also expect the army to live off the territory (domestic or foreign) on which it operates, or the fleet to support itself by acts of piracy.[7]

Subsequently, however, as armies and navies turn into more permanent institutions, and become larger and more expensive, the relationship between military requirements and the domestic economy needs to be put on a sounder footing. In the eighteenth century, for instance, Prussia supported the relatively large standing army it could not afford not to have chiefly by means of a new system of taxation, based on so-called excises. Its administrative apparatus, largely run by and for the military, on the one hand managed to extract considerable resources from a relatively primitive economy, and on the other developed sophisticated budgeting practices and (through administrative practices collectively designated as Polizey) began to take some responsibility for protecting and developing the country's economic base.

Subsequently, it became increasingly clear that a country's military effectiveness depends on the strength of the economy at large, and particularly of its industrial sector. This dependency is both indirect – a modernized economy is more capable of bearing a sizeable fiscal burden or of financing a war effort through public loans – and direct – the productive equipment and the managerial and working skills typical of modern industry can be put to use more easily in fitting out the country for offence and defence in case of war; in due course, they can also repair more promptly whatever material damages war operations may leave in their wake.

On both counts, even rulers and statesmen particularly committed to the distinctiveness and supremacy of specifically political interests are increasingly forced to attend, through the apparatus of rule, to the needs of the domestic economy, and seek to foster its international standing. In their view, the economy should not only just allow itself to be milked for political purposes, but should become a primary factor in the power game states are forced to play with one another. In the second half of the twentieth century, a country's domestic economy was expected to play such a political role not only in the context of military competition and conflict, but also by demonstrating the validity and workability of the model of economic and social development each larger power sought to represent, with respect to one another or with respect to the underdeveloped countries. On all these accounts, the state imposes upon its domestic economy, for the sake of its own power pursuits, a claim – that it should be as strong, as internationally competitive as possible.

Accommodations between economic power and the state

One can easily see that this political objective is liable to generate a massive convergence of interests between economic and political power. Indeed, some of the forms of benevolent intervention which, in the previous chapter, I have treated as the state's response to claims put forward by the economic elites, can now be seen to result also from its own, autonomously conceived interest in a strong, modernized, developed economy. Among other things, one can make sense along these lines of the extensive cooperation and understanding between Hitler and the German business elite, *without* viewing Nazism chiefly as a political instrumentality of embattled financial capital: what took place was a massive convergence of interests between two parties seeking in principle rather different goals.

Yet, such a convergence cannot be taken for granted always and anywhere. Although both political and economic elites consider 'a strong economy' a highly desirable target of public policy, they may mean considerably different things by that expression. It may even happen that the economic powers that be are not quite sure that they *want* a strong economy, if strengthening the existent economic system means having to change markedly the ways they operate. A previous chapter has already referred to an instance of this: in the latter half of the nineteenth century the infrastructure of the Italian industrial system began to be created chiefly on the initiative of political, military and administrative leaders – an initiative that at first found little response on the part of the newly unified country's economic elites, unused to the challenges of innovation and enterprise.[8]

A somewhat different example is suggested by some of Max Weber's early writings, as well as by his inaugural lecture at Freiburg University (1895). Weber emphasized the contrast between two ways of managing the grain-producing estates in the German territories bordering on Poland. In one case, the chief criterion was how to maximize grain production while minimizing the labour force involved in it; in the other case, how to maximize the population regularly settled on those territories. The first pattern fostered the progressive uprooting of the German peasantry, its flight into the cities, and its replacement by a workforce chiefly composed of Polish rural workers. This made sense purely from an economic view-point, but by weakening the German component in the region's population it exposed the eastern frontier of the nation to the grave political risk of what was elegantly called *Polonisierung* ('Polonization'). The second pat-tern took that risk into account, and sought to counter it, at some cost to the economic viability of the estates. According to Weber, only that second pattern made sense from the overriding standpoint of the country's power interests.[9]

In other terms, the intervention of the state in the economy should not be considered exclusively as an accommodating response to interested claims imposed upon it from economic power; it is a more complex phenomenon than that. In some forms, to some extent, in some circum-stances, it may express more the state's own interest in maximizing the power it yields in the international context (to begin with, in military terms) than its responsiveness to the holders of economic power.

The costs of consensus

A different but parallel argument refers to another of the state's concerns – securing some degree of consensus on the part of the population at large. This concern is not as vital as the ability to defend and to police the state's own territory by means of organized coercion, and thus to uphold its very existence as a sovereign political entity. Nor is it a constant in the history of the modern state. Although reportedly an early modern French king aspired for all his subjects to afford chicken on Sundays, many rulers seem to have had little or no sense that they should (or could) pay attention to the population at large as a source of either political support or political demand.

At any rate, from a certain point on (the timing varies from place to place), most modern states are led by a number of considerations – including military ones – to attend to the circumstances and the feelings of the population, and to seek to generate in it some acknowledgment of their legitimacy, of the validity of their arrangements for rule. In a previous chapter we have seen how creative intellectuals serve this goal, consciously or otherwise, by no longer just exalting the rulers, but by projecting an image of the state as the political expression of an encompassing social entity, the nation. Affiliation with and service to the nation, those works suggest, confer meaning on the existence of individuals at large, attributing to them a shared, glorious history and a shared, worthy destiny. The political project of these intellectual and artistic activities is to induce in individuals a less constrained, more willing compliance with the demands imposed on them by the state's policies, motivated by a sense of identification with the community and of moral responsibility for it. That project takes institutional form primarily by conferring some political capacities and entitlements on individuals *qua* citizens.

But there is another aspect to this project, which consists in giving individuals a more or less significant stake in the material fortunes of the nation, making them benefit from belonging to it. Appropriate state policies can foster the individuals' well-being, their sense of security, their expectation of an improvement in the economic circumstances of each new generation, and thus bind them more solidly to the polity. Many of these policies do so indirectly, by variously assisting and regulating the economic process – which largely means, as we have seen in the last chapter, by acceding to the claims of the economic power holders. For in the end it is mostly the historically unique productivity of the industrial system that underwrites the public expectation of sustained or increasing welfare for the population at large; and this imparts a special authority to the claims for state action voiced by the more significant captains of industry.

More directly, however, the state confers upon citizens welfare entitlements of a material nature, to be met by various publicly funded arrangements: from schools to hospitals, from old-age pension schemes to retraining facilities for individuals who have recently lost a job or a limb. The economic system on the one hand benefits from this, by undertaking to produce for profit, say, school buildings or heart valves. On the other hand, the economically powerful deplore (and oppose) the fact that, once more, the state finances the welfare system by drawing (once more) on resources that it does not produce, Rather, it commandeers them, whether by raising the taxation level, or by absorbing through loans savings that might otherwise become private investments.

They also deplore the fact that those arrangements are enjoyed by individuals to the extent of their need or, as in the case of higher education, of their proven capacity to learn. They thus have an equalizing effect, for individuals may qualify for the related benefits or expectations purely as citizens – as against acquiring them at the going rate by expending their own private resources. The availability to citizens of some free state services or their access to a share of public resources makes them less dependent on the market, both as a supplier of the things they want and as a place in which to sell their capacities on their own initiative.

This phenomenon is said to have various negative consequences. For instance, it may lessen the individuals' motivation to sharpen those capacities, make them excessively reliant on public support, and induce them to claim more and more handouts from the state, disconnected from any specific obligation towards it. Since many public benefits are distributed as 'use values' to the beneficiaries, these are under no pressure to establish binding priorities between their needs *and* to decide precisely how much satisfaction of any one need to trade off for how much satisfaction of all other needs. Thus, there is no guarantee that the 'public hand' will allocate the resources it controls in such a way as to maximize the society's welfare (understood as the sum total of the utilities enjoyed by all individuals). Also, the location of a given individual within the society's stratification system, not being exclusively dictated by the market, does not reflect closely how much other individuals would choose to pay for whatever goods or services that individual might sell them.

This last point shows to what extent the contemporary critique of 'statalism' rests on untenable assumptions – in this case, for instance, the assumption that, left to itself, the market process would allocate its rewards on the basis of the contribution all individuals, including those belonging to the middle and upper classes, make to the functioning of the economy, without economic *power* structuring that process and limiting its effective reach. In spite of this, in its recent formulations that critique has had the merit of reopening the question (of long standing) of *which* goods and services are best provided by *which* mechanism – the state or the market (though some current formulations put forward the notion of a third mechanism, embracing volunteer services and the so-called 'philanthropic sector').

This is no place to review (much less assess) the literature dealing with that question. In our context, what matters is the fact (undeniable in my view) that the state by and large tends to increase its own share of the resources produced and processed within the economic system and to deploy that share in order (among other things) to fulfil its need for social consensus, for a broad popular recognition of its own legitimacy. Many practitioners of conventional economic thinking complain that this strategy of the state has unbearable or at any rate highly burdensome economic consequences. Whatever one makes of this, that strategy does present difficulties from a political standpoint. Two such difficulties deserve mention.

First, as the old saying 'guns *or* butter' (public policy can maximize either the state's might or the population's well-being) suggests, it is very difficult for a state to levy enough resources *both* to pursue power politics and to buy the populace's consent without overstraining the economic system; at the very least, some trade-offs between those two objectives are necessary. It is true that in the past some polities have tried to finance through the proceeds of war (especially colonial wars) a share of the bounty bestowed on domestic populations. But while such operations may have paid off very handsomely for some specific groups – directly involved, say, in producing armaments or in exploiting colonial resources – it seems doubtful that they systematically paid off for the domestic economies and the metropolitan populations at large.

By and large, a strong commitment to power politics and military might has costs which in the judgement of governing politicians render unafford-able, so to speak, a generous welfare system, as the case of the United States in the last part of the twentieth century indicates. (However, sometimes there are synergies between the two objectives. In the US itself, recent work by Theda Skocpol suggests,[10] one of the impulses behind some early federal welfare policies came from the existence of strong veterans' organizations. In Britain, one of the objectives of a public housing programme undertaken after World War I was rhetorically formulated as that of building 'houses fit for heroes' – the heroes in question being, again, returning warriors.)

The second main difficulty arises specifically from the state's policy of buying consensus through welfare expenditures. Even though the chief vehicle of this policy is often an expansion of the content of citizenship, and the latter is in principle an equalizing institution, states must still choose which specific needs to meet through each successive expansion – whether to give priority, for instance, to the needs of the older or those of the younger generations, to material or 'post-material' needs.[11] Such choices make the state the target of pressures from lobbies and organized interest groups, and sometimes of heated and divisive public contentions which activate conflicting social movements. Even when the resulting controversies concern relatively straightforward policies (for instance the issuing of new regulations of industrial activities or the establishment of specialized agencies), and even when the state can afford to be relatively generous toward many claimants, the very best it can produce among the public at large is what Raymond Aron once called 'une satisfaction querelleuse'. When the focus is on whether the state should allow and pay for abortions, or whether it should expressly extend its legal blessings to homosexual preferences and practices, policy choices are likely to arouse even fiercer passions. To a greater or lesser extent, the resulting divisions of opinion tend to become associated with different parties; in this fashion (and otherwise) they diminish the state's ability to form and execute policies aimed at overriding, general concerns; according to one line of argument, they deprive the state of its sovereignty.

In any case, the historical trend towards the expansion of the content of citizenship contributes to the fact that, as we have seen, the state commandeers and disposes of a larger and larger share of the national product, allocating it according to the rules of the political game rather than those of the market. In my view it is preposterous to conceive of this process, in its contemporary forms, as a variant of the old-fashioned phenomenon of the 'predatory state'; as I have indicated in this chapter and the previous one, much in the state's involvement in the economic system sustains its health and stability, both directly and indirectly. The state has a nonpredatory relationship to the domestic economy not only because it knows better than to kill that famous goose, but because of the multiple inputs it makes into its survival.

However, the imagery of predation remains credible in many circumstances, especially when applied to a certain level of the political system – that where political parties operate. By its very nature, the modern party system tends to be led and run by people who mostly, whether or not (in Weber's terminology) they live *for* politics, are bound to live *off* politics.[12] In the last decades of the twentieth century, a series of scandals revealed

that this relationship entailed, for instance in Italy and in Japan, a spectac-
ularly huge, systematic, ever increasing 'take', which (among other things)
party leaders and functionaries levied on various kinds of economic units.
It is true that in some cases a two-way exchange of political advantage for
monetary 'contributions' was taking place; but other cases looked much
more like instances of extortion and racketeering. In any case, a colossal,
hidden diversion of resources from productive to unproductive uses was
taking place, at the expense of consumers, taxpayers and the domestic
economy at large, whose international competitiveness was sometimes
affected.

Even aside from these (and related) financial gains which political parties
can derive from the state's interventions in the economic process, the
mechanism itself of inter-party competition tends to foster further interventions, and the related forms of 'extraction'. Parties may bid for votes from
relatively large sectors of the population (or for that matter for other kinds
of support for otherwise significant groups) by sponsoring new interventions which favour them. Other social groups are positively interested in
the expansion of the share of economic resources controlled by the state –
chiefly, occupational groups, which are, so to speak, nested within the
sprawling complex of structures through which the state operates, aspire to
build a nest of their own within that complex, or otherwise seek to convert
increased public expenditures into income flows for themselves. (Think of
the question currently discussed in the United States, as to whether the
health services to be funded, to this or that extent, from the public purse,
should include those of therapists.[13] Or consider the consultants who stand
to gain from a public university's decision to establish or expand a
'sensitivity training' programme in order to reduce the occurrence of
politically incorrect conduct on the part of the faculty.)

Whether or not one should label the relationship of such groups to the
economic system 'predatory' is largely a matter of judgement (or prejudice).
Clearly, the adoption of a new target for administrative action, the creation
of new units or the enlargement of old ones, the assignment to a given
programme of a higher priority in the expenditure of public funds are all
political decisions (whatever their merits from other standpoints) that make
a lot of difference to the opportunities for employment, security, career
advancement and professional prominence of the members of the groups in
question, who can be expected to vote, lobby, pressurize politicians and
write letters to editors in order to enhance those opportunities.

Furthermore, the output of many public agencies is hard to measure, for
they do not sell their goods and services on the market and are not
supposed to show a profit from their production or distribution. As a
consequence, there is a tendency to treat measures of input (how much
money was spent on a programme, the size of an agency's budget, the
number of its employees, how many field units it operated) as proxies for
measures of output.

Thus, the dynamics of state expenditure are to some extent the product of the convergence of diverse interests: those of direct beneficiaries, be they firms receiving subsidies or welfare claimants; those of providers, be they bureaucrats, generals, or other professionals; those of parties, keen to improve their standing within the electorate and / or to increase their own 'take' from public disbursements; finally, those of economic units whose output (pharmaceutical drugs or weapon systems) is paid for prevalently or exclusively from public funds.

This last point is a reminder of a larger one. Earlier, I have mentioned a basic contradiction in the relationship between politics and economics: political activity consumes resources that it cannot itself provide. One implication of this contradiction (or, if the reader doubts that such a contradiction exists, an implication of Jacobs's contrast between the respective 'moral syndromes') is that many historically significant patterns in that relationship, even when they are essentially predatory, require some economic operators to function as brokers between the two realms. Such operators provide the economic know-how without which a narrow-mindedly extractive attitude of the political elite would quickly become un- or counter-productive; they associate themselves with the extractive activities of that elite, manage them, and profit from them. They embody a kind of economic power, although one characterized (contaminated, if you wish) by its proximity to and sometimes its overlap with political power. For instance, if we consider pre-modern Western polities, we often find rulers making systematic use of tax farmers, of bankers, of experts in currency and financial manipulation, of financial specialists who arranged domestic or foreign loans, of court personnel or ministers who possessed strategic economic knowledge and information. (A rather special example of the latter, in fact, is constituted by the Old Testament's – and Thomas Mann's – Joseph, whose remarkable career at Pharaoh's court was built on his divinely assisted insights into forthcoming economic events. Had he not been something of a saint, one might suspect Joseph of having profited from speculating on futures on the side.)

But the extractive practices of *ancien régime* polities did not simply reward brokers and overseers standing between the ruler and the domestic or the international economy. Increasingly, they required the assistance also of personnel directly involved in the production process. For instance, a significant role in mercantilist economic policy was played by the local elite of towns, including the heads of craftsmen's and tradesmen's guilds, whom rulers empowered to control prices, regulate the craft production process and police the market. These practices of rulers, of course, by conferring on them advantages of a political nature, induced economic practitioners to engage in what is today labelled 'rent-seeking'.

Schematically speaking, under later forms of economic policy economic elites cease to constitute, so to speak, a hinge between the political and the economic systems; rather, they emerge and operate within the latter, according to market rules. Correspondingly, the extractive process takes chiefly the form of taxation, that is, of legally authorized, impartially administered levies of resources which seek to interfere in, and to distort, the productive and commercial process as little as possible.

In fact, this conceptualization is schematic to the point of being fanciful, chiefly because it ignores the international context in which states operate, and *its* implications for economic policy. Even modernized polities inherit from the mercantilist past, while discarding its obsession with bullion, a preoccupation to ensure that the domestic economy is relatively self-sufficient and possibly maintains a positive balance of trade; often, they continue to pursue colonialist designs on the parts of the world not yet modernized; and they are increasingly concerned to develop, within the domestic economy, the industrial sectors more significant from a military standpoint. As we have already seen, such preoccupations lead to a considerable involvement of the state in the economic process, with the result of privileging certain economic power groups (including sometimes, for limited purposes, certain labour unions) over others.

Vilfredo Pareto and Max Weber shared a concern with one question in particular: *which* economic interests are systematically favoured by *which* economic policy? Pareto, however, emphasized one aspect of economic policy, the decision for or against free trade; as an admirer of free-trading England, he was antagonized by the protectionist policies rife in late nineteenth- and early twentieth-century Europe, and chiefly blamed them (often in vituperative language) for the corruption of both economic and political life engendered by those policies, particularly in his native Italy.

The economic system of Weber's Wilhelmine Germany was largely the product of a *successful* experiment in state-protected industrial development; perhaps for this reason, and on account of his commitment to the political values that had inspired the experiment, Weber did not share Pareto's infatuation with free trade and his detestation of policies that violated it. Rather, he sought to conceptualize the whole range of associations between *types* of economic policy (and of extractive strategy) and *types* of favoured economic elites. He also emphasized the contrast between political capitalism and properly commercial and industrial capitalism. The first he saw represented chiefly in the economic history of antiquity, and most particularly of Rome; the second he considered a specifically modern phenomenon, whose dominance in contemporary economies did not, however, exclude either the recurrence of forms of political capitalism or the emergence of novel forms of speculative capitalism.

Thanks to its broad typological scope, Weber's treatment of relations between political and economic power suggests a further corrective to the simplistic view that, when all is said and done, the first preys upon the second. Let us review some objections to that view. First, even a political elite chiefly intent upon predation must become aware of the risks of pursuing it too narrow-mindedly and impatiently – lest (once more!) it kills the goose that lays the golden eggs. Second, most political elites do not seek just to avoid damaging the economy, but seek positively to foster and protect it, in the light of two key political concerns: to maintain the polity's military might, a key asset in the context of power politics; and to secure the compliance and if possible the allegiance of the domestic population. Also, as we have seen in the last chapter, under modern conditions the state makes a critical contribution to the very existence of the economic system by laying down an institutional framework – and sometimes a material framework – for its functioning. Finally, as we have just seen, many significant ways in which the state intervenes in the economic process, beginning with the form it gives to its extractive activities, tend to be managed by distinctive types of economic elites, or at any rate to foster distinctive forms of economic activity.

If there is a grain of truth to the view that the politically powerful relate to the economy chiefly by preying upon it – or, otherwise put, that all extraction is predation – it is the following: all state intervention *in* the economy, as against those political activities strictly necessary to provide a framework *for* the economy, diminishes the economic system's ability to generate its own equilibria through the mutual adjustment of its own internal variables. But this is *barely* a grain of truth, since:

- the above statement is essentially tautological;
- its chief referent – the economic system, understood as a self-contained, self-sufficient set of purely economic givens – does not exist on the ground;
- what exists on the ground – *really existent capitalism*, to modify a fortunate expression originally referring to socialism – is itself a system largely structured by economic power relations;
- these power relations continually seek to assert and reinforce themselves by influencing the state and selecting its interventions in the economy.

Of course, the economically powerful (which in advanced industrial countries are chiefly corporate entities) are by no means the only forces seeking to influence the state; nor is state policy exclusively the product of influences from economic or other power actors; it has interests of its own that affect and shape in turn, among other things, its interactions with the economy as well as with other social realms and the respective power structures.[14] For all this, the state's relationship to economic power has some claim to having constituted *the* chief issue within much of modern and contemporary history. In particular, the East / West conflict, which constituted the chief theme of world history between 1917 and 1989, can be said to have revolved around that issue.

The Soviet experience

The way in which the East (or the Soviet bloc, as it came to be called after World War II) dealt with that issue was utterly peculiar, for it consisted in the total subsumption of economic under political power. Indeed, if one reserves the expression 'relationship' for circumstances in which there are at least two entities, each with some standing independent of the other, in the East there did not *exist* a relationship between economic and political power. The suppression of private property in the means of production rendered it impossible for the economic system to establish its institutional distinctiveness, and to be structured by the emergence of specifically economic power.

The denial of the autonomy of the economic system was already signalled by Lenin's slogan 'Communism is Soviet power plus . . . electrification', if for 'Soviet power' we understand 'power of the Communist Party'. The term 'electrification' implied that the processes going on in the economic sphere were essentially technical, and that the political leadership could easily take charge of them. Several years later, under Stalin, the adoption of centralized planning as an instrument for developing and managing the whole Soviet economy remained coherent with that solution (or, rather, *dis*solution) of the problem of how to relate economic to political power.

Stalin on the one hand recognized that the attendant problems were more demanding than Lenin's 'electrification' suggested, for the planning machinery he set about establishing was vast and complex, and was meant to operate according to specifically economic, not just technological, criteria. On the other hand, that machinery was totally subordinated to the political power structure (meaning, at the time, Stalin's own dictatorship), and the autonomy of the economic sphere continued to be denied. Essentially, the whole Soviet economy was to be run as a single *oikos*, where both production and distribution were controlled from the top by political and administrative means. In due course the same formula was imposed, with various modifications, on all countries of the Soviet bloc.

In the second half of the twentieth century, it became apparent that the resultant suppression of economic rationality had disastrous consequences – political, economic and social – which ultimately spelled the doom of the whole system. Subsequently, a key problem for the countries in question came to be how to re-establish economic power in the respective societies, and what its relationship to political power should be. This problem is a key aspect of the broad project, to extend to the countries of the previous Soviet bloc the institutional design of the Western ones. Here a secular process of differentiation between economic and political power had triumphed in the nineteenth century; for this same reason, as Franz Neumann suggested in a text already quoted, a major issue of public life had become how the two powers would relate to one another; or, phrased otherwise, what aspects of social life would be controlled primarily through the market, and which by the state.

The settlement of that issue varied fairly widely over time and from country to country. In the middle of the nineteenth century, the *Communist Manifesto*'s characterization of government as 'the executive committee of the bourgeoisie' was fairly appropriate to a number of European countries and to the United States. A few decades later, it was rather less applicable, say, to the newly established German Reich. In the twentieth century, two contrasting trends affect the relationship, and, again, which trend prevails varies with time and place. On the one hand, more and more aspects of social life, from warfare to cultural production and consumption, are decisively transformed by capitalism, and fall under the sway of the capitalist power structure (increasingly dominated by large-scale corporations). On the other hand, the functioning itself of the capitalist economies requires (according to an argument reviewed in chapter 7) a greater and greater involvement of the state, which is pushed in that direction also by developments internal to the political sphere (as argued previously in this chapter).

In the second half of the twentieth century, for a few decades the expansion of the content of citizenship signalled the prevalence of the second trend; but subsequently the legitimacy and the sustainability of that trend became again a matter of contention. In the 1990s, in particular, the breakdown of the Soviet system eliminated a significant reason for the economic power structure to accept that trend. Neither market nor state can do without one another; but, it is claimed, the state should intervene in the market only to support its workings, or to supplement them, in keeping with the 'subsidiarity principle'. On behalf of the Western business elites, the World Bank and the International Monetary Fund are seeking to apply that principle also to the less developed countries, where, previously, political mechanisms (including the transfer of financial resources from more developed countries) had been allowed a somewhat greater sway in the economic process.

Globalization

In the course of these same few decades, the capitalist system has been undergoing a huge transformation, mostly referred to as its 'globalization'. The most significant units of the system operate now on a world-wide scale, both producing and disposing of their product in a large number of countries. A number of them have progressively detached themselves from their original heartland in a specific domestic economy and from their dependency on local resources, while others have from the beginning constituted themselves, so to speak, 'offshore'.

The globalization of the industrial economy represents a wholly new chapter in the long history of the relationship between economic and political power. Its significance is strikingly conveyed by the title of a recent Italian book: *Nazioni senza ricchezza. Ricchezza senza nazione* ('Nations Without Wealth. Wealth Without Nation').[15] This title is, so to speak, a nostalgic pun on that of Adam Smith's masterpiece, *The Wealth of Nations*. Smith assumed that the economic process went on both within and between a number of locales, each politically controlled by a different (nation) state. This, among other things, allowed the state to tap the wealth being processed by means of taxation. In classical fiscal theory taxation is often depicted as something which 'strikes' (in Italian: *percuote*) an economic actor, be it the possessor of a patrimony, a producer, or a consumer. But one might wonder how the state is to strike the major economic actor of today, the business corporation, if it won't stay put.

Globalization has increasingly taken the economic process out of its previous political context, the state; more and more aspects and phases of it are now placed outside the jurisdiction of any single state. In some cases they have been dispersed between a variety of states, but sometimes they exist in a kind of extra-territorial space. Huge flows of financial resources are currently generated, invested, shifted, dispersed and destroyed, by means of computer networks operating again world-wide, sometimes via artificial satellites. The diverse activities (from capital acquisition to research to manufacturing) conceptually central to the most significant forms of contemporary business – for instance, software production, or the media – are sometimes carried out in the organizational periphery of the respective units, far from the corporate headquarters on whose decision it depends whether, where and how those activities are to continue. And those headquarters themselves have become relatively mobile, or their major functions have been decentralized.

Corporate strategies take into account the plurality of actual or potential locales in which the corporation operates, and bargain from a position of advantage with the respective political units, which compete with one another to induce the corporation to invest in their territory. In any case, even when the corporation's activities remain stably localized, some aspects of them can be placed outside the scope of a given state's operations. Often, major corporations which have a serious quarrel with one another no longer submit themselves to the jurisdiction of the state in which they both exist, or to that of an international court if they exist in different states: they turn for arbitration to a quasi-judicial private body which they themselves set up and whose decision they agree to accept. The opening statement in *Nazioni senza ricchezza. Ricchezza senza nazione*, to which I have referred above, deserves to be quoted at length:

> Once, their control of the territory sufficed to the states in controlling wealth, since wealth found in the territory its natural centre of gravity, allowing states to exercise their political monopolies: to coin money, to exercise jurisdiction, to levy taxes. But the connection state–territory–wealth is now broken. Its control of the territory no longer suffices for the state to control wealth, which to a greater and greater extent and with accelerating speed merely passes over the territory. A new kind of 'law merchant' which does not originate from the state binds together the great economic forces. Fiscal law – whereby the state coins money and levies taxes – is of diminishing significance: there is a supranational money, currently constituted by the dollar, and the currently dominant form of wealth, financial wealth, escapes the state's monopoly of taxation, since it can choose where and how to pay taxes. National sovereignty now chiefly expresses itself through welfare law, but this too is losing significance, for it expresses a social solidarity typical of social-democratic political systems which in turn presupposes economically strong states.

For some time after World War II, it seemed as if states were in their turn making arrangements that bound them together into broader units, which could conduct some of the fiscal and regulatory activities previously carried out by single states, and thus match the growing geographic scope of key economic forces. But this development seems to have peaked with the consolidation of the European Union, an entity whose specifically *political* faculties and facilities are not that significant, and in any case do not operate on the global scale. Besides, in the last decades of the twentieth century the dominant trend was if anything towards an increasing number of smaller and smaller states, rather than the aggregation of existent states into larger ones.

Given these trends, it looks as if in the early twenty-first century the new turn imparted by economic globalization in the ancient 'dialectic of the ruler and the trader' will see the state on the defensive *vis-à-vis* ever larger, more mobile, politically more autonomous and self-reliant aggregations of economic power.

10

Military Power

Three power forms – plus one?

Early on in this book I raised the question of how many forms of social power we should think of as existing in relative independence of one another, and argued at some length what may be called the 'trinitarian formula', according to which only political, ideological / normative and economic power deserve that status. In that context, however, I mentioned that different answers have been given to that question; in particular, one significant contemporary author, Michael Mann, has organized his remarkable work in progress, *Sources of Social Power*, around a 'quadripartite formula', with military power as the fourth component. In doing so Mann disconnects conceptually political power from the phenomenon of organized violence – he sees it instead as grounding the identity of military power – and construes it as having primarily to do with administration and territoriality.

I did not follow Mann's conceptual lead in this book because I find it difficult to define political power *otherwise* than with reference to organized violence; it is the command over this resource that allows one group, for example, to 'run things' over a given territory. Also, the standard sociological definition of the state, formulated by Max Weber, confirms the intimate relationship of all political power with the phenomenon of organized violence, by emphasizing two aspects of that relationship. First, in the state (as well as in other forms of institutionalized political power) the violence in question is seen as legitimate; that is, the threat or exercise of it are seen as constituting not a merely factual affair, but the realization of a normative claim demanding assent. Second, such violence can only be threatened or exercised by the state's agents; and this *monopoly* over legitimate, organized violence is peculiar to the state itself.

In chapter 3 I briefly discussed this conceptual connection between politics – especially but not exclusively the politics of states – and violence; but I would like to illustrate it further by means of a few quotations, in order to lay the background for an argument I shall make in this chapter – an argument that apparently *concedes* Mann's point.

First, various authors have emphasized what may be called the genetic aspect of the politics–violence connection, by arguing that, to quote the title of a chapter of a recent book by Charles Tilly, 'war made states and viceversa'. As Tilly says in that chapter, 'War wove the European network of national states, and preparation for war created the internal structures of states within it.'[1] A considerably older book, by Bertrand de Jouvenel, makes that same point somewhat more diffusely:

The intimate tie between war and power is a constant feature of European history. . . . If a feudal monarchy succeeded in getting financial aids from the vassals at more and more frequent intervals and could thus increase the number of mercenaries in its employ, the others had to copy it. If in the end these aids were consolidated into a permanent tax for maintaining a standing army, the movement had to be followed. For, as Adam Smith remarked, 'Once the system of having a standing army had been adopted by one civilized nation, all its neighbours had to introduce it; security reasons made it inevitable, for the old militias were quite incapable of resisting an army of this kind.[2]

But that genetic connection is not a prerogative of European states, reflecting exclusively their origins in the feudal political systems of the late Middle Ages. It can be found in a political system – that of the United States of America – operating in a very different environment, and originally fashioned with the express intent of transcending the European experience. A recent book by R. F. Bensel, *Yankee Leviathan*, emphasizes the role played by the Civil War in fostering the progress of central political institutions both in the US and in the Confederacy. Paradoxically, in spite of the fact that the Confederacy had emerged in defence of 'states' rights', that role was even more significant in it than it was in the Union: 'The South created in the Confederacy a central state at least as strong as the one that guided Union war mobilisation. . . . The South jettisoned states' rights and built a central state much stronger than either pre-bellum or post-reconstruction federal government.'[3] Furthermore, the connection between politics and violence is not simply genetic, but also structural; it does not simply reveal itself in the making of the state, but affects (and indeed, one might say, constitutes) its very nature. According to the German institutional historian Otto Hintze, 'all state constitution is originally military constitution, army constitution'.[4] The American sociologist Collins makes this point strongly:

What we mean by the state is the way in which violence is organised. The state consists of those people who have the guns or other weapons and are prepared to use them; in the version of political organisation found in the modern world, they claim monopoly on this use. . . . The state *is*, above all, the army and the police.

This tough-minded view of the state is barely softened when Collins explains what he means by 'politics':

What we shall deal with here is the ways in which violence has been organised in society. . . . In this fashion we can deal with all questions that might arise about politics. . . . Politics, in this approach, involves both outright warfare and coercive threats. Most of what we refer to as politics in the internal (but not external) organisation of the modern state is a remote version of the latter. . . . Much politics does not involve actual violence but consists of manoeuvering around the organisation that controls the violence.[5]

The expression 'the organisation that controls the violence' has some implications worth teasing out. First, 'organization' implies in the first instance a readiness, a capacity to exercise (or threaten) violence; the violence exercised or threatened is a product, a manifestation of pre-constituted, abiding arrangements. Second, 'organization' implies that these arrangements constitute an expressly contrived, differentiated, relatively self-standing aspect of a broader social reality. Third, the notion of 'control over violence' suggests that, from the standpoint of that broader reality, the phenomenon of violence has costs (including the risk of being challenged and overcome by greater violence, or the risk of being overused) which it is the task of organization to curb.

The institutionalization of political power in general and, more specifically, the development of the state point up the complex and sometimes paradoxical relationships between these implications. We have already seen the paradox in Hobbes: political power arises as a remedy to fear, but operates chiefly by making people fearful. Similarly, institutionalized political power tends to restrict the play of diffuse violence in the society; and the state, in particular, *pacifies* society, in two closely related ways. It declares illegitimate much of the violence people would otherwise indulge in – *much*, not all; as feminist critics have pointed out, the violence exercised and threatened by men in their dealings with women has mostly *not* been considered illegitimate. And it tries, more or less consistently and successfully, to reserve to itself the social and material devices that make violence more formidable – from uniforms to military and police command systems, to weapons.

This last is the critical process in the curbing of domestic violence (Collins, in fact, chooses to ignore the other one, the outlawing of diffuse violence). Through that process the political centre vests in a part of itself, specifically organized to deal with it, an overwhelmingly superior capacity for violence. Thus individuals or groups which might otherwise attempt to engage in violence on their own behalf are persuaded to cease and desist from such attempts. What pacifies society, thus, is not the disappearance or the utter rarity of social and material devices for restraining, killing, maiming, destroying, but the fact that these are vested, in principle, only in the political system, which entrusts them in turn to a specialized part of itself. To the extent that this happens, Hobbes's paradox is confirmed: as the *potential* for violence increases, its *actual* exercise (or the threat of it) diminishes. (The Roman saying 'Si vis pacem para bellum' – 'If you wish for peace, make yourself ready for war' – seeks to transpose this paradox from the realm of relations *within* polities to that of relations *between* them. Time and again in history, this transposition has not worked – an indication, perhaps, of the structural disjunction between politics within and politics between states.)

Now, that paradoxical effect can only be obtained if the part of the political system entrusted with the potential for violence is – to return to an expression I have previously emphasized – an 'organization', that is, a purposefully contrived and coherently controlled set of practices, people and resources, specialized in building up and maintaining that potential. The political system must ensure that the organization in question packs enough of a punch to 'pacify' the social process at large and, when necessary, to keep outside political forces from interfering with it. It must also ensure that the potential for violence it vests in the organization does not become dispersed into the rest of society by a kind of osmosis or entropy. Finally, the organization itself should not, as a whole or in its parts, exercise or threaten to exercise violence on its own behalf, against the larger society or the political system itself.

Let us restate this argument. The larger society can be secured against internal disorder and external aggression only if, through its political system, it possesses itself a potential for violence which is *formidable* – in the etymological sense of the expression, meaning 'such as to evoke fear'. Organization serves this aim, for it entails that violence will be primarily (indeed, as far as possible, exclusively) engaged in an effective, workman-like fashion by trained, competent specialists. It also serves the aim of differentiating institutionally the business of violence from the remainder of the social process.

Here comes the tricky part. Exactly that institutional differentiation creates an awkward possibility: the specialists in question may use their own exclusive guardianship of a critical social resource (organized violence) to affect the definition of public interest with which are charged other parts of the political system, and the related policies. The organization they inhabit may become self-absorbed, relatively unresponsive to the require-ments and expectations of the rest of society. It can foster its own autonomy of other parts, increase its claims upon the resources they produce and manage, or seek to impose on the rest of the political system a self-interested understanding of what the larger society, taken as a whole, can and should do. These possibilities are enhanced by the fact that an organization built around violence tends to have a strongly hierarchical structure; this, on the one hand, allows it to confront promptly and effectively the contingencies requiring violence to be threatened or exer-cised; on the other hand, it allows the top levels of the structure to deploy the organization's resources in a coherent and unitary fashion; thus the organization can present more of a challenge *also* to other parts of the political system.

This means that, *pace* Michael Mann, organized violence constitutes the bottom line of the whole political process, and should be conceived as an integral part of the political system. By the same token, it should not be considered as a distinctive form or source of social power, standing on the same conceptual level as (in our own vocabulary) normative / ideological or economic power, *and* political power itself; instead, it is a dimension or part of the latter. However, under certain conditions the guardians and practitioners of organized violence may deal with the rest of the system *as if* from the outside, disregarding or subverting their own subordination to other parts, including those instituted to stand for the whole of the political system. In this fashion, the relationship between organized violence and political power, although it is a part-to-whole relationship (which is what my previous quotes from Tilly, Jouvenel and Collins were intended to establish),[6] may come to resemble those we have already discussed, between normative / ideological or economic power on the one hand, and political power on the other.

Mann's emphasis on conditions where this occurs, as well as his sensitivity to the historical significance of technical military innovation, induce him to plead for a fourfold partition of social power, giving military power 'equal status'. As I have reminded the reader, I subscribe instead to the trinitarian formula. But to an extent this book deviates from it, and adopts a modified version of Mann's conceptual quartet, because of its prevalent concern with the institutional horizon of the modern West. Here, the differentiation of organized violence from other aspects of political power has been carried a long way, and has *sometimes* engendered a situation similar to the one Mann, as I read him, conceptualizes as general.

In this, my position is closer to that of Giddens, when he writes that 'the "separation" of military from political power within the state's territory is . . . as distinctive of the European nation-state as is that of the political from the economic'.[7] Once more, I do not consider this a conceptually valid parallel, for I envisage the relationship of economic to political power as one of part to whole rather than as (so to speak) a relationship between peers. However, I acknowledge that frequently, in the modern state, the guardians of violence have pressurized, manipulated and challenged the whole of which they were meant to constitute a part. In fact, one might argue that within the modern state a development of this nature has sometimes seen as the antagonist of political leadership not only the military, but also another, much less frequently discussed, aggregation of organized violence – the police.

However, this final chapter discusses only the military, and disregards the police. It assumes, in so doing, that there is a clear differentiation between them: while both are organizations specialized in building up and if necessary deploying legitimate violence, they differ in their respective institutional missions. The military is chiefly intended to guard, so to speak, the outside slope of the state's territory, bringing to bear the exercise or the threat of organized violence (offensively or defensively) on the relations *between* states. The police operates within the state's inside slope, and deals with domestic affairs *within* the state, securing public order and the enforcement of laws. Of course this neat division of labour between the military and the police took time to develop, and even after it became institutionalized it was often violated or compromised, and occasionally it still is. However, within the historical horizon of the Western state, a fairly clear separation between military and police allows us to consider only one of these entities in its relationship to 'civilianized' political power.

Military elites

I generally assume, for the purposes of this book, that there exists, as the embodiment of political power within each state – constitutional states of the type existing in the West since the eighteenth century – a public institution we shall call 'the military': a distinctive body of personnel, availing itself of its control over a complex of material resources, and engaging in a particular set of social practices, that is expressly concerned with the following task and considers it exclusively its own. On behalf of the state, it makes ready and keeps ready a capacity for organized, armed violence, so that, if necessary, it may prevail in the conflict with other states whose policies threaten the state's own security, and primarily its exclusive political control over its own territory. Thus, it is directly and accountably concerned with activities that the state may occasionally want performed on its own behalf as a matter of policy, and the *possibility* of whose performance by the military all other state institutions normally take for granted.

Materially, these activities culminate in warfare, that is, basically in the organized, systematic, technology-assisted infliction of death and bodily harm on individuals and the destruction of their resources; typically, they have as immediate target the armed forces of another state defined as foe; therefore, they are carried out in the face of similar acts of hostility on the part of *its* armed forces. On this account, such activities involve, for those that carry them out, a high degree of *very material* risk. At the collective level, in particular, the course of warfare may reveal the foe's military superiority, allowing it to impose its own policy, in the end, on the defeated contender; at the individual level, the risk is that, in the context of a given armed encounter (whatever its larger outcome), any one individual, on either side, may be killed, or experience grievous physical or moral suffering.

Increasingly, over the last two centuries, such risks (and related ones) have affected a state's population at large, for civilians have all too often become the target of murderous military violence, and modern warfare typically mobilizes a large share of the resources (beginning with the man- and woman-power) of the whole domestic economy, and requires the ideological indoctrination of the whole population. But we can leave this aside, and consider some consequences of the elementary facts of political, and military, life (and death) restated above. The consequence we are chiefly interested in is that the top personnel in the military institution often act as significant contenders in the struggle over policy at large, and raise imperious claims *vis-à-vis* the state's political leadership.

There is of course great diversity in the extent to which the top-level military personnel act as a semi-independent elite, in the nature of the claims they advance, and in the content of the arguments by which they support those claims.[8] Some countries have occasionally experienced the outright usurpation of political power by military leaders, in others these have successfully blackmailed the political elites into undertaking policies (sometimes of no direct military significance) different from those they had intended to pursue, in still others the military have merely been a pressure group seeking to increase or maintain its share of the state's budget.

In spite of this variety, it is possible to identify a set of recurrent issues in the relationship that I have reluctantly agreed to characterize as one between two powers, political and military. In advancing their own position on those issues, military power has mostly played upon two big themes: on the one hand, how significant, in the context of political experience in general, is the problem of war and of the preparedness for it; on the other, how necessary is it that the institution specifically committed to handling that problem be granted a large amount of autonomy. I will comment briefly on these themes.

War as the touchstone of political experience

In the context of the modern state, and particularly in the West, the first theme – the persistent significance of war – has had a complex career. On the one hand, in the nineteenth century the war phenomenon, from time immemorial the central issue and the central instrumentality in the relations between states, acquired a monumental, ominous dimension, first fully displayed in the mass carnage of the American Civil War; and in the first half of the twentieth century two world wars enormously amplified and deepened that experience. Through most of the second half of the century, the capitalist West and the collectivist East stood in a relationship that some claimed to be akin to war, and which occasionally seemed to push them towards the brink of an unprecedented kind of warfare of total mutual annihilation. Besides, a distressing number of highly murderous wars took place outside the areas directly occupied by the blocs, and without involving them in direct military confrontation, though many of those wars were related to the blocs' policies.

On the other hand, in our own time war seems to have become something of a dirty secret, at any rate for Western nations, which have preferred to emphasize political issues related to economics. Even in the West / East contest, it was widely felt that the key issue was not the military might of the two blocs, but the productive capacities of the respective socio-economic systems, and their ability to promote industrial growth both in the countries of each bloc and in the Third World. Only in the

USA and the USSR (especially, perhaps, in the latter) were the military elites spared the suspicion that their role in the politics of the respective countries had become a recessive one.

Naturally enough, this was for them a painful experience, to which they often reacted by arguing that, for all appearances to the contrary, war unavoidably remained the overriding concern of states, and organized, armed might their ultimate sanction. In some cases, military elites acknowledged that all-out war (not just nuclear, but also conventional) had become a highly improbable option; however, they began to prospect alternative uses for their own distinctive competences, and developed a set of neologisms and euphemisms for such uses – for instance, counter-insurgency measures, low-intensity military operations, peacekeeping interventions, aid to civil authority. They also saluted, almost with glee, the occasional opportunities – for instance, the Falklands (Malvinas) War, in the case of the British armed forces – to proclaim anew the critical significance of a country's military capacity.

Furthermore, in the USA, and to a lesser extent in smaller powers of the Western bloc, military power sought to reassert itself by establishing close connections with what it perceived as the dominant social power – that embodied in large-scale industrial corporations. If the redoubtable infatuation of contemporary Western publics with technological and industrial advance could not be ignored, the military elites could try and join the chief protagonists and beneficiaries of that infatuation; they claimed for instance that the public expenditure on military research and development (and on related undertakings, such as space exploration) had a huge fallout effect for the industrial economy at large, benefiting in the end also the private consumer.

In 1973, the first oil shock revealed to the Western publics to what extent facilities and amenities to which they were thoroughly addicted – such as the car, central heating, air-conditioning, plastic goods – depended on foreign petroleum. Its continuing supply, it was realized, could be contingent, among other things, on the willingness of Western states to contemplate (and to prepare themselves for) 'resource wars'. (The Gulf War of 1991 was the biggest although not the first of these. Very likely, it will not be the last.) Also, this development allowed military elites to point up the synergy between their own competences and those of economic elites, and more generally to stress that even societies thoroughly hooked on economic concerns and used to making politics revolve around them cannot afford to neglect the centrality of war and of armed might to political business.

Such centrality is not, however, the sole theme to which military elites connect their claims. Another is the necessity that, for many intents and purposes, the military institution should be run according to criteria exclusive to it, and that it should enjoy a high degree of autonomy with respect to other political and social institutions. In order to understand this requirement, we may consider the utter peculiarity of the core activity of fighting soldiers, which (when all is said and done) consists in seeking to kill people who at the same time seek to kill *them*.

Soldiers are supposed to carry out this activity in a peculiar frame of mind, which is well conveyed by the meaning of the expression 'mission' in the military context. This entails that one is *sent* to accomplish a task not of one's own, but in the accomplishment of which one is to invest all one has and is. 'Mission' also suggests that the task in question is a distinct phase or aspect of a broader project, of which one may not be even aware. The responsibility of formulating and assigning the task, and of co-ordinating it with other phases or aspects of the same project, falls to others. The connection between one's specific activity and those of others assigned the same mission, between that mission and other missions, can only be ensured by prompt and thorough obedience to commands. Command and obedience are the key mechanisms because they operate at all levels and unite all levels in a military enterprise, however huge and complex – as the expression 'chain of command' suggests.

The chain of command is of interest here because, due to it, a country's armed forces, no matter how large and internally diverse, can be treated as one single social entity in the hands of a small group of men who hold the chain's uppermost links and through it manoeuvre the whole enterprise. Take for instance the directive that the joint chiefs of staff of the US armed forces issued to General Eisenhower, in order to activate, through the chain of command, a huge undertaking – the invasion of Normandy and the subsequent Western campaign against Germany: 'You will enter the Continent of Europe and, in conjunction with the United Nations, undertake operations aimed at the heart of Germany and the destruction of her armed forces.'[9]

The *same* chain of command reaches down to the last private, and summons his obedience. However, the execution of commands by a soldier, while (so to speak) *oriented* by obedience, must also be *motivated* by a sense of personal engagement. It would not be safe for this to be provided exclusively by the soldiers' attachment to their own personal survival, for all too often this might induce soldiers to flight rather than to fight. (In French, *sauve-toi*, literally 'save yourself', also means 'run away'.) An additional, and sometimes an overriding, motivational ingredient must instead be solidarity – a keen sense that one has a significant personal stake also in the survival and bodily integrity of others with whom one is closely associated. One might say that obedience provides a vertical tie between the individual soldier's conduct and that of his or her superiors, and solidarity a horizontal linkage between the individual soldier and his or her peers. A further emotional requirement is that, in the combat situation, soldiers should feel called upon to *prove themselves* in the face of an extremely testing and threatening situation.

What soldiers are to prove about themselves used to be characterized as manliness; if this notion is to be disposed of because of its sexist connotations, one should replace it with another one bearing the same complex semantic freight. This embraces the capacity, in extremely stressful situations, to give and execute commands, to demonstrate solidarity toward one's associates, to perform complex activities, to endure deprivation, suffering and the prospect of painful death; it also encompasses a willingness to engage in violent, armed aggression and to overcome resistance to it of others.

In the context of a more or less modernized society, such psychical dispositions tend to be rare, as well as potentially dangerous. Their inculcation, therefore, requires a specialized environment, which insulates those who impart them, as well as those in the process of acquiring them, from the rest of society, and thereby both protects the society itself and maximizes the probability of having those dispositions duly learned and tested. The insulation is both symbolic (for instance, the wearing of uniforms, the ceremonies of induction of soldiers) and physical. (As an Italian saying goes, the reason army barracks are guarded by sentinels is to keep common sense out.) Above all, it is institutional; that is, a set of publicly acknowledged, sanctioned practices structure military life differently from all other forms of social life, for instance by valuing obedience, solidarity and various aspects of what one used to call manliness, over contrasting attitudes and dispositions rewarded by the larger society. (Jacobs's contrast between the commercial and the guardian moral syndromes is enlightening also in this context.)

There are two further, overlapping reasons why military elites seek to maximize the distinctiveness and autonomy of their own realm. First, military operations have a greater probability of success when the enemy knows little or nothing about where, when, by which forces or in what ways they are or will be carried out. There is thus a premium on secrecy in the military business, and in order to protect secrecy it pays to mark as clearly as possible the boundaries between those directly involved in that business and those not so involved. Second, in modern societies war is a relatively infrequent occurrence, yet (in the views of military leaders, at any rate) the possibility of it is a permanent condition, which must be continuously taken into account. While it does not make sense to maintain the whole society constantly on a war footing, the armed forces themselves must continuously sustain their material and cultural readiness for war, and can best do so when they are acknowledged (and funded, and honoured, and governed) as a distinctive, significant institutional realm. That is, in a given country social life may go on as if war were not a possibility, *only if* in a specialized part of that society all of social life goes on all the time as if war were an impending possibility, a continuous threat.

The understandable preoccupation of military elites with the autonomy of *their* institution, if taken by itself, might lead to the construction of an exclusively professional army, utterly distinct from the rest of society. Apart from the political implications of such an arrangement, it does not make much military sense, in view of some aspects of modern warfare. In the first place, this often requires the fielding of mass armies, and thus the involvement in military activities of a relatively high proportion of the population at large. Even when this does not obtain, modern warfare requires the commitment of huge industrial resources, which the domestic economy must commit to the armed forces. Furthermore, particularly since World War II the conduct of military operations has required the direct involvement of many men and women who do not cease to be civilians, but work side by side with professional officers and soldiers. In fact, the 'officering' itself of contemporary armies requires knowledge and skills of a technical and managerial nature extraneous to the traditional formation of the officer class; and in practising command, at any rate outside the immediate combat situation, officers increasingly assume that their subordinates are largely guided and motivated by dispositions not very different from those typical of any employees, rather than by dispositions characteristic of 'trained killers'. Such considerations suggest that military elites, in dealing with their political counterparts, must develop a rather sophisticated and qualified version of the argument for the institutional autonomy of the armed forces, and acknowledge the necessity for some mutual adjustment between the forces and the larger society.

Also, the argument for the continuing significance of war as a central fact of political life can be given a sophisticated and qualified formulation. Even Clausewitz's classical definition of war as 'the continuation of politics with the intervention of other means' assumes that politics, central as war may be to it, is larger than war. In the twentieth century, a major theoretical attempt was made to invert the relationship, considering politics as the continuation of war; but characteristically the man who made that attempt was not a military thinker, but a political and constitutional theorist, Carl Schmitt.[10] By and large, military thinking takes Clausewitz's own position, which entails that war, when all is said and done, has an instrumental relationship to politics, does not define its essence but constitutes a realm of 'means' applicable to it. The elites in charge of that realm must soft-pedal somewhat their tune about the supreme importance of war, lest their political counterparts accept their argument but qualify it by suggesting, as Georges Clemenceau once said, that war is *too* important to be left to generals.

Constraints on military elites in their relationship with civilian leaders

In any case, military elites (at any rate in contemporary Western polities) act within two sets of constraints. On the one hand, they are constitutionally subordinate to political elites whose modes of selection and operation are mostly quite unmilitary. On the other hand, they are appointed to serve societies which are mostly rather unbellicose in temper (among other reasons, because they are aware how destructive and murderous modern warfare is).

Note that these are historically evolved and fairly loose constraints. The

first has taken very varied institutional forms; for instance, within constitutional monarchies, where the monarchs themselves had learned 'to rule
but not to govern', armies often cherished some direct connection with the
crown which bypassed the normal apparatus of government, for instance
via the monarch's own 'military cabinet';[11] or there might be a convention
that only a general could be appointed minister of war or of defence. Also,
the second constraint (the relatively non-bellicose temperament of Western
nations) is subject to considerable variation and qualification, among other
reasons because it can be rapidly and seriously modified by the media. For
instance, Britain, on the occasion of the Falklands (Malvinas) War, witnessed a considerable upsurge of good old 'hooray' emotions within certain
sectors of opinion. More generally, the publics of even fairly unmilitarily
disposed Western countries sometimes do not seem to notice, or to mind,
that a given country foments and supports 'wars by proxy' between a client
state of its own and that of another state, or that its domestic economy is
heavily into the arms export business.

In any case, constraints are just that – more or less fixed boundaries
which the custodians of various forms of social power need to take into
account as they seek to affect public policy that addresses problems in
which they have a stake. In the case of the military institution, take for
instance the problem of how to recruit its rank and file. Within the
historical experience of the constitutional Western state, the solutions of
that problem observe fairly simple and constant rules; for instance, there
may be exceptions (such as the French Foreign Legion, or the British
Gurkha regiments), but normally only a country's citizens will be its
soldiers; their military engagement may only be long-term during wartime
or when it is volunteered and / or professionalized.

However, consider how much variation these rules allow. For instance,
in the last few decades the question of whether the opportunity and / or the
obligation to serve as soldiers should be extended to women has been
widely debated and variously settled. Of much longer standing is the issue
of how to structure the recruitment of a country's army, an issue that
directly affects the nature of the army itself. This issue has been surveyed
by Eliot Cohen, in a book on which I draw for the following schematic
presentation.[12]

There are three basic approaches to recruiting, training and fielding a
mass army, that is, 'armed forces composed of a large proportion (say, a
quarter or more) of the young male population, and composed primarily
of soldiers ready for war':

- the *cadre / conscript approach*, whereby 'a cadre of professional NCOs
  and officers trains and leads conscripts who then become part of the
  nation's standing forces'; this was practised, for instance, in the United
  States between 1948 and 1973;
- the *militia approach*, whereby '[m]en, selected by a number of possible
  methods, train sporadically during the year (e.g., one weekend per

month) while pursuing civil careers. These men perform active duty
only in time of invasion or general war. [Within this approach the]
armed force ... exists as such only in time of war.' The classical
exemplar of this arrangement is the Swiss Army;
- the *expansive/selective service*, whereby 'a cadre of professional
  soldiers prepares in peacetime to train large numbers of conscripts or
  volunteers in War'. An example is the German *Reichswehr* during the
  Weimar Republic.

Note that according to Cohen the current US army, characterized as an 'all
volunteer force', falls outside this framework, not being a *mass army* by
the previous definition. His book details the broader political implications
of the various arrangements, not just their respective strengths and weaknesses in strictly military terms, and makes a strong case that 'a system of
military service has functions beyond providing sufficient armed forces
adequately trained and equipped. It flourishes and withers only in part
because of its military utility.' For instance:

> militia systems are peculiarly vulnerable to subversion of discipline, through
> political interference and other means. The former was a particular problem
> for the National Guard in the U.S., where appointments and promotions often
> depended on cronyism. At a more subtle level, the informality of militia units
> occasionally subverts the need for discipline that war requires; an officer
> whose men call him by his first name rather than 'Sir' can, in most cases,
> expect less compliance with his instructions than can his professional
> counterpart.

This last passage points to a question of similar significance and complexity: how the military provides itself not with rank-and-file soldiery but with
a body of officers and non-commissioned officers, both in peace and in
wartime. Particularly recurrent and significant issues have been, for
instance, how officers should be recruited and trained, to what extent
professional officers should be distinguished from reserve ones, what
privileges either category should enjoy with respect to the rank and file.

Questions of this kind have been much on the mind of military elites
whenever the political situation has allowed them some play within what I
have called the constitutional constraints upon their position in the political
system and in society. Note that other power groups have had their own
preferences, which might or might not coincide with those of the military.
For instance, from a military standpoint a great deal may be said for
constituting units that recruit their soldiery each from a different, relatively
small part of the country, as is shown by the history of many English and
Scottish regiments. However, for reasons of its own, the political elite may
seek to reduce the saliency of regional affiliations within its citizenry, and
thus may prefer each army unit to assemble soldiers from a variety of
locales. In this manner, while these serve under arms, their local attach-
ments can to some extent be transcended by a 'nationalization' of their

attitudes and orientations, and by a greater sense of their belonging together.

Or consider the question of how to train appropriate skills and inculcate appropriate dispositions into a body of recruits drawn from the population at large, in order to make them both militarily apt and politically reliable, for the duration of their service and possibly afterwards. One issue here is: what *are* those appropriate skills and dispositions? Should they be chiefly those of devoted subjects and brave fighters, ready to obey orders and if necessary to kill and get themselves killed for their country, or should they be (also) those of politically conscious, responsible citizens? Under most conditions, the military elites can be expected to stand for the first solution (whether or not they make that preference explicit); consequently, it prefers to recruit young men (and perhaps women) for relatively long periods, during which their distance from civilian life is emphasized by subjecting them to uncomfortable circumstances and harsh discipline; furthermore, even after their discharge trained soldiers are to keep themselves available for retraining, and so forth.

But these preferences may not suit other power players. Some economically powerful groups, for instance, may not mind this treatment being applied to the children of the lower orders, but object to their own scions being subjected to it; or they may feel that if the military experience of the masses is so arranged, those undergoing that experience will find it difficult, successively, to acquire instead the habits and dispositions of the relatively sophisticated, skilled workforce the economic system may need.

Furthermore, middle-class groups with traditions of civism and of active political participation will consider unacceptable the claim of the military elites that the country's young men and women, when serving under arms, must unreservedly submit to the military hierarchy, and surrender many rights of citizenship. Cohen phrases that claim as follows:

> Military service means participation in a total institution, an institution that can control every minute of a man's waking hours and every facet of his behavior. This total institution differs greatly from normal liberal-democratic society. Whereas such a society tolerates diversity of dress and behavior, the armed forces must insist on uniformity of both. Whereas society frowns upon or prohibits violence and killing, a military organisation must prepare men for them. Whereas free societies tell their members that one citizen is the equal of any other, the military must insist on rank, order, and deference.[13]

On the other hand, more conservatively disposed groups may find these features of the military experience quite acceptable, and indeed expect them to have positive long-term effects upon each successive cohort of citizens, by instilling in young people a healthy respect for authority, an aversion towards subversive politics, a love of country. This preference resolved a certain ambivalence originally felt by European conservative circles towards the military innovations introduced by the French revolutionary armies, and particularly in respect of the phenomenon of mass soldiering. On the one hand, those circles were concerned that this amounted to 'putting rifles in the hands of the lower orders'; on the other hand, they could not deny its military necessity. They reconciled these two contrasting considerations by arguing that if handled properly (that is, according to the preferences of the military elite) the induction of the masses into the military experience could have the positive effects listed above. After all, as a nineteenth-century German dictum had it, 'Gegen Demokraten helfen nur Soldaten' ('Against democrats only soldiers are of use').

The diverse, recurrent tensions between the preferences, respectively, of the military and of other social elites can to some extent be obviated by the fact that a modern army is a very complex body, highly differentiated both functionally and hierarchically. On this account, it can (and perhaps it must) acknowledge that different bodies of military personnel require different patterns of recruitment, training and operation in the field. Thus those patterns may match the preferences of different social elites, and keep everybody happy. During the reconstruction phase following World War II, for instance, the Italian car manufacturer Fiat willingly hired as low-level managers young men whom the military police corps (the *Carabinieri*) had trained as privates (sometimes as commissioned or non-commissioned officers) and then discharged, for such people could be relied upon to adopt with relish the firm's harsh disciplinary posture towards its workforce. Later, as Fiat began to introduce electronics into its cars, it found particularly useful, instead, the training in avionics and informatics that the Italian Air Force was giving to its men. Currently, the increasing 'managerialization' of the military profession, and the increasingly technological content of the training of enlisted personnel, has increased the compatibility between military and civilian practices, and made experienced military personnel a preferred target of the hiring policies of some industrial firms.

Economic aspects of the relationship

Another significant, recurrent issue to be settled within what I have called the first constraint concerns the economic resources that the state allocates to what is referred to, sometimes euphemistically, as 'defence', and which it places under the direct control of military power. In chapter 9 I expanded somewhat on the dictum 'C'est l'argent qui fait la guerre', and on the reasons why this fact imposes upon public funds a heavy and (under certain conditions) increasing burden. The issue concerns not only the absolute size of the military allocation, but also two other aspects of it.

The first aspect is the *way* in which the allocation is made and funds are then administered. For instance, in Wilhelmine Germany, the military successfully insisted on being funded on a longer than yearly basis; this protected the army from what it considered as excessive parliamentary scrutiny and other forms of public auditing,[14] and allowed it greater freedom to plan the expenditure of those funds on the basis (allegedly) of purely military criteria. Even in political systems less generous toward their armed forces, a persistent concern is to maintain some degree of secrecy, for security reasons, on how military funds are to be expended. For this reason, the military elite has sometimes insisted on excluding from the deliberations of the competent parliamentary committees, or of the related administrative units, individuals entitled to take part in those deliberations but whom the top brass considered as security risks.

The second aspect concerns the way in which the allotted funds are sub-allocated between the various components of the armed forces; we may adopt American usage and call them 'the services'. It is a persistent weakness of military power in general that the services, while operating jointly to induce political elites to maintain and increase the military budget as a whole, often become each other's fiercest rivals over the question of how to divide those funds among themselves.[15] How open inter-services rivalries become, and how they are resolved, varies a great deal from system to system. In any case, they have two contrasting effects. On the one hand, they tend to increase the total size of the military allocation, for in this as in other distributive struggles the easiest solution consists in giving something to everybody, thus masking the fact that somebody is getting a great deal, and somebody else not nearly as much. On the other hand, sometimes the rival services carry on their fight by attacking each other's technical rationales for increased or protected funding. If politicians and/or the public become aware of such attacks, these may discredit the claim that cogent, unanswerable reasons lie behind the military's push for greater funding in general, and suggest that those alleged rationales are in fact self-serving and merely a pretext. Sometimes it is also doubtful to what extent military funds, in general, are expended purely in maintaining or improving the lifestyle and the working conditions of the officer corps, instead of financing actual improvements in the services' capacity to fight, which might require new equipment or a better treatment of the rank and file. Or it may be doubtful whether military expenditures establish the right ratio between keeping the existent forces in good trim on the one hand, and developing new fighting resources and skills on the other.

A further issue concerns the concrete meaning to be attributed, within a given state, to the Clausewitzian formula according to which (as I interpret it) politics is larger than war, and war stands in an instrumental relationship to politics. In my view, the constitutional subordination of military to political elites – which I have referred to above as the first constraint upon military power – is in keeping with that formula. But sometimes the military attempts to loosen that constraint and increase its own autonomy by (explicitly or implicitly) questioning that formula, or at any rate problematizing its meaning in given circumstances.

Such an attempt may seek justification in a sequence of statements such as the following. Any given state, as one sovereign political entity among others, is inescapably committed to maintaining and increasing its own power; sometimes that power can only assert itself through military might; in the end, such might can only prove itself by prevailing over that wielded against itself by another state. *Whether* it prevails, on the one hand is the master political question, and on the other depends exclusively on the sheer effectiveness of a given state's fighting forces. To that extent, proving in fact that effectiveness (when necessary) may well be seen as a *technical* matter; building up and wielding the relative capacity may well be seen as an activity *instrumental* to the larger political enterprise; the elites dealing with that activity may well be *subordinated* to other political personnel. *But* that activity remains, by its very nature, absolutely central to politics at large. In other words, constitutionally the top brass may well be 'just technicians', *but* the basic issue of all politics, on which ultimately hangs the existence itself of any given sovereign state, is itself a technical one: whether the amount of violence (potentially or actually) streaming out of that state is bigger or smaller than that streaming out of another.

Using such a line of thinking, without directly attacking the Clausewitzian formula, the custodians of military power within a state have often attacked, instead, Clemenceau's dictum 'War is too important to be left to generals'. They have retorted (not, as far as I know, in these very words) that politics is too important to be left to politicians; that all of politics ought to reflect the absolute priority of the question whether the political entity, confronted with the challenge of war, is capable of prevailing militarily. Accordingly, the personnel constitutionally entrusted with direct responsibility for military affairs ought to play a large role in the conduct of political affairs at large. Even assuming that the question of whom the country should fight does not fall within their responsibility, the question of how to fight definitely does, and it is so important (as previous considerations suggest) that the search for an effective solution of it should constitute a major, constant constraint also upon the solutions of political questions not directly concerned with war; in fact, a constraint upon the whole political management of a country's society.

Even a constitutional framework subordinating military to civilian elites may allow some leeway for an argument along the lines of that rehearsed above. In other terms, even within such a framework military elites may make a push toward militarism, if by militarism one understands the systematic prioritizing of technical military considerations in the conduct of politics. Of course foreign policy is the first referent of this claim; but given the assumption of the *Primat der Außenpolitik*, the primacy of foreign over domestic policy – one can expect domestic policy, too, to be strongly affected.

The 'military mind'

A significant aspect of militarism thus understood is the extent to which the 'military mind', whether openly or covertly, downgrades politics as usually understood, and denigrates its protagonists, the politicians. From the military perspective, 'normal' politics appears to be all about *division*: it is structured by the antagonism between parties over governmental office and its spoils; its chief theme is the distribution of the gross national product (via the welfare state, the regulation of economic activities, and so on). Bottom-line politics, however – the kind military leaders declare themselves exclusively concerned with – requires and protects the *unity* of the state, pursues interests that the state's constituency (generally conceived as 'the nation') shares, and which are threatened from outside. Military leaders may also criticize the short time perspective of normal politics, the preoccupation of politicians with temporary gains and losses, with continually shifting interests, and emphasize their own professional preoccupation with abiding, long-term interests. 'Normal politics' appears to be all about superficial change; bottom-line politics about deep continuities, resting ultimately on the geopolitical circumstances of a given country and of its possible opponents.

Also, normal politics is too much a matter of *words* – words from the parties' ideological platforms, words at the hustings, words in the legislative chambers, words in the statutes, words in administrative circulars and decrees, words in judicial decisions. Through words the protagonists of normal politics make a case for their party, win the electorate, hand down administrative rulings, argue court decisions, achieve compromises, allocate resources. However, as a hoary old American dictum has it, winning battles is all a matter of 'gitting thar' fustest with the mostest'. In the context of battle – thus, in the context of war – words only matter as commands, and it is the deeds those commands activate, their execution on the ground, that are decisive. In that execution, timing is everything – whereas in normal politics words tend to be produced and consumed at some leisure, often delaying the resolution of problems rather than facing up to them. Livy said it all, long ago: 'Dum ea Romani parant consultantque, iam Saguntum summa vi oppugnabatur' – 'While the Romans were thus planning and deliberating, Saguntum was already being besieged with the greatest vigour'.[16]

Military elites often feel on all these counts that the holders of political power have largely lost contact with the ultimate issues of political life. They work for party rather than country; they operate chiefly through words; they waste time; they have no commitment to authentic, abiding political interests, no taste for the prime political resource, organized violence, no sense of its significance or understanding of its requirements. Thus, military leaders often see their mission as guarding and asserting the forgotten, unwelcome truth about politics and statesmanship, and perform that mission in various ways. They insistently remind politicians of that truth; pound the desks of those in office and plead the urgency of the needs of the armed forces; denounce politicians who resist those pleas as irresponsible, irredeemably partisan, or traitorous; court the support for their cause of organs of opinion less committed to the *status quo*; associate themselves, sometimes covertly, with unconventional political figures (generally from the extreme right wing) who share their vision; and project new uses to which a country could put its armed forces.

Sometimes the military elites conspire among themselves to induce the appropriate state organs to make favourable legislative or budgetary responses to their claims, or to circumvent unfavourable ones. On other occasions, they go over the brink and challenge their constitutional subordination to civilian personnel, proclaiming that it jeopardizes supreme political interests of which only military elites are aware and to which that personnel is regrettably blind. In 1952, for example, General MacArthur tried to forestall President Truman's move to replace him as commander of the US forces in Korea by objecting to 'a new and heretofore unknown and dangerous concept that the members of our armed forces owe primary allegiance or loyalty to those who temporarily exercise the authority of the executive branch of government rather than to the country and the constitution which they are sworn to defend'.[17] Nothing much came of this particular attempt to assert the autonomy of the military elites. But in other circumstances they may have their way; they may for instance insist that individual political leaders be replaced by others who 'enjoy the confidence' of the armed forces, or even that a whole civilian cabinet be replaced wholesale by a number of such figures. They may even themselves take over all key government offices, though they generally claim to do so on a temporary basis, and with the intent of returning them in due course to civilians.

Over the last few pages I have discussed several ways in which military power both adapts and reacts to what I called the first major constraint on its relationship to political power: the constitutional subordination of military elites to the civilian political institution. I will deal more briefly with what I consider a second constraint – the fact that, particularly in the contemporary West, publics are (relatively speaking) not bellicose, and the prevalent culture tends to discount the legitimacy and the moral significance of military violence.

Of course, in such societies the machinery of mass killing and destruction has become exceedingly advanced, and it is duly tended and cherished by the armed forces; it is perhaps chiefly for this reason that our societies need not continually concern themselves with such machinery, much less celebrate its presence and contemplate gleefully its potential uses. As I have already suggested, another reason may be the awareness, however dim, of the unspeakably murderous and destructive nature of any war in which such machinery is employed. Perhaps for this reason the disgracefully numerous and popular electronic games and films that play on the theme of high-tech war mostly set it in a science-fiction context, feature mainly non-human, perhaps post-human protagonists, and do not directly invoke the conventional national identities of participants and spectators.

For those reasons or others, little in contemporary Western societies (it seems to me) resembles the fascinated public concern with the theme of war, much less the expectant anticipation of an armed conflict between the chief world powers, which directly preceded World War I. Consumption, sexuality, personal identity, the elaboration and projection of an image of oneself, the relationship with one's body and with others, seem currently much more pervasive concerns of the individual; such concerns unfortunately can accommodate and activate much violence, but this is mainly interpersonal, expressive violence, rather than the collective, organized, instrumental violence of war. As I have indicated above in evoking the military elites' perturbed perception of it, most of contemporary politics seems to be made exclusively of words, the dominant theme of which consists in routine administrative practices more or less related to the economic well-being (or 'ill-being') of the individual. All of this leaves little space and energy, in the public mind, even for revisiting and entertaining the symbolic imagery of the country's military might and of its warlike past, let alone for concerning itself seriously with its current military affairs.

Confronted with what it considers the public's irresponsible lack of awareness of its own professional concerns (which in its view continue to be of foremost political significance), the military elite would very much like to present the military experience as an opportunity to re-educate the public and especially to correct and improve the new generations' moral temper through the army's recruitment and training practices.

An acute sensitivity to these themes is a characteristic feature of the military mind, where it complements a set of attitudes apparently at odds with it. Earlier, I have evoked the emphasis that the phenomenon of war unavoidably places on brutal physical realities, on the ability to prevail in the field, ultimately on the armed forces' organized, machine-assisted capacity to kill en masse. But this emphasis on *hard* facts is often counterbalanced by an emphasis on the *soft* requirements of the military experience, and particularly of battle – an emphasis on mental and moral habits and dispositions, on sheer qualities of character, on the individual's ability to overcome fear and egoism, to endure danger and deprivation, to suppress rather than express his or her own capacity for judgement, to discipline his or her own aggression.

According to Michael Howard, the phenomenon of militarism itself refers largely to these moral implications of the war experience; he defines the phenomenon as:

> an acceptance of the values of the military subculture as the dominant values of society; a stress on hierarchy and subordination in organisations, on physical courage and self-sacrifice in personal behaviour, on the need for heroic leadership in situations of extreme stress; all based on the acceptance of armed conflict within the states-system and the consequent need to develop the qualities necessary to conduct it.[18]

The military elite's stress on these factors sometimes imparts an odd moralistic turn to their view of human affairs; and this has two closely related effects. On the one hand, it adds to the elite's feeling of estrangement from a society and a culture it perceives instead as having turned its back on virtue, or as rewarding all the wrong moral dispositions (such as hedonism, individualism, love of comfort and well-being). On the other hand, it frequently leads the military elite to form close associations with other groups which lament the moral poverty of the current society and culture, even when those groups pursue projects (for instance, a return to old-time religion) with moral messages different from those implicit in the military's own complaints.

This tendency is reinforced by the military's high evaluation of tradition, of continuity with the past, and by the frequent adoption of a 'what is the world coming to?' mind-set. An aspect of this is an almost anguished rejection of modern images of the genders and of the associated changes in the patterns of sexual experience. This escalates to a sense of outrage when politicians, yielding to certain currents of opinion, seem to use the army as a proving ground for particularly offensive new developments, such as first introducing women into the army, then allowing them to take part in combat, or allowing gays to maintain and express their sexual identity while serving in the army. The revulsion of the military elites towards these developments is one component of a syndrome that we can call, with Barrington Moore, jun., 'catonism'. An important aspect of this is that often it induces the military elites to associate themselves, overtly or covertly, with right-wing political forces, and sometimes to hatch or favour political projects where the motifs of *re*vival, *re*storation, *re*turn to ancient values and institutions are predominant.

It should be noted, however, that in most circumstances such a posture is not likely to be taken (at any rate expressly) by *top* military leaders, for two convergent reasons. First, their appointment is generally the prerogative of the civilian holders of constitutional offices, who in exercising that prerogative do not favour individuals particularly likely to challenge or embarrass them. Second, even the processes of leader selection internal to the military elite must attach some positive significance to the political acceptability of candidates for top posts, to what is known about their contacts with politicians, their ability to work together with them, and so forth. As a result, unless the military elite is particularly strong, it is not likely to be represented at the very top by people any of whom is widely considered 'a soldier's soldier', for such a person is expected to embody in a particularly visible fashion the catonism endemic among his peers, or an intolerant and insubordinate attitude towards 'normal politicians'.

The concerns of civilian elites

These, in turn, have typical attitudes of their own towards the military institution in general and in particular towards its leaders. In the first place, they resent their failure to adapt to changing circumstances. For instance, the military leaders justify the privileges the armed forces enjoy, or claim, by pointing to the particular risks they take when the chips are down and armed conflict begins; yet, for quite some time now warfare has extended its murderous reach well beyond the circle of professional soldiers to the civilian population at large; death in war is no longer the prerogative, so to speak, of soldiers.

Besides, there are armies, say in South America, that have not fought wars for generations, and nevertheless claim special treatment and consideration from other political institutions, and act in a particularly insubordinate and threatening manner towards 'normal politicians'. There is also some evidence that, within its professional sphere itself, the military elite is particularly resistant to innovation: it adheres uncritically to its inherited doctrines and practices, refuses to consider or to adopt new technological developments and isolates and frustrates those of its members who promote them. As an old saying goes, generals, at any rate at the beginning of a war, tend to replay the *last* war, and sometimes have to be forced by the enemy, and / or by the politicians themselves, to acknowledge and transcend the limitations of their professional knowledge.

Furthermore, the armed forces' traditionalism has social and political aspects that can also be bothersome to politicians, and especially those seeking to promote greater equality and the modernization of a country's social structure. For many decades after the end of the *anciens régimes*, for instance, European armies, in selecting their officers and in promoting those destined to the more significant positions, continued to favour systematically (though in most cases covertly) young aspirants to a military career who hailed from the aristocracy, and discriminated systematically against those having a middle-class (not to mention a Jewish or a lower-class) background. It took a long time (and a great deal of pressure from progressive politicians and from enlightened opinion circles) before the military calling became in fact what it had long been said to be – 'une carrière ouverte aux talents'. Also, other practices through which the army defends its institutional autonomy – for instance those concerning the training of recruits – had long been (and sometimes remain) anathema to politicians, giving them some grounds for considering the army 'a bulwark of reaction', and a persistent threat to republican and / or democratic values.

Finally, politicians often complain how expensive it is to maintain a modern army, air force, or navy, particularly since the hardware they claim to need tends to become obsolete rather fast, and somehow the new hardware always seems to cost even more. As President Eisenhower pointed out at the end of his second mandate, a coalition between the makers and purveyors of new weapons on the one hand and their potential users on the other – the so-called 'industrial-military complex' – tends to place particularly ruinous burdens on public resources and thus on a country's economy. Politicians who can think of better, civilian uses to which to turn some of the funds the armed forces claim for themselves find arrayed with the top brass and against themselves not just the organs of conservative opinion but (sometimes) the leaders of the technologically most advanced industrial sectors, and sometimes those of the unions organizing their workforce. As a result, the so-called 'peace dividend' some Western nations anticipated from the end of the cold war has failed to materialize.

While there have been and there are grounds for systematic friction between political and military elites, contemporary states remain by and large very reluctant to disown that considerable aspect of their historical heritage, the extent to which, to quote Tilly again, 'war made states and viceversa'. True, even their foreign policy – the field in which war has always constituted a most significant option – is more and more preoccupied with complex arrangements relating to financial and industrial matters. Yet a critical concern of even the *trade* policy of many an advanced industrial state remains the promotion of its domestic arms industry; and the thinking on other aspects of foreign policy remains informed by geopolitical concepts intrinsically connected with strategic issues. Major international crises continue to evoke responses with a more or less pronounced military component, and military elites thrive on the continuing significance of the resources they guard. At the end of the twentieth century, for instance, the destabilization of political relations in eastern Europe has indeed engendered much concern with peacekeeping; but the imagery connected with that in the public mind still centres on uniformed men carrying weapons, rather than, say, on citizens' movements.[19] Above all, in the current processes of state-making – and un-making – warfare has brutally reasserted itself as the chief political instrumentality, and the day-by-day chronicles of some parts of the world are turning Tilly's backward-looking generalization into a description of the present and a sad prescription for the future.

Epilogue

I bring to a close a relatively long book with a very brief restatement of its main argument.

Society is structured *also* by power relations. That is, the groups routinely interacting within a given territorial framework differ, among other things, in the extent to which some of them are able to determine or condition what the others undertake, accomplish, forbear to do or have done to them. A given group is or is not in a position to do so in its relation to the others depending chiefly on whether it does or does not find itself in possession of a resource from which it can exclude those other groups and which it can employ to put pressure on them.

The resources significant enough to play this role are those that put at stake three distinct vulnerabilities of human beings: the difficulty they find in forming an idea of what the world is like and in attributing a meaning to their own position and their own destiny; the insecurity to which they are exposed by the scarcity of the resources and energies on which they depend if they are to make their own survival possible; and the fragility of their bodies, their susceptibility to physical constraint, suffering and death.

'Social power' means on the one hand that a given group can make a significant difference to the extent to which other individuals actually experience those vulnerabilities, relieving or heightening the anxieties that they arouse; on the other hand, it means that it can make that difference depend on what those individuals do or abstain from doing. As Hobbes pointed out long ago, the sovereign relieves the subjects from the experience of fear by means of his own capacity to awaken fear. Those vulnerabilities differ from one another; they concern different aspects of the constitution of humans. The corresponding resources also differ; and in the intent of securing them and availing themselves of them, groups develop different dispositions, tendencies, sensitivities and acquire different identities – as indicated by the concept of 'moral syndrome' which I have borrowed from Jane Jacobs. On this account, the search for and the exercise of social power turn into a complex game.

On the one hand, different contenders confront each other starting from different positions of advantage, each downplaying the other's priorities, trying to decrease their leverage on the situation they share, denigrating their identities. On the other hand, each power group must to some extent take into account the existence of alternative power bases, seek to exercise some influence on the ways other power forms are acquired and put to use, and in the end acknowledge the constraints their existence places upon the form it has made its own. This necessity engenders a restless dynamic in which are undertaken and adjusted to one another diverse strategies of each given power form: from its attempt to take over or to suppress other forms, to more or less stable and explicit ways of coming to terms with the existence of others and to attain a compromise with them.

The open-ended, highly contingent character of the resulting relations between power forms does not exclude that some trends may develop and become relatively stable and reliable. I have mentioned two such current trends: the erosion undergone by the secular embodiments of ideological / normative power in their autonomy and significance, particularly as concerns those I have called creative intellectuals; the challenge constituted for the state's authority, rooted in the control of the territory, by the globalization of the economic process and by the fact that the greatest agglomerations of economic power present in our own times are increasingly constituted, or at any rate operate, *offshore*.

I hope I am overstating somewhat the significance, and above all the durability, of these trends. I hope that the 'power games' in the foreseeable future will not be seriously impoverished by a reduction in the name of the players, by the consolidation of a stable and imposing hierarchy between them, and above all by a thoroughgoing unification of the social power forms. While I am unable to place any confidence in the prospect, attractive in itself as it might be, of a world without power(s) – for I remain convinced that the power phenomenon cannot be eliminated from the social world – I find less incredible, and thus more disquieting, the prospect of a significant, lasting elimination of any of the major forms that that phenomenon takes. The damage to human values – a close approximation to such a condition – has been amply demonstrated, in our own times, by the experience of the Soviet Union. Today, what could be called 'the marketing of pretty much everything' constitutes a less visible and threatening, but in some ways analogous, phenomenon, which might also, in the long run, jeopardize significant human values.

Notes

Chapter 1 Homo Potens

1 See for example B. Barnes, *The Nature of Power*, Polity Press, Cambridge (1988); S. Clegg, *Frameworks of Power*, Sage, London (1989); S. Lukes, *Power: a Radical View*, Macmillan, London (1974); D. Wrong, *Power: Its Forms, Bases, and Uses. With a New Preface*, University of Chicago Press, Chicago (1988); D. Rueschemeyer, *Power and the Division of Labour*, Polity Press, Cambridge (1986).

2 See for example M. Olsen, ed., *Power in Societies*, Macmillan, New York (1970); S. Lukes, ed., *Power*, Blackwell, Oxford (1985).

3 Lukes, *Power: a Radical View*.

4 The expression was coined by the British philosopher W. B. Gallie; see his 'Essentially contested concepts', *Proceedings of the Aristotelian Society*, vol. 56 (1955–6): 67–98.

5 H. Rosinski, *Power and Human Destiny*, Praeger, New York (1965).

6 A. Gehlen, *The Human Being: His Nature and Place in the World*, Columbia University Press, New York (1988).

7 Rosinski does not refer to Plessner. In fact, he refers to very few authors – chiefly 'classics' of the rank of Hegel or Marx – and (perhaps because it was left unfinished) his book has no apparatus of notes and little explicit discussion of arguments similar or opposed to its own. This, come to think of it, may have been one reason why the book failed to attract attention.

8 R. N. Adams, *Energy and Structure: a Theory of Social Power*, University of Texas Press, Austin (1975).

9 A. Gehlen, *Man in the Age of Technology*, Columbia University Press, New York (1980): 5–7.

10 Quoted in R. Jhering, *Lo scopo nel diritto*, Einaudi, Turin (1978): 229 fn. 1.

11 Rosinski, *Power and Human Destiny*: 22.

12 W. H. McNeill, 'The peasant rebellion of our times', in B. Rothblatt, ed., *Changing Perspectives on Man*, University of Chicago Press, Chicago (1969): 227–43.

13 A. Gehlen, *Urmensch und Spätkultur*, Athenaeum, Bonn (1973).

14 Rosinski, *Power and Human Destiny*: 19.

15 Ibid.: 21.

16 Ibid.: 25.

17 N. Luhmann, *Macht*, Enke, Stuttgart (1968): 21.

18 R. Michels, *Political Parties*, Free Press, Glencoe, Ill. (1953).

19 'Move over, I'm taking your place!' Consider also the refreshingly straightforward statement of the French revolutionary leader Danton of what the revolution was about: 'We are at the bottom, we want to get on top.'

20 N. Luhmann, 'Reflexive Mechanismen', in his *Soziologische Aufklärung I*, Westdeutscher, Cologne (1992): 92–112.

21 See M. Crozier, *The Bureaucratic Phenomenon in France*, University of Chicago Press, Chicago (1964).

22 G. Simmel, *Soziologie*, Suhrkamp, Frankfurt am Main (1992): 161.
23 L. Coser, 'The notion of power: theoretical developments', in L. Coser and B. Rosenberg, eds, *Sociological Theory: a Book of Readings*, 4th edn, Macmillan, New York (1976): 154.
24 M. Weber, *Wirtschaft und Gesellschaft*, 5th edn, Mohr (Siebeck), Tübingen (1972): 28, 531.
25 Ibid.: 542.

Chapter 2   Power Forms

1 L. Coser, 'The notion of power: theoretical developments', in L. Coser and B. Rosenberg, eds, *Sociological Theory: a Book of Readings*, 4th edn, Macmillan, New York (1976): 152.
2 M. Weber, *Wirtschaft und Gesellschaft*, 5th edn, Mohr (Siebeck), Tübingen (1972): 28.
3 Ibid.: 531.
4 K. Davis and W. Moore, 'Some principles of stratification', repr. in Coser and Rosenberg, eds, *Sociological Theory: a Book of Readings*, 4th edn, Macmillan, New York (1963): 414.
5 For a sophisticated treatment of the notion of 'resource' as the basis of various aspects of inequality, but especially of status inequality, see M. Milner jun., *Status and Sacredness: a General Theory of Status Relations and an Analysis of Indian Culture*, Oxford University Press, New York (1994).
6 Weber, *Wirtschaft und Gesellschaft*: 544.
7 K. O. Hondrich, *Theorie der Herrschaft*, Suhrkamp, Frankfurt am Main (1978): 34ff.
8 H. Popitz, *Phänomene der Macht*, Mohr, Tübingen (1985): 69.
9 E. Gellner, *Plough, Sword and Book: the Structure of Human History*, Collins-Harvill, London (1988).
10 I. Kant, *Werkausgabe*, vol. VIII, Suhrkamp, Frankfurt am Main (1968): 751.
11 N. Bobbio, 'Politica', in N. Bobbio et al., eds, *Dizionario di politica*, 2nd edn, UTET, Turin (1983): 828.
12 T. H. Rigby, 'Stalinism and the mono-organisational society', in R. Tucker, ed., *Stalinism: Essays in Sociological Interpretation*, Norton, New York (1978): 53–76.
13 J. C. Scott, *Weapons of the Weak: Everyday Forms of Peasant Resistance*, Yale University Press, New Haven, Conn. (1987).
14 B. Moore jun., *Injustice: The Social Bases of Obedience and Revolt*, Macmillan, London (1978).
15 A. O. Hirschman, *The Passions and the Interests: Political Arguments for Capitalism before its Triumph*, Princeton University Press, Princeton, NJ (1977).

Chapter 3   Political Power

1 B. de Jouvenel, *Power: the Natural History of its Growth*, Hutchinson, London (1948): 110.
2 D. Hume, 'On the first principle of government', in D. Hume, *Political Essays*, Cambridge University Press, Cambridge (1987): 16.
3 H. Popitz, *Phänomene der Macht*, Mohr, Tübingen (1986).
4 G. Ferrero, *Potere: i geni invisibili della città*, Sugarco, Milan (1981): 36–7.
5 Ibid.
6 T. Mann, *Joseph und seine Brüder: III: Joseph in Ägypten*, Fischer, Frankfurt am Main (1983): 599.
7 Popitz, *Phänomene der Macht*: 72–3.
8 Ibid.: 76.
9 Ibid.: 77.

10   Ibid.: 78.
11   M. Weber, *Wirtschaft und Gesellschaft*, 5th edn, Mohr (Siebeck), Tübingen (1972): 30.
12   T. Hobbes, *Leviathan*, Cambridge University Press, Cambridge (1991): 70.
13   Popitz, *Phänomene der Macht*: 38–9.
14   Ibid.: 48.
15   Ibid.: 91–2.
16   C. Meier, *Die Entstehung des Politischen bei den Griechen*, Suhrkamp, Frankfurt am Main (1983).
17   I am grateful to François Hartog for discussing these matters with me, and allowing me to see the draft of his essay 'Cité: histoire d'un concept'.
18   P. Berger, *Invitation to Sociology*, Doubleday, Garden City, New York (1969): 75.
19   See Hartog, 'Cité: histoire d'un concept': 2.
20   Quoted in S. Lukes, ed., *Power*, Blackwell, Oxford (1974): 96.
21   N. Luhmann, *Macht*, Enke, Stuttgart (1968): 17.
22   Quoted from L. Coser, 'The notion of power: theoretical developments', in L. Coser and B. Rosenberg, eds, *Sociological Theory: a Book of Readings*, 4th edn, Macmillan, New York (1976): 159.
23   S. Huntington, *Political Order in Changing Societies*, Yale University Press, New Haven, Conn. (1973): 1.
24   D. Rueschemeyer, *Power and the Division of Labour*, Polity Press, Cambridge (1986): 6.
25   Luhmann, *Macht*.
26   Quoted from Jouvenel, *Power*: 103.
27   R. Michels, *Political Parties*, Jerrold, London (1915).
28   Jouvenel, *Power*: 95.
29   R. Unger, *Politics*, Cambridge University Press, Cambridge (1987): vol. III.
30   G. Poggi, *The State: Its Nature, Development and Prospects*, Polity Press, Cambridge (1991): 73–4.

Chapter 4   Ideological / Normative Power

1   V. Pareto, *The Mind and Society: A Treatise in General Sociology*, Harcourt Brace, New York (1935).
2   M. Mann, *The Sources of Social Power*, vol. I, Cambridge University Press, Cambridge (1986): 22–3.
3   G. M. Otto, *Frühe politische Ordnungsmodelle*, Kösel, Munich (1970): 22.
4   M. Douglas, *Implicit Meanings: Essays in Anthropology*, Routledge, London (1975): xiv.
5   F. de Coulanges, *La Cité antique*, as quoted in F. Hartog, *Le XIXe Siècle et l'histoire*, PUF, Paris (1988): 26.
6   Quoted in R. N. Bellah, 'Durkheim and history', repr. in P. Hamilton, ed., *Émile Durkheim: Critical Assessments*, vol. VII, Routledge, London (1995): 43.
7   M. Weber, *Wirtschaft und Gesellschaft*, 5th edn, Mohr (Siebeck), Tübingen (1972): 688.
8   A. de Tocqueville, *De la démocratie en Amérique*, vol. II, Vrin, Paris (1990): 33.
9   Quoted from J. Delumeau, *Le Peché et la peur: la culpibilisation en Occident (XIIIe– XVIIIe siècles)*, Fayard, Paris (1983): 19.
10   Ibid.: 88.
11   É. Durkheim, *Règles de la méthode sociologique*, PUF, Paris (1997): 68.
12   H. Gerth and C. W. Mills, *From Max Weber: Essays in Sociology*, Routledge, London (1947): 287.
13   F. Heer, *Die dritte Kraft: der europäische Humanismus zwischen den Fronten des konfessionellen Zeitalters*, Fischer, Frankfurt am Main (1959).

Chapter 5   Religious Power and the State

1   N. Bobbio, 'Dispotismo', in N. Bobbio et al., eds, *Dizionario di politica*, 2nd edn, UTET, Turin (1983): 242.

2   See for instance the discussion of classical China and ancient Egypt in G. M. Otto, *Frühe politische Ordnungsmodelle*, Kösel, Munich (1970): chs 2 and 3.

3   See A. Watkins, 'State II: the concept', in D. Sills, ed., *International Encyclopedia of the Social Sciences*, Free Press, New York (1968): vol. 15.

4   R. N. Bellah, 'Religious evolution', in his *Beyond Belief: Essays on Religion in a Post-Traditional World*, Harcourt Brace, New York (1970).

5   G. Brennan, *The Spanish Labyrinth*, 2nd edn, Cambridge University Press, Cambridge (1970): Preface.

6   M. Weber, *Wirtschaft und Gesellschaft*, 5th edn, Mohr (Siebeck), Tübingen (1972): 689.

7   A. de Tocqueville, *De la démocratie en Amérique*, Vrin, Paris (1990), vol. II: 34.

8   A. Dansette, *Histoire religieuse de la France contemporaine*, Flammarion, Paris (1952): ch. 1.

9   D. E. Smith, *India as a Secular State*, Princeton University Press, Princeton, NJ (1963): 4.

10   R. Sohm, cited in P. Krämer and H. Frost, 'Kirchenrecht', in *Staatslexikon*, 7th edn, Herder, Freiburg, (1987), vol III: 435.

11   F. Ruffini, *Relazioni tra stato e chiesa*, Mulino, Bologna (1974).

Chapter 6   Creative Intellectuals and the State

1   A Gouldner, *The Future of Intellectuals and the New Class*, Macmillan, London (1979).

2   P. Zanker, *Augustus und die Macht der Bilder*, Beck, Munich (1987): 107.

3   J. Linz, 'State building and nation building', *European Review*, 1 (1993), 4: 355.

4   See M. Tanner, *The Last Descendants of Aeneas: the Hapsburgs and the Mythic Image of the Emperor*, Yale University Press, New Haven, Conn. (1993).

Chapter 7   Economic Power

1   M. Weber, *Wirtschaft und Gesellschaft*, 5th edn, Mohr (Siebeck), Tübingen (1972): 541–5.

2   F. Perroux, 'The domination effect and modern economic theory', in K. W. Rothschild, ed., *Power in Economics*, Penguin, Harmondsworth (1971): 56–73, here 56–7.

3   For Böhm-Bawerk's argument to this effect, see the essay by Preiser cited below.

4   Quoted in R. L. Heibroner, *The Nature and Logic of Capitalism*, Norton, New York (1985): 41.

5   E. Preiser, 'Power, property and the distribution of income', in Rothschild, ed., *Power in Economics*: 119–40, here 136–7. The last part of the quotation is from p. 37, fn. 16.

6   Heibroner, *The Nature and Logic of Capitalism*: 66–7.

7   Ibid.: 544.

8   See G. Poggi, *Calvinism and the Capitalist Spirit: Max Weber's 'Protestant Ethic'*, Macmillan, London (1983): 20–2.

9   F. Parkin, *Marxism and Class Theory: a Bourgeois Critique*, Tavistock, London (1979): 53.

10   Heibroner, *The Nature and Logic of Capitalism*: 38–9.

11   A. Gouldner, *The Coming Crisis of Western Sociology*, Heinemann, London (1971): 309.

12   K. Marx, 'Randglossen zum Programm der deutschen Arbeitspartei', in K. Marx and F. Engels, *Werke*, vol. 19, Dietz, Berlin (1978): 15.

13   F. Neumann, 'Approaches to the study of political power', in his *The Authoritarian and the Democratic State*, Free Press, Glencoe, Ill. (1954): 3–21, here 13.

14 A. Gouldner, *The Future of Intellectuals and the New Class*, Macmillan, New York (1979): 22.
15 Ibid.: 21.
16 R. Blau, *Exchange and Power in Social Life*, Wiley, New York (1965).
17 K. Marx, *Das Kapital*, Dietz, Berlin, vol. I (1979): 96, fn. 33.
18 É. Durkheim, *De la division du travail social*, 2nd edn, PUF, Paris (1967): Preface.
19 M. Mann, *The Sources of Social Power*, vol. I, Cambridge University Press, Cambridge (1986): 24.
20 A. de Tocqueville, *De la démocratie en Amérique*, Vrin, Paris (1990), vol. II: 141.
21 Ibid.: 258.
22 Ibid.: 260.
23 Ibid.: 11–12.
24 J. Jacobs, *Systems of Survival: a Dialogue on the Moral Foundations of Commerce and Politics*, Random, New York (1992): 45–6.

Chapter 8 Business and Politics

1 A. Gouldner, *The Coming Crisis of Western Sociology*, Heinemann, London (1971): 307.
2 F. Parkin, *Marxism and Class Theory: a Bourgeois Critique*, Tavistock, London (1979): 52.
3 J. C. Coleman, *Power and the Structure of Society*, Norton, New York (1974).
4 M. Albert, *Capitalism vs. Capitalism*, Four Walls Eight Windows, New York (1993).
5 D. C. North and R. P. Thomas, *The Rise of the Modern World: a New Economic History*, Cambridge University Press, Cambridge (1973).
6 Ibid.: 91.
7 A. O. Hirschman, *The Passions and the Interests*, Princeton University Press, Princeton, NJ (1977).
8 See the discussion of the 'reform cycle' in R. Unger, *False Necessity: an Anti-Necessitarian Social Theory in the Service of Radical Democracy*, Cambridge University Press, Cambridge (1987).
9 F. Neumann, 'Approaches to the study of political power', in his *The Democratic and the Authoritarian State*, Free Press, Glencoe, Ill. (1957).
10 M. De Cecco, 'Keynes and Italian economics', in P. Hall, ed., *The Political Power of Economic Ideas: Keynesianism across Nations*, Princeton University Press, Princeton, NJ (1989).
11 See A. Shonfield, *Modern Capitalism: the Changing Balance of Public and Private Power*, Oxford University Press, Oxford (1969).
12 K. Borchardt, 'Zur Theorie der sozial-ökonomischen Entwicklung der gegenwärtigen Gesellschaft', in T. W. Adorno, ed., *Spätkapitalismus oder Industriegesellschaft?*, Enke, Stuttgart (1969): 29–47, here 35–6.
13 P. Wills, *Learning to Labor: How Working Class Kids Get Working Class Jobs*, Columbia University Press, New York (1977).
14 C. Lindblom, *Politics and Markets: the World's Political-Economic Systems*, Basic Books, New York (1977).

Chapter 9 The Economic Costs of the State

1 M. Weber, *Wirtschaft und Gesellschaft*, 5th edn, Mohr (Siebeck), Tübingen (1972): 114–17.
2 M. Levi, *Of Rule and Revenue*, University of California Press, Berkeley (1988).
3 A. de Jasay, *The State*, Blackwell, Oxford (1985).
4 S. N. Eisenstadt, *The Political System of Empires*, Free Press, Glencoe, Ill. (1963): 151–2.
5 R. Unger, *Plasticity into Power*, Cambridge University Press, Cambridge (1987).

6   Weber, *Wirtschaft und Gesellschaft*: 57.

7   E. W. N. McNeill, *The Pursuit of Power: Technology, Armed Forces, and Society since AD 1000*, Blackwell, Oxford (1983).

8   De Cecco in P. Hall, ed., *The Political Power of Economic Ideas: Keynesianism across Nations*, Princeton University Press, Princeton, NJ (1989).

9   W. Hennis, 'Il significato della avalutatività. Occasione e motivi del "postulato" di Max Weber', *Materiali per una Storia della Cultura Giuridica*, XXIII, 1 (June 1993): 159–77.

10   T. Skocpol, *Protecting Soldiers and Mothers: the Political Origins of Social Policy in the United States*, Harvard University Press, Cambridge, Mass. (1992).

11   R. Inglehart, *The Silent Revolution: Changing Values and Political Styles among Western Publics*, Princeton University Press, Princeton, NJ (1977).

12   M. Weber, 'Politics as a vocation', in H. Gerth and C. W. Mills, *From Max Weber: Essays in Sociology*, Routledge, London (1947): 53ff.

13   J. Nolan, *The Therapeutic State: Justifying Government at Century's End*, New York University Press, New York (1998).

14   H. Leipold, *Wirtschafts- und Gesellschaftssysteme im Vergleich*, 4th edn, Fischer, Frankfurt am Main (1985): 132–3.

15   F. Galgano et al., *Nazioni senza ricchezza. Ricchezza senza nazione*, Mulino, Bologna (1993).

Chapter 10   Military Power

1   C. Tilly, *Coercion, Capital and European States AD 990–1990*, Blackwell, Oxford (1976).

2   B. de Jouvenel, *Power: the Natural History of Its Growth*, Hutchinson, London (1947): 12.

3   R. F. Bensel, *Yankee Leviathan: the Origins of Central Authority in America 1859–1877*, Cambridge University Press, Cambridge (1991): 13.

4   O. Hintze, 'Staatsverfassung und Heeresverfassung', in his *Staat und Verfassung*, Vandenhoeck & Ruprecht, Göttingen (1970): 53.

5   R. Collins, *Conflict Sociology*, Academic Press, San Francisco (1975): 351, 353.

6   On the dynamics of part–whole relationships, see A. Gouldner, 'Reciprocity and autonomy in functional theory', in L. Gross, ed., *Symposium on Sociological Theory*, Row, Peterson, Evanston, Ill. (1959): 241–70.

7   A. Giddens, *The Nation-State and Violence*, Macmillan, London (1985): 228.

8   For a general discussion of this problem, see S. Finer, *Man on Horseback: the Role of the Military in Politics*, 2nd edn, Westview, Boulder, Colo. (1988).

9   Quoted in J. Ehrman, *Grand Strategy*, vol. V, HMSO, London (1956): 281.

10   C. Schmitt, *The Concept of the Political*, University of Chicago Press, Chicago (1995).

11   G. Ritter, *The Sword and the Sceptre: the Problem of Militarism in Germany*, vol. I, Allen Lane, London (1973).

12   E. Cohen, *Citizens and Soldiers: the Dilemmas of Military Service*, Cornell University Press, Ithaca, NY (1985).

13   Ibid.: 34.

14   Cf. G. Eley, 'Army, state and civil society', in his *From Unification to Nazism*, Allen and Unwin, Boston, Mass. (1986): 89ff.

15   See for instance D. Mackenzie, *Inventing Accuracy: a Historical Sociology of Nuclear Missile Guidance*, MIT Press, Cambridge, Mass. (1990).

16   T. Livy, *Ab urbe condita*, trans. B. O. Foster, Loeb Library edn, Heinemann, London (1929), bk XXI, 7: 16.

17   Quoted in Finer, *Man on Horseback*: 26.

18   M. Howard, *War in European History*, Oxford University Press, Oxford (1976): 109.

19 M. Grundmann and K. Pothoff, 'Konversion des Militärs: eine Bedingung für "Schützen, Helfen, Retten"', *Jahrbuch Frieden 1994*, Beck, Munich (1993): 180–93; C. M. Merkel, 'Methoden ziviler Konfliktbewältigung: Fragen an eine kriegserschütterte Welt', *Jahrbuch Frieden 1994*: 35–48.

Select Bibliography

Adams, R. N., *Energy and Structure: a Theory of Social Power*, University of Texas Press, Austin, 1975.

Albert, M., *Capitalism vs. Capitalism*, Four Walls Eight Windows, New York, 1993.

Barnes, B., *The Nature of Power*, Polity Press, Cambridge, 1988.

Bellah, R. N., *Beyond Belief: Essays on Religion in a Post-Traditional World*, Harcourt Brace, New York, 1970.

Bellah, R. N., 'Durkheim and history', repr. in P. Hamilton, ed., *Émile Durkheim: Critical Assessments*, vol. VII, Routledge, London, 1995.

Bensel, R. F., *Yankee Leviathan: the Origins of Central Authority in America, 1859–1877*, Cambridge University Press, Cambridge, 1991.

Berger, P., *Invitation to Sociology*, Doubleday, Garden City, New York, 1969.

Blau, R., *Exchange and Power in Social Life*, Wiley, New York, 1965.

Bobbio, N., 'Dispotismo', in N. Bobbio et al., eds, *Dizionario di politica*, 2nd edn, UTET, Turin, 1983.

Bobbio, N., 'Politica', in N. Bobbio et al., eds, *Dizionario di politica*, 2nd edn, UTET, Turin, 1983.

Borchardt, K., 'Zur Theorie der sozial-ökonomischen Entwicklung der gegenwärtigen Gesellschaft', in T. W. Adorno, ed., *Spätkapitalismus oder Industriegesellschaft?*, Enke, Stuttgart, 1969.

Brennan, G., *The Spanish Labyrinth*, 2nd edn, Cambridge University Press, Cambridge, 1970.

Clegg, S., *Frameworks of Power*, Sage, London, 1989.

Cohen, E., *Citizens and Soldiers: the Dilemmas of Military Service*, Cornell University Press, Ithaca, New York, 1985.

Coleman, J. C., *Power and the Structure of Society*, Norton, New York, 1974.

Collins, R., *Conflict Sociology*, Academic Press, San Francisco, 1975.

Coser, L., 'The notion of power: theoretical developments', in L. Coser and B. Rosenberg, eds, *Sociological Theory: a Book of Readings*, 4th edn, Macmillan, New York, 1976.

Coulanges, F. de, *La Cité antique*, in F. Hartog, *Le XIXe Siècle et l'histoire*, PUF, Paris, 1988.

Crozier, M., *The Bureaucratic Phenomenon in France*, University of Chicago Press, Chicago, 1964.

Dansette, A., *Histoire religieuse de la France contemporaine*, Flammarion, Paris, 1952.

Davis, K., and Moore, W., 'Some principles of stratification', repr. in Coser and Rosenberg, eds, *Sociological Theory: a Book of Readings*, 4th edn, Macmillan, New York, 1963.

De Cecco, M., 'Keynes and Italian economics', in P. Hall, ed., *The Political Power of Economic Ideas: Keynesianism across Nations*, Princeton University Press, Princeton, NJ, 1989.

Delumeau, J., *Le Peché et la peur: la culpibilisation en Occident (XIIIe–XVIIIe siècles)*, Fayard, Paris, 1983.

Douglas, M., *Implicit Meanings: Essays in Anthropology*, Routledge, London, 1975.

Durkheim, É., *De la division du travail social*, 2nd edn, PUF, Paris, 1967.

Durkheim, É., *Règles de la méthode sociologique*, PUF, Paris, 1997.

Ehrman, J., *Grand Strategy*, vol. V, HMSO, London, 1956.

Eisenstadt, S. N., *The Political System of Empires*, Free Press, Glencoe, Ill., 1963.

Eley, G., 'Army, state and civil society', in his *From Unification to Nazism*, Allen and Unwin, Boston, Mass., 1986.

Ferrero, G., *Potere: i geni invisibili della città*, Sugarco, Milan, 1998.

Finer, S., *Man on Horseback: the Role of the Military in Politics*, 2nd edn, Westview, Boulder, Colo., 1988.

Galgano, F., et al., *Nazioni senza ricchezza. Ricchezza senza nazione*, Mulino, Bologna, 1993.

Gallie, W. B., 'Essentially contested concepts', *Proceedings of the Aristotelian Society*, vol. 56 (1955–6).

Gehlen, A., *Man in the Age of Technology*, Columbia University Press, New York, 1980.

Gehlen, A., *Urmensch und Spätkultur*, Athenaeum, Bonn, 1973.

Gehlen, A., *The Human Being: His Nature and Place in the World*, Columbia University Press, New York, 1988.

Gellner, E., *Plough, Sword and Book: the Structure of Human History*, Collins-Harvill, London, 1988.

Gerth, H., and Mills, C. W., *From Max Weber: Essays in Sociology*, Routledge, London, 1947.

Giddens, A., *The Nation-State and Violence*, Macmillan, London, 1981.

Gouldner, A., 'Reciprocity and autonomy in functional theory', in L. Gross, ed., *Symposium on Sociological Theory*, Row, Peterson, Evanston, Ill., 1959.

Gouldner, A., *The Future of Intellectuals and the New Class*, Macmillan, New York, 1979.

Gouldner, A., *The Coming Crisis of Western Sociology*, Heinemann, London, 1971.

Grundmann, M., and Pothoff, K., 'Konversion des Militärs: eine Bedingung für "Schützen, helfen, retten"', *Jahrbuch Frieden 1994*, Beck, Munich, 1993.

Hall, P., ed., *The Political Power of Economic Ideas: Keynesianisms across Nations*, Princeton University Press, Princeton, NJ, 1989.

Hartog, F., 'Cité: histoire d'un concept', unpublished manuscript.

Heer, F., *Die dritte Kraft: der europäische Humanismus zwischen den Fronten des konfessionellen Zeitalters*, Fischer, Frankfurt am Main, 1959.

Heibroner, R. L., *The Nature and Logic of Capitalism*, Norton, New York, 1985.

Hennis, W., 'Il significato della avalutatività. Occasione e motivi del "postulato" di Max Weber', *Materiali per una Storia della Cultura Giuridica*, XXIII, 1 (June 1993).

Hintze, O., 'Staatsverfassung und Heeresverfassung', in his *Staat und Verfassung*, Vandenhoeck and Ruprecht, Göttingen, 1970.

Hirschman, A. O., *The Passions and the Interests: Political Arguments for Capitalism before its Triumph*, Princeton University Press, Princeton, NJ, 1977.

Hobbes, T., *Leviathan*, Cambridge University Press, Cambridge, 1991.

Hondrich, K. O., *Theorie der Herrschaft*, Suhrkamp, Frankfurt am Main, 1978.

Howard, M., *War in European History*, Oxford University Press, Oxford, 1976.

Hume, D., *Political Essays*, Cambridge University Press, Cambridge, 1987.

Huntington, S., *Political Order in Changing Societies*, Yale University Press, New Haven, Conn., 1973.

Inglehart, R., *The Silent Revolution: Changing Values and Political Styles among Western Publics*, Princeton University Press, Princeton, NJ, 1977.

Jacobs, J., *Systems of Survival: a Dialogue on the Moral Foundations of Commerce and Politics*, Random, New York, 1992.

Jasay, A. de, *The State*, Blackwell, Oxford, 1985.

Jhering, R., *Lo scopo nel diritto*, Einaudi, Turin, 1978.

Jouvenel, B. de, *Power: the Natural History of Its Growth*, Hutchinson, London, 1947.

Kant, I., *Werkausgabe*, vol. VIII, Suhrkamp, Frankfurt am Main, 1968.

Krämer, P., and Frost, H., 'Kirchenrecht', in *Staatslexikon*, vol. III, 7th edn, Herder, Freiburg, 1987.

Leipold, H., *Wirtschafts- und Gesellschaftssysteme im Vergleich*, 4th edn, Fischer, Frankfurt am Main, 1985.

Levi, M., *Of Rule and Revenue*, University of California Press, Berkeley, 1988.

Lindblom, C., *Politics and Markets: the World's Political-Economic Systems*, Basic Books, New York, 1977.

Linz, J., 'State building and nation building', *European Review*, 1 (1993).

Livy, T., *Ab urbe condita*, trans. B. O. Foster, Loeb Library edn, Heinemann, London, 1929, bk XXI.

Luhmann, N., *Macht*, Enke, Stuttgart, 1968.

Luhmann, N., *Soziologische Aufklärung I*, Westdeutscher, Cologne, 1992.

Lukes, S., ed., *Power*, Blackwell, Oxford, 1974.

Lukes, S., *Power: a Radical View*, Macmillan, London, 1974.

Mackenzie, D., *Inventing Accuracy: a Historical Sociology of Nuclear Missile Guidance*, MIT Press, Cambridge, Mass., 1990.

Mann, M., *The Sources of Social Power*, vol. I, Cambridge University Press, Cambridge, 1986.

Mann, T., *Joseph und seine Brüder: III: Joseph in Ägypten*, Fischer, Frankfurt am Main, 1983.

Marx, K., 'Randglossen zum Programm der deutschen Arbeitspartei', in K. Marx and F. Engels, *Werke*, vol. 19, Dietz, Berlin, 1978.

Marx, K., *Das Kapital*, vol. I, Dietz, Berlin, 1979.

McNeill, E. W. N., *The Pursuit of Power: Technology, Armed Forces, and Society since AD 1000*, Blackwell, Oxford, 1983.

McNeill, W. H., 'The peasant rebellion of our times', in B. Rothblatt, ed., *Changing Perspectives on Man*, University of Chicago Press, Chicago, 1969.

Meier, C., *Die Entstehung des Politischen bei den Griechen*, Suhrkamp, Frankfurt am Main, 1983.

Merkel, C. M., 'Methoden ziviler Konfliktbewältigung: Fragen an eine kriegserschüttelte Welt', *Jahrbuch Frieden 1994*, Beck, Munich, 1993.

Michels, R., *Political Parties*, Free Press, Glencoe, Ill., 1953, and Jerrold, London, 1915.

Milner, M., jun., *Status and Sacredness: a General Theory of Status Relations and an Analysis of Indian Culture*, Oxford University Press, New York, 1994.

Moore, B., jun., *Injustice: the Social Bases of Obedience and Revolt*, Macmillan, London, 1978.

Neumann, F., *The Democratic and the Authoritarian State*, Free Press, Glencoe, Ill., 1957.

Nolan, J., *The Therapeutic State: Justifying Government at Century's End*, New York University Press, New York, 1998.

North, D. C., and Thomas, R. P., *The Rise of the Modern World: a New Economic History*, Cambridge University Press, London, 1973.

Olsen, M., ed., *Power in Societies*, Macmillan, New York, 1970.

Otto, G. M., *Frühe politische Ordnungsmodelle*, Kösel, Munich, 1970.

Pareto, V., *The Mind and Society: a Treatise in General Sociology*, Harcourt Brace, New York, 1935.

Parkin, F., *Marxism and Class Theory: a Bourgeois Critique*, Tavistock, London, 1979.

Perroux, F., 'The domination effect and modern economic theory', in K. W. Rothschild, ed., *Power in Economics*, Penguin, Harmondsworth, 1971.

Poggi, G., *Calvinism and the Capitalist Spirit: Max Weber's 'Protestant Ethic'*, Macmillan, London, 1983.

Poggi, G., *The State: its Nature, Development and Prospects*, Polity Press, Cambridge, 1991.

Popitz, H., *Phänomene der Macht*, Mohr, Tübingen, 1986.

Preiser, E., 'Power, property and the distribution of income', in K. W. Rothschild, ed., *Power in Economics*, Penguin, Harmondsworth, 1997.

Rigby, T. H., 'Stalinism and the mono-organisational society', in R. Tucker, ed., *Stalinism: Essays in Sociological Interpretation*, Norton, New York, 1978.

Ritter, G., *The Sword and the Sceptre: the Problem of Militarism in Germany*, vol. I, Allen Lane, London, 1973.

Rosinski, H., *Power and Human Destiny*, Praeger, New York, 1965.

Rueschemeyer, D., *Power and the Division of Labour*, Polity Press, Cambridge, 1986.

Ruffini, F., *Relazioni tra stato e chiesa*, Mulino, Bologna, 1974.

Schmitt, C., *The Concept of the Political*, University of Chicago Press, Chicago, 1995.

Scott, J. C., *Weapons of the Weak: Everyday Forms of Peasant Resistance*, Yale University Press, New Haven, Conn., 1987.

Shonfield, A., *Modern Capitalism: the Changing Balance of Public and Private Power*, Oxford University Press, Oxford, 1969.

Simmel, G., *Soziologie*, Suhrkamp, Frankfurt am Main, 1992.

Skocpol, T., *Protecting Soldiers and Mothers: the Political Origins of Social Policy in the United States*, Harvard University Press, Cambridge, Mass., 1992.

Smith, D. E., *India as a Secular State*, Princeton University Press, Princeton, NJ, 1963.

Tanner, M., *The Last Descendants of Aeneas: the Hapsburgs and the Mythic Image of the Emperor*, Yale University Press, New Haven, Conn., 1993.

Tilly, C., *Coercion, Capital and European States AD 990–1990*, Blackwell, Oxford, 1976.

Tocqueville, A. de., *De la démocratie en Amérique*, vol. II, Vrin, Paris, 1990.

Unger, R., *Plasticity into Power*, Cambridge University Press, Cambridge, 1987.

Unger, R., *Politics*, vol. III, Cambridge University Press, Cambridge, 1987.

Unger, R., *False Necessity: an Anti-Necessitarian Social Theory in the Service of Radical Democracy*, Cambridge University Press, Cambridge, 1987.

Watkins, A., 'State II: the concept', in D. Sills, ed., *International Encyclopedia of the Social Sciences*, vol. 15, Free Press, New York, 1968.

Weber, M., 'Politics as a vocation', in H. Gerth and C. W. Mills, *From Max Weber: Essays in Sociology*, Routledge, London, 1947.

Weber, M., *Wirtschaft und Gesellschaft*, 5th edn, Mohr (Siebeck), Tübingen, 1972.

Wills, P., *Learning to Labor: How Working Class Kids Get Working Class Jobs*, Columbia University Press, New York, 1977.

Wrong, D., *Power: Its Forms, Bases, and Uses. With a New Preface*, University of Chicago Press, Chicago, 1988.

Zanker, P., *Augustus und die Macht der Bilder*, Beck, Munich, 1987.

Index

accumulation of power 4–6, 39
Adams, R. 4
aesthetic practices
   commodification of 112
   and creation of national identity
      106–7, 168
   as public good 114
   self-referential 121
   state support for 111–14, 121
   see also creative intellectuals;
      meaning, norms, aesthetic and
      ritual practices
Africa, predatory rulers 163–4
Agnew, S. 115
agrarian reform 143
alienation 65
allocation of resources
   and market mechanism 22, 154
   outside market mechanism 153,
      169–71
   and social power 17–19, 21
American Civil War 181, 186
appropriation 129
Archilocus 37
Archimedes 13
Arendt, H. 121
armed forces
   autonomy of military institutions
      187–90
   chain of command 188
   and industrial-military complex
      165–7, 174–5, 201
   inter-service rivalry 195
   recruitment and training 191–4, 199,
      201
   traditionalism 199–200, 201
   see also military elites; military

   expenditure; military power;
      war
Aron, R. 171
art
   services to the state 103–4
   see also aesthetic practices
asymmetries
   between clergy and faithful 71–3
   in employment relationship 127–9,
      130–2, 141, 151–2
   in political power 29–30, 33–7,
      47–9
   in social power 10–14
   see also inequality
Augustus 77, 103, 119
autonomy, military 187–90, 201

Bagehot, W. 90
Bastiat, F. 133, 161
bellicosity
   lack of 190–1, 198–9
   prior to World War I 198
Bensel, R. F. 181
Bismarck, O. E. L. von 81
Blau, R. 131–2
Bobbio, N. 20, 31
Böhm-Bawerk, E. von 128
Bolingbroke, Viscount 52
Borchardt, K. 150
Brennan, G. 81
Buddhism 67
bureaucratization 135, 137
business confidence, and social policy
   153–4
business, and politics
   claims of economically powerful on
      state 144–7, 148–53, 154–6

business, and politics (*cont'd*)
  constraints on public policy 143–7,
    148
  interaction between elites 156–8
  maintenance of stability 151–3
  post-war developments 150–1
  and protection of property rights
    141–5
  restoration of 'business confidence'
    153–4
  state intervention favouring business
    interests 148–53
  trade policy 147
  see also economic power; political–
    economic relationships

'caesaropapism' 94
canon law 91, 110
capital
  asymmetric relations with labour
    127–8, 130–2, 141, 151–2
  Gouldner's definition 131
capital mobility 146
capitalism
  and domination of corporations 177
  Marx on 135
  rationality and modern 135–6, 176
  Rhenan and Anglo-Saxon models
    143
  Weber on 135–6, 137
cartels 160
Catholicism
  concordats 86, 96
  hierarchical nature of 70–1
  Inquisition 10, 91, 110
  relationships with state 86–7, 92–3
  see also Christianity
'catonism' 200
censorship 111
charisma
  and desacralization of ideological/
    normative power 97–100
  Weber's political and magical 65–6,
    69–70, 76
Chernobyl disaster 5
China 33, 87
Christianity
  complex nature of 86–9, 91–3
  and Islam compared 78

and political–religious dualism
    78–80, 93
  suffering and salvation 83
  and transient nature of life 67
  see also Catholicism
Church of England 88
Cicero 5
citizenship
  expansion of content of 171–2, 177
  well-being 169–71
civil religion, USA 90
civil society
  demarcation between state and
    145–6
  and disestablished religion 92–3
  position of church in 95
  as production of creative intellectuals
    106–7
civilian elites, attitude towards military
    elites 200–2
civilianization of government 46, 57
classes
  Marx on 17, 22, 136
  as stratification units 21
  Tocqueville's industrial aristocracy
    136–7
  Weber on 16–19, 22–3, 137
Clausewitz, K. von 190, 195, 196
Clemenceau, G. 190, 196
coercion
  defence of state by 168
  economic institutions and 124, 141,
    148
  and fear 30–1
  in labour relationship 127
  property protected by political
    sanction of 141–3
  see also violence
Cohen, E. 191–3
Cold War 186
collective bargaining 128, 143, 153
collective identity
  built by creative intellectuals 106–7,
    168–9
  business interests and creation of
    152–3
  political use of religious 83–4
Collins, R. 181–2, 184
command

allocation of resources by 18, 19, 22
command/obedience interaction
29–30
military chain of 188
in St Luke's 'centurion episode'
29–30, 31–2
command economies 139, 175–7
commodification
of aesthetic practices 112
and exchange value 135
communication, creative intellectuals
and 101–2, 107
Communism 45, 176–7
competition
between creative intellectuals 101–2,
113, 121
economic power under perfect 125
in economic systems 125, 135
imperfect 126
international 167
concepts and definitions of power
energy-focused 3–4
and future 11–12
generic 1–2
Parsons on 13
relational 12–14
Rosinski on 2–4
Weber on 12–14, 15–16
Concordat (1929) 86
conflict
business interests and social 151–2,
153–4
power-related 21–8: around
resources 21–4; between forms of
social power 24–5, 203–4; and
powerless 25–8
contracts
employment 128–9, 142, 143–4
institutional enforcement 148
control
of social conflict 151–2, 153–4
of violence 41–2, 43–7, 50–3, 182–3
corporations
domination by 177
and globalization 178–9
military power connections with 187
as products of public policy 143,
146–7
Coser, L. 11, 16

costs of entry 126
Council of Trent 71
creative intellectuals 100–22, 204
association with party politics 101,
109–10, 116, 117
as awkward customers 115–19, 122
commitment to higher values 117–18
and communication 101–2, 107
competition between 101–2, 113,
121
and construction of new political
communities 105–7
and creation of collective identity
106–7
differentiation 100–2, 120–1
as distraction from political matters
108–9
as easy mark 119–22
financing 112–14
and legitimation 104, 105, 111,
168
nature of 100–2
relationships with other power
centres 118–19
and state see politics–creative
intellectuals relationship
see also aesthetic practices
cults 71
custom, allocation of resources by 18,
22

dance see aesthetic practices
Dansette, A. 87, 88, 92
Dante, A. 68–9, 110
Davis, K. and Moore, W. 17
De Cecco, M. 149
defence of state, by coercion 168
Delaware, incporporation in 147
delusion 62–3
democratization 135
depersonalization of power
relationships 42
deprivation, in social power
relationships 10–12, 14
Descartes, R. 9
despotism 76–7
dialects 106
differences, power as 'ability' to make
3–4, 8–10, 11–12

differentiation
  of creative intellectuals 100–2,
    120–1
  institutional 53–5: religious 69–70
  Jacobs's 'moral syndromes' 138–9,
    189
  modern 99–100
  within economic system 127
distribution, social 151–2
division of labour 24
  differentiation as 54
division of powers 45–7
domination
  by virtue of authority 123–4, 129
  by virtue of a constellation of
    interests 123–4, 129, 138
  Perroux's domination effect 126
Douglas, M. 62–3
Durkheim, É. 50–1, 58, 63, 64, 65

East India Company 146
economic institutions 134
  and coercion 124, 141, 148
  and demarcation between state and
    civil society 145–6
  for growth 146–7, 148
  incorporation as 143, 146–7
economic power 18–21, 123–40
  claims on state 144–7, 148–53,
    155–6
  and commercial moral syndrome
    138–9, 173
  domination by virtue of a
    constellation of interests 123–4,
    138
  exchange 131–2
  inequalities of 125–6
  military power connections with 187
  and political parties 155
  property and 129–31
  significance in classical social theory
    134–8
  social consequences of 132–4
  as social power 124, 136–8
  theoretical absence of 124–7
  see also business, and politics;
    political–economic relationship
economic systems 123–6
  command economies 139

competition 125, 135: imperfect 126
  institutional requirements of 145–7
  internal differentiation 127
  plurality of actors 124, 126–8,
    131–2, 141
  political requirements of 141–3
  Soviet denial of autonomy of 176
  state intervention favouring business
    interests 148–50
  theoretical absence of power in
    124–7
economics, theory and practice 126–7,
  129
education 85, 86, 111–12, 152–3, 169
Eisenhower, D. D. 188, 201
Eisenstadt, S. N. 164
Eliot, T. S. 85
elites
  civilian 200–2
  interaction between political and
    business 156–8
  military see military elites
  social 193–4
employment
  asymmetric relationship in 127–9,
    141
  full 153
  unequal contractual partners 128–9,
    142, 143–4
empowerment
  by institutionalization of political
    relations 51–2
  of society through ideological/
    normative power 60–1
England, property rights and taxation
  revenue 145
Enlightenment
  and despotism 76–7
  and plurality of self-standing states
    77–8
European Union 179
exchange
  allocation of resources by 18–19,
    22
  asymmetric relationships and aspects
    of 36
  and existence of economic power
    131–2
exchange value 135

exclusion
  ability of groups to enforce 60–1
  from property 129–30
Exxon Valdez wreck 5

Falklands (Malvinas) War 187, 191
fascism 45, 90–1
fear
  of God 69
  Hobbes's paradox 182, 203
  and political power 30–1, 40
  religious institutions and 67–9
Ferrero, G. 31, 32
Fiat 194
financing
  creative intellectuals 112–14
  economic costs of state 159–79:
    predatory extraction of resources
    160–7, 171–2, 173–5; Weberian
    typology 159–60, 174
  religious institutions 86
firms, as profit seekers 127
fiscal policy 145, 148, 149, 153
  and globalization 177–8
foreign policy 202
formalization of power relationships
  42–3
Foucault, M. 13
France 145
free trade 147, 174
French Revolution 79, 88, 90
future 11–12

Galileo, G. 111
Geertz, C. 61
Gehlen, A. 2, 4, 7
Gellner, E. 20
Germany
  business–politics relationship in
    Reich 176–7
  German intellectual tradition 2–3
  Polonization of border territories
    167–8
  recruitment and training of armed
    forces in Weimar Republic 192
  state-protected industrial
    development 167, 174
Giddens, A. 184
globalization 177–9, 204

Goffman, E. 123
Golding, W. 21–2
Gouldner, A. 130, 131, 142
Greece, ancient 43–4, 48, 133, 161
groups
  Mann's distinctive 60–1, 74–5, 97
  non-religious 97–100
  Weber's status 16–19, 21
growth
  institutions for 146–7, 148
  and property rights 146–7
Guizot, F. 162
Gulf War 187

Hartog, F. 48
Heibroner, R. L. 128
hierarchy
  of creative intellectuals 101–2
  in religious institutions 69–73
Hintze, O. 181
Hobbes, T. 1, 9, 31, 32, 39
  paradox of fear 182, 203
  power and the future 11, 12
homo potens 3
Hondrich, K. O. 19
hope, religious monopoly of 67
Horace 68
households, as economic units 127
Howard, M. 199
Huguenots 111
human beings
  and deprivation of human values
    14
  power over nature 3–7, 9
  production as interaction between
    nature and 161–2
  self-determination of 3
Hume, D. 30
Huntington, S. 51–2

identity
  national collective 106–7, 168
  personal 61, 62
  political use of collective religious
    83–4
  ideological/normative power 18–21,
    58–73
    creative intellectuals and 100
    desacralization of 97–100

ideological/normative power (*cont'd*)
  empowerment of society through
    60–1
  Mann's argument about 60–1, 62–4,
    97
  objections to concept of 58–63
  see also religious power
imperfect competition 126
imperium (political authority)
  145–6
industrial economy, and military power
  165–7, 174–5, 201
inequality
  asymmetry and equality in nature
    33–7
  of economic power 125–6
  justification of political 31–7
  and layering relationships 35–6
  and population as constituency
    44–5, 48
  stratification of power and 17–18
  see also asymmetries
innovation 125, 135–6
Inquisition 10, 91, 110
institutionalization of political power
  42–7
  empowerment by 51–2
institutions
  autonomy of military 187–90,
    201
  and control of violence 41–2
  economic *see* economic institutions
  as embodiment of power 1–2
  military 187–90
  religious *see* religious institutions
  support of state for intellectual 111
  tensions and contrasts between 55
integration, systemic 26–8
intellectuals
  sacred or profane 98–9, 110
  struggle between church and secular
    110–11
  see also creative intellectuals;
    politics–creative intellectuals
    relationship
International Monetary Fund 177
Ireland 84
Islam 78
Italy 86, 90–1, 149, 172

Jacobs, J., 'moral syndromes' 138–9,
  162, 173, 189, 203
Japan 172
Joseph, divine insight 173
Jouvenal, B. de 29–30, 52–3, 181, 184
Joyce, J. 86, 100
'jurisdictionalism' 95
justification, of political asymmetries
  31–7, 47–9

Kant, I. 20, 98
Knights Templar 91
Krauss, K. 68

labour, asymmetric relations with
    capital 127–8, 130–2, 141, 151–2
labour market
  and education 153
  state intervention 143–4, 149
laissez-faire 148
language
  and dialects 106
  and order 62
law
  canon 91, 110
  civil and commercial 148
  legitimacy of state grounded in 89
  norms and 97–8
  quasi-sacredness of judges and
    lawyers 100
  Rhenan and Anglo-Saxon models of
    143
  struggle between church and secular
    intellectuals 110–11
layering
  of political power 35–6
  of religious institutions 69
leadership, political and religious
    aspects of 74–5
  see also rulers
legal positivism 98
legitimacy/legitimation
  grounded in validity of law 89
  of institutionalized structures 50
  non-religious forms of 89–90
  of state: by religion 82–3, 87–8, 105;
    creative intellectuals and 104, 105,
    111, 168; popular
    acknowledgment of 168

struggle between church and secular intellectuals to provide 110–11
Weber's concern with 36, 83, 89
Lenin, V. I. 31, 46, 176
liberal democracy 153–4, 155
libertinism 119
Lindblom, C. 155
literacy 111
Longarone flood 6–7
Luce, H. 11
Luhmann, N. 8, 9, 52–5
Luther, M. 73, 83

MacArthur, Gen D. 198
Machtpolitik (power politics) 56, 170–3, 174–5
McNeill, W. H. 6
manliness 188, 189
Mann, M. 2
  economic power 136
  ideological power 60–1, 62–4, 74–5, 84, 97
  military power as fourth power 21, 180, 184
Mann, T. 21, 34–5, 173
market
  allocation of resources by 22, 154
  allocation of resources outside 153, 169–71
  business and politics and operation of 149–50, 151, 153–4, 177
  creative intellectuals and 111–14
Marlowe, C. 20
Marx, K. 65
  class 17, 22, 136
  economic power 129, 130, 133–4, 135–7, 161
  ideology 59–60
  religion 67, 83
  stratification of power 16–17, 22–3, 27–8
Mead, G. H. 62
meaning, norms, aesthetic and ritual practices
  and charismatic qualifications 97–100
  Mann's distinctive groups' monopoly of 60–1, 74–5, 84, 87–8
  sacred or profane 98–9, 110

media
  creative intellectuals and 102, 112
  role in modern politics 108–9
Michels, R. 8, 53
militarism 196–7, 199
military elites 185–200
  attempts to usurp political power 186
  attitude of civilian elites to 200–2
  attitude towards politicians 196–200
  and centrality of war 186–7
  constraints on 190–4, 197–200
    civilian appointment of 200
    constitutional subordination 190–1, 192, 195–6, 198
  militarism 196–7
  preoccupation with tradition and morality 199–200, 201
  recessive role 186–7
  see also armed forces; military power; political–military relationship
military expenditure 150, 165–7, 174–5, 185–6, 190, 194–5
  allocation 194–5
  property rights and 144–5, 146
military power 180–202
  commitment to power politics and 170–1, 174–5
  connections with economic power 187
  and development of modern states 56–7, 144–5, 146, 165–7, 181
  and industrial-military complex 165–7, 174–5, 201
  and institutional autonomy 187–90, 201
  as key political concern 165–6
  as Mann's fourth power 21, 180, 184
  and organized violence 180–5
  resources expended on 150, 165–7, 174–5, 185–6, 194–5
  see also armed forces; political–military relationship; violence; war
minimum wage legislation 128
Mirabeau, Vicomte de 87, 92
modernity, and secularization of the state 80

modernization, and marginalization of religion 105–6
monetary policy 148, 149
money
  and economic exchange 124
  and political power compared 51, 52
  social role of 134
Money–Commodity–Money cycle 135
monopoly
  legitimate violence by state 55–7, 180
  of meaning, norms, aesthetic and ritual practices 60–1, 74–5, 84, 87–8: not religious 97–100
  political power and granting of 125, 160
  religious: of hope and truth 67, 70–1; of moral authority 66–7
  of resources in power games 70
Moore, B., jun. 200
Moore, W. see Davis, K. and Moore, W.
'moral syndromes' 138–9, 173
morality, military preoccupation with 199–200
music see aesthetic practices

nations
  creative intellectuals and nation-building 106, 168–9
  and well-being of citizens 169–71
  see also state
nature
  human power over 3–7, 9
  production as interaction between human beings and 161–2
  subjective and objective aspects 7
Nazism 90–1, 167
Near East, political and religious empires 76
Netherlands 145
Neumann, F. 130–1, 137, 139–40, 148, 176
night-watchman state 148
normative power see ideological/normative power
norms 60, 97–8
  see also meaning, norms, aesthetic and ritual practices

North, D. C. and Thomas, R. P. 144–5, 146, 148

oath, as religious ritual 82
obedience
  interaction with command 29–30
  Jesuit and Prussian form 10
  military 188
oil shock 187
'order', meanings of 61–2
original sin 69
Ovidius Naso (Ovid) 119

Pareto, V. 49, 60, 174
Parkin, F. 129, 142–3
Parsons, T. 9, 13, 58
  Gouldner's polemic against 130, 142
  political power 13, 49–51, 52–5
parties
  church-sponsored 88–9
  as stratification units 21
  Weber on 16–19
party politics
  creative intellectuals and 101, 109–10, 116, 117
  and diversion of resources 171–2
  and economic power 155
Pascal, B. 62, 63
patents 125
'peace dividend' 201
Perroux, F. 126
philosophy 97, 98
Plessner, H. 2
poetry see aesthetic practices
Poland 84, 93, 167–8
police, and legitimate violence 184–5
policy see fiscal policy; monetary policy; public policy; social policy; trade policy
polis 43–4, 48
political organizations 159–60
political power 18–21, 29–57
  compared with money 51, 52
  comparison of amount of 50–2
  and division of powers 45–7
  as enforceable commands 53
  and fear 30–1, 40
  and 'guardian' moral syndrome 138–9, 173

institutionalization of 42–7
justification of inequality of 31–7
layering relationships 35–6
Parsons/Luhmann alternative view
    49–55
'power over' or 'power to' 49–54
uncoupling 45
violence as core of 38–9, 43, 57,
    180–5
political–economic relationships
    accommodations 138–40, 167–8
    'c'est l'argent qui fait la guerre' 161,
        165–6
    classical views on 136–8
    confrontational 138–40, 164–5
    and development of industrial
        economy 166–8, 174–5
    and globalization 177–9
    international context 167, 168, 174
    and non-market allocation of
        resources 169–71
    power politics and social consensus
        trade-off 170–3
    predatory extraction of resources
        160–7, 171–2, 173–5: constraints
        on 163–7
    Soviet 175–7
    see also business, and politics; state
        expenditure; state intervention
political–military relationship
    attitude of civilian elites to military
        elites 200–2
    attitude of military towards
        politicians 196–200
    civilian appointment of top military
        personnel 200
    constraints on military 190–4,
        197–200: constitutional
        subordination 190–1, 192, 195–6,
        198; popular distaste for war
        190–1, 198–9
    economic aspects 194–6
    political role of military 186, 196
    separation of political and military
        power 183–4
    see also armed forces; military elites;
        military expenditure; military
        power
political–religious relationships 74–96

benefits of church to state 82–4
benefits to church from state 84–9
Christian dualism 78–80, 93
church-sponsored parties 88–9
and moral authority of church 85–6
in Near East 76
political use of church organization
    82–3
process of mutual accommodation
    80–1, 93–6
religious legitimation of state 82–3,
    87–8, 89, 105
state violence to support religion
    91–2
typology of 93–6
variable nature of 74–6
Western versions 76–80
see also religion; religious
    institutions; religious power
politicians
    attitudes of business towards 156–8
    attitudes of military elites to
        196–200
politics
    as Greek invention 43–4
    parasitical on production 161–3,
        165, 169, 173
    see also business, and politics
politics–creative intellectuals
    relationship 105–14
    benefits expected by creative
        intellectuals 109–14
    benefits offered to state 102–9
    state support for creative intellectuals
        111–14, 121
    state as target for influence of
        creative intellectuals 102–4
    strains in 115–22
Polonization 167–8
Pope 34
Popitz, H. 19–20, 31, 42–4, 47
    on violence 37–9, 40, 47
'potentiality' 11–12
power see accumulation of power;
    concepts and definitions of power;
    economic power; ideological/
    normative power; military power;
    political power; power forms;
    social power; structures of power

power forms 15–28, 203–4
  accommodation between 25–8
  conflict between 24–5, 203–4
  Mann's quadripartition of 21, 180,
    184
  power-related conflicts 21–8
  tripartition of 18–21
  vertical and horizontal relations 26
  Weber's multiplicity 19
power politics 56, 170–3, 174–5
powerless 25–8
Preiser, E. 128
price makers and takers 125–6
production
  Greek and Roman 133, 161
  as interaction between human beings
    and nature 161–2
  Marx on primacy of 161
  not created by political activity
    161–3, 165, 169, 173
  ownership of means of see capital;
    property
profit
  innovation and search for 135–6
  maximization by firms 127
property
  or appropriation 129, 161
  dominium right of 145–6
  exclusion and withholding 129–30,
    131
  as means of production 161
  power of 129–31
  Soviet supressiom of private 176
  state protection for 141–5
Protagoras 44
protection, state
  of intellectual institutions from
    religion 111
  of private property 141–5
psychoanalysis 68
public good 114
public ownership 150–1
public policy
  and business interests 143–53
  choice of intervention policies 154–6
  constraints on 143–7
  corporations as products of 143,
    146–7

public sphere, creative intellectuals and
  101–2
punishment 10–12

rationalization, capitalism and modern
  state 135–6, 176
reciprocity
  between clergy and faithful 72–3
  between state and church 87
recruitment, armed forces 191–4, 199
Reformation 71, 79, 95
relationships see business, and politics;
    political–economic relationships;
    political–military relationship;
    political–religious relationships;
    politics–creative intellectuals
    relationship
religion
  American civil 90
  church-sponsored parties 88–9
  civil society and disestablished 92–3
  fear and 67–9
  marginalization of 105–6
  political use of collective identity
    83–4
  and reciprocity between clergy and
    faithful 72–3
  and state protection of intellectual
    institutions 111
  support of political authority for
    85–6, 91–2, 110
  variable relationships between state
    and 74–6
religious institutions
  canon law and structure of 91
  division into churches and sects 86
  financing 86
  'going political' 91
  hierarchical ordering of 69–73
  non-political violence and 92
religious power 63–6
  asymmetry between clergy and
    faithful 71–3
  despotism and 76–7
  legitimation of state 82–3, 87–8, 89,
    105
  monopoly of meaning, norms,
    aesthetic and ritual practices 60–1,
    74–5, 84, 87–8

moral authority of 66–7
and social power 63–5
spiritual nature of 66–7, 77–9, 83–4
Weber's political and magical
    'charisma' 65–6, 69–70, 76
see also ideological/normative power;
    political–religious relationships
Renaissance 71
rent-seeking 173
repression 153–4
resources
    allocation of 18–19, 22: outside
        market mechanism 153, 169–71
    commitment to military power 150,
        165–7, 174–5, 185–6, 190,
        194–5
    diversion by political parties 171–2
    economic 141
    of power 16, 17–19
    resource wars 187
    state's increasing share of 170, 171,
        177
Rigby, H. 22
rites of passage 82
ritual 60, 64
    see also meaning, norms, aesthetic
        and ritual practices
Robespierre, M. M. I. de 87, 92
Rome 133, 161, 163
Rosinski, H. 2–4, 5, 7–8, 9, 27
Rouvroy, C.-H., Comte de Saint-Simon
    162
Rouvroy, L., Duc de Saint-Simon 33
Ruffini, F. 93–6
rulers
    benefits offered by creative
        intellectuals 103–4
    and Christian dualism 78–9
    'colouring them sacred' 75
    masking the power of 33–4, 75
    predatory extraction of resources
        161–7, 171–2, 173–5:
        compensatory benefits 163–4;
        constraints on 163–7
    reciprocity between people and 87
    religious authority of 77
    use of church organization 82–3
    see also leadership
rulership

conflicts around 23–4
as resource of power 19, 21
Russell, B. 12
Russian Orthodox Church 83

'sacredness' 64–5, 75
    desacralization of ideological/
        normative power 97–100
    and social change 99–100
Saint-Simon see Rouvroy, C.-H.;
    Rouvroy, L.
salvation 83
Sartre, J.-P. 116, 120–1
Scelba, M. 115
Schmitt, C. 162, 190
science 97
secularization of the state 80, 88
security
    and ideological/normative power
        61
    need of individual for moral 67
Serlo of Wilton 67
sexuality 85, 86
Shakespeare, W. 33–4, 36
Shelley, P. B. 117
Silone, I. 37
Simmel, G. 9–10
skills, learning new 6–7
Skocpol, T. 170–1
slavery 133
Smith, A. 127–8, 177, 181
social conflict, state control of 151–2,
    153–4
social consensus
    and political–economic relationships
        168–75
    and welfare expenditure 169–71
social elites 193–4
social policy
    and business confidence 153–4
    and business interests 151–2
social power 8–14, 203
    ability to make differences 8–10
    aoristic 13–14
    asymmetries in 10–14
    dilemmas and contradictions in 8–10
    economic power as 124, 136–8
    role of punishment and deprivation
        in 10–12

social theory
  economic power in classical 134–8
  tough- or tender-minded views
    59–60
society
  empowerment through ideological/
    normative power 60–1
  religion and early development of
    64–5
  role of economic activities 133–4
  sacralization of 65
Sohm, R. 91
solidarity, military 188–9
sovereignty 56, 77
  and globalization 178–9
Soviet Russia 175–7
Spain 145
  Spanish Civil War 81
Stalin, J. 176
state
  boundaries of sovereign 56
  capitalism and modern 135–6, 176
  claims of economic power on 144–7,
    148–53
  coercion and defence of 168
  and creative intellectuals see politics–
    creative intellectuals relationship
  demarcation between civil society
    and 145–6
  development of modern 54–7: and
    military power 56–7, 144–5, 146,
    165–7, 181
  distinction between *imperium* and
    dominium 145–6
  and economic power see business,
    and politics; political–economic
    relationships
  financing economic costs 159–79:
    Weberian typology 159–60
  increasing share of resources 170,
    171, 177
  myth of laissez-faire 148
  night-watchman 148
  plurality of self-standing states 77–8,
    79
  popular acknowledgment of
    legitimacy of 168
  protection of private property 141–5
  relations between 56

and religion see political–religious
    relationships
  secularization of 80, 88
  support for intellectual institutions
    111
  see also nations
state expenditure 168–75
  achieving popular consensus 168–75
  business dislike of non-market
    allocation of resources 169–71
  increasing share of national product
    170, 171, 177
  power politics and social consensus
    trade-off 170–3
  and well-being of citizens 169–71
state intervention
  composition of government and
    choice of policy 155
  and control of social conflict 151–2,
    153–4
  and education system 152–3
  favouring business interests 148–50
  labour market 143–4, 149
  and market mechanism 149–50, 151,
    153–4, 177
  objections of business community to
    153–4
  policy choices 154–6
  and political parties 171–2
  in wartime economy 150
status
  conflicts around 23
  as power resource 18, 21
status group
  as stratification unit 16–19, 21
  Weber on 16–19
stratification of power
  three dimensions of 17–18, 21
  Weber and Marx compared 16–18,
    19, 22–3
structures of power 13
subsidiarity principle 177
suffering 83
Switzerland 191–2

taxation
  as extractive process 173–4
  and financing political organizations
    160

and globalization 177–8
and industrial development 144, 148
property rights and revenue from 144–5
theocracy 94–5
Thomas, R. P. *see* North, D. C. and Thomas, R. P.
Three Mile Island incident 5
Thurber, J. 5
Tilly, C. 181, 184, 202
Tocqueville, A. C. H. C. de 66–7, 83–4, 134–5, 136
Torrey Canyon wreck 5
Toscanini, A. 120
trade policy 147, 148, 149, 174, 202
traditionalism, military 199–200, 201
training, armed forces 191–4, 199, 201
tripartition of power forms 18–21
Truman, H. S. 198
trust 61

unemployment benefits 128
unions 143, 149, 153–4
United Kingdom, houses fit for heroes 171
United States
    business–politics relationship 176
    civil religion in 90
    Civil War 181, 186
    recruitment and training of armed forces 191
    religion and Constitution 85
    welfare policies 170–1
use value 135

value
    exchange 135
    use 135
violence 37–42, 180–5
    against women 182
    boundlessness 38, 40
    confined to periphery 40–1
    control of 41–2, 43–7, 50–3: organization for 182, 183
    as core of political power 38–9, 43, 57, 180–5
    devices vested in political system 182
    differentiated from political power 183–4

graduation of 37–8
and Hobbes's paradox 182–3
institutionalized 41–2, 43–7, 50–3: church requests for support of 91–2
irrationality 39, 40
military power and organized 180–5
and predatary rulers 162, 163
in religious institutions 92
restrictions on 40–2
separation of military and civil use of 56–7, 184–5
state monopoly of legitimate 55–7, 180
technology of 38
see also armed forces; coercion; military power; police

war
    American Civil War 181, 186
    centrality of 186–7
    'c'est l'argent qui fait la guerre' 161, 165–6
    Cold War 186
    Falklands (Malvinas) War 187, 191
    Gulf War 187
    political significance of 186–90
    popular distaste for 190–1, 198–9
    resource wars 187
    resources committed to 150, 165–6, 185–6
    Spanish Civil War 81
    World Wars 150, 198
    see also armed forces; military power; violence
wealth
    conflicts around 23
    as resource of power 18–19, 21
Weber, M.
    capitalism 135–6, 137
    classes 16–19, 22–3, 137
    definitions of power 12–14, 15–16, 128
    economic power 123–4, 129, 135–6, 137
    Herrschaft 29
    on legitimacy 36, 83, 89
    political and magical 'charisma' 65–6, 69–70, 76

Weber, M. (*cont'd*)
  relations betweeen political and
    economic power 167–8, 174–5
  resistance inherent in power relations
    9, 15–16, 128
  stratification of power 16–18, 19,
    22–3
  typology of financing of political
    organizations 159–60, 174
  on violence 38, 40, 180
  war economy 165–6
welfare expenditure 169–71
well-being
  of citizens 169–71
  human need for moral 61

as justification of inequality
  49
West India Company 146
West, political–religious relationships
  76–80
women
  in armed forces 192
  violence against 182
World Bank 177
World Wars 150, 198
writing 76

Yangtze River dams 6

Zanker, P. 103, 119